edexcel

Edexcel GCSE

ICT

Student

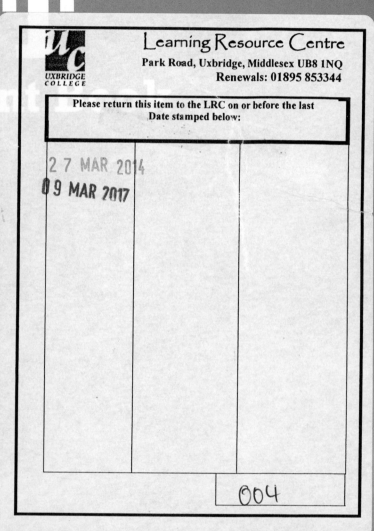
Written by R.S.U. Heathcote, Naveed Latif,
Monica Mason and David Waller

A PEARSON COMPANY

Published by Pearson Education Limited, a company incorporated in England and Wales, having its registered office at Edinburgh Gate, Harlow, Essex, CM20 2JE. Registered company number: 872828

www.pearsonschoolsandfecolleges.co.uk

Edexcel is a registered trademark of Edexcel Limited

Text © Rob Heathcote, Naveed Latif, Monica Mason and David Waller, 2010

First published 2010

14 13 12 11
10 9 8 7 6 5

British Library Cataloguing in Publication Data
A catalogue record for this book is available from the British Library.

ISBN 978 1 846906 14 5

Developed by Melanie Birdsall
Edited by Susan Ross
Typeset by Phoenix Photosetting, Chatham, Kent
Original illustrations © Pearson Education Ltd and Clive Goodyer, 2010
Illustrated by Clive Goodyer and Oxford Designers & Illustrators Ltd
Picture research by Kathy Kollberg
Printed in the Malaysia (CTP-VP)

Acknowledgements
The authors and publisher would like to thank the following for their kind permission to reproduce their photographs:

(Key: b-bottom; c-centre; l-left; r-right; t-top)

Alamy Images: Mike Booth 191tl, Cultura 223, ICP 86br, Johner Images 37-38, Vario Images GmbH & Co. KG 66, Angela Hampton Picture Library 3-4, First Light 85-86, ONOKY – Photononstop 139, Fredrik Renander 48, Alex Segre 122, Stockbroker 92, 159, Michael Ventura 140; **Construction Photography:** Buildpix 201; **Corbis:** Gene Blevins / LA Daily News 12br, Reuters / Fred Prouser 68, Fancy / Veer 207; **Courtesy of Cadbury plc:** 112; **David Waller:** 49, 52; **Digital Stock:** 151; **Emotiv Systems Inc:** 60tl; **Getty Images:** Max Oppenheim 34, PhotoDisc 164, Taxi 119; **iStockphoto:** Grigory Bibikov 185t, Blackbeck 184tl, 184tr, Dtsuneo 183bl, 183bc, Alex Slobodkin 102; **NAU:** 59br; **Ovei Ltd:** 59tr; **Pearson Education Ltd:** Clark Wiseman, Studio 8 185b, Steve Shott 115, Ian Wedgewood 32; **Photolibrary.com:** Imagestate 195; **Rex Features:** Action Press 44; **Science Photo Library Ltd:** Johnny Greig 59cl; **Solo Syndication / Associated Newspapers Ltd:** Mark Richards 60cr; **Sony Ericsson:** 8, 12tc, 12tr, 12cr

All other images © Pearson Education

Every effort has been made to trace the copyright holders and we apologise in advance for any unintentional omissions. We would be pleased to insert the appropriate acknowledgement in any subsequent edition of this publication.

The authors and publisher would like to thank the following individuals and organisations for permission to reproduce copyright material:

p. 9 Table of memory card capacities © 2009, Lexar Media Inc. All rights reserved. Used with permission; p. 21 Logo copyright 2010 Bebo, Inc. Used with permission; p. 21 Logo used with permission from myspace.com; p. 23 Email statistics used with permission of the Radicati Group; p. 70 Logo used with permission from BT; p. 70 Logo used with permission from Telefónica O2 UK Limited; p. 70 Logo used with permission from Virgin Media; p. 97 Adobe product box shot reprinted with permission from Adobe Systems Incorporated; p. 109 40% statistic © Forrester Research; p. 109 83% statistic © NetSmart Research; p. 112 The "Rowntrees Randoms" brand name and image is reproduced with the kind permission of Société des Produits Nestlé S.A.; p. 128 Amazon security certificate; © 2010 Amazon.com Inc. and its affiliates. All rights reserved. p. 136 Amazon privacy notice © 2010 Amazon.com Inc. and its affiliates. All rights reserved. p. 162 image of London Eye © 2009 TripAdvisor LLC All rights reserved, used with permission; p. 191 top food image © Sid Khullar, www.chefAtlarge.in; p. 191 middle food image courtesy of eHow.com – Clear Instructions on How to Do (just about) Everything. http://www.ehow.com/; p. 191 bottom food image beckyhiggins.com; p. 202 Energy Savers Report used with permission from British Gas; p. 219 Figure 2.26 by permission of TV Licensing;

The authors and publisher would like to thank the following individuals and organisations for permission to reproduce screen shots from their websites:

p. 24 VLP screen shot used with permission from RM ; p. 41 interrailnet.com screen shot used with permission from InterRail, part of Eurail.com; p. 43 Google; p. 52 Picasa from Google; p. 53 Google maps © Google – Map data © 2009 Tele Atlas; p. 53 Google Earth © 2009 Europa Technologies © 2009 Tele Atlas; p. 78 BBC iPlayer screen shot used with permission from BBC Photo Library; p. 100 screen shot used with permission from OpenOffice.org; p. 106 top screen shot used with permission from Zen Internet; p. 106 bottom screen shot HSBC; p. 107 screen shot © Inter IKEA Systems B.V. 2009; p. 109 © 2010 Amazon.com Inc. and its affiliates. All rights reserved. p. 110 Google; p. 120 screen shot used with permission from My Virtual Model Inc.; p. 123 Ebay; p. 124 Ebay; p. 125 Ebay; p. 126 Ebay; p. 126 Sign in page from Google Mail; p. 127 screen shot used with permission from Amicode.com; p. 129 screen shot used with permission from The Co-operative Bank plc; p. 171 Google and The Collaroy Centre; p. 174 Wiltshire Farm Foods, part of apetito Ltd, Canal Road, Trowbridge BA14 8RJ; p. 181 Transport for London; p. 190 Smilebox Inc; p. 204 Figure 2.7 copyright Quayside Clothing Limited; p. 231 Figure 3.5 Bang & Olufsen; p. 234 Figure 3.9 Pearson Education Limited.

All screen shots of Microsoft products used with permission from Microsoft. All screen shots of the sample Controlled Assessment Brief for Unit 2 and the Sample Assessment Materials for Unit 1 used with permission from Edexcel Limited.

Every effort has been made to contact copyright holders of material reproduced in this book. Any omissions will be rectified in subsequent printings if notice is given to the publishers.

Websites
There are links to relevant websites in this book. In order to ensure that the links are up to date, that the links work, and that the sites are not inadvertently linked to sites that could be considered offensive, we have made the links available on the Heinemann website www.heinemann.co.uk/hotlinks. When you access the site, the express code is 6145P. Alternatively, you can access them from the ActiveTeach CD-ROMs.

Disclaimer
This material has been published on behalf of Edexcel and offers high-quality support for the delivery of Edexcel qualifications.

This does not mean that the material is essential to achieve any Edexcel qualification, nor does it mean that it is the only suitable material available to support any Edexcel qualification. Edexcel material will not be used verbatim in setting any Edexcel examination or assessment. Any resource lists produced by Edexcel shall include this and other appropriate resources.

Copies of official specifications for all Edexcel qualifications may be found on the Edexcel website: www.edexcel.com.

Contents

Introduction

Welcome to Edexcel GCSE ICT!

Our GCSE in ICT is designed to help you become a confident user of ICT. We have chosen interesting topics that are relevant to your life, and placed more emphasis on 'doing' rather than just 'writing about' ICT. You will learn how to use ICT knowledgeably, effectively and safely in all aspects of your daily life. Nowadays being a savvy user of ICT is non-negotiable and this GCSE ICT will give you the edge. We hope you will enjoy taking this course and have fun showing what you can do. Good luck!

Ann Weidmann, Head of ICT, Edexcel

A note for students

How will I be assessed?

This book supports Unit 1 Living in a Digital World and Unit 2 Using Digital Tools of the Edexcel specification.

- Unit 1 makes up 40% of your final marks and will be assessed by a 90-minute written exam. The exam contains five compulsory questions made up of different question types including multiple-choice, short answer, open-ended short answer and extended writing questions.
- Unit 2 makes up 60% of your final mark. You will have up to 40 hours to complete a Controlled Assessment task. The brief for this task is provided by Edexcel. The task is broken down into a number of activities and will include research and information gathering, modelling, digital publishing and evaluation.

A note for teachers

These resources have been written to support Edexcel's new specification for GCSE ICT (for first teaching in 2010). The Student Book covers Units 1 and 2 of the specification, which make up the Single award.

Written by experienced authors and examiners, and packed with exam tips and activities, the Student Book includes lots of engaging features to enthuse students and provide the range of support needed to make teaching and learning a success for all ability levels.

The *Edexcel GCSE ICT Teacher Resource with ActiveTeach CD-ROM* is a powerful electronic teaching and learning resource designed to support the Student Book. The Teacher Resource contains two CD-ROMs: a student one and a teacher one. The student CD-ROM is a networkable CD which will allow your students to access all the electronic resources (worksheets, files, interactive activities, weblinks, video tutorials) referred to in the Student Book from selected Student Book pages. The teacher CD-ROM is a full ActiveTeach product and you can see details of what it includes below under the heading 'What's in the Teacher Resource?'

As required by the QCDA, Functional ICT Skills are embedded within the Edexcel GCSE ICT specification, however, assessment is separate and students would need to take a different test to achieve a Functional Skills qualification.

In this Student Book, Skills builder activities give students the opportunity to practise both Functional Skills and those skills they need for the GCSE ICT Unit 2 Controlled Assessment Brief.

What's in the Teacher Resource?

The student CD-ROM contains links to all the electronic resources referred to in the Student Book. The teacher CD-ROM includes all lesson plans on screen, as well as:

- an electronic copy of the Student Book within the planning tab
- a glossary
- schemes of work
- editable lesson plans
- editable worksheets
- chapter overview, learning outcome and teaching presentations

- peer and self assessment presentations
- engaging interactive activities
- video tutorials
- useful weblinks

- ResultsPlus activities which combine exam-type questions with examiner insight and advice
- ExamZone which provides revision support.

What's in this Student Book?

In each chapter of this book you will find the following features:

- *An introductory spread* which introduces the theme of the chapter.
- *An overview spread* which lists the topics covered, the learning outcomes, the relevant Functional Skills criteria and all the electronic files you will need in the chapter (see Electronic components below for more details).
- *Topic spreads* containing the following features:
  - › *Learning outcomes* for the topic.
  - › *Key terms* emboldened for easy reference – a full glossary can be found on both the Teacher Resource and the Student CD-ROM.
  - › A range of activities including:
    - – *Starter activities* to get students thinking about the topic.
    - – *Tasks* in Unit 1 that allow students to practice what they have learned and extend their knowledge further.
    - – *Skills builders* require students to complete more practical ICT activites that are more closely linked to the types of activities they will complete in Unit 2 and in the Controlled Assessment Brief (CAB).
    - – *Knowledge checks* in Unit 1 to reinforce learning and to highlight any areas that need more work.
    - – *Discussion and exam-style questions* provide stimulating tasks for the classroom and for homework.
  - › *Be safe/be efficient* tips to raise awareness of health and safety risks and to encourage students to use devices responsibly and safely.
  - › *In practice* boxes give helpful tips on using ICT in the real world.
  - › *Did you know* features provide interesting ICT facts and figures.
  - › *ResultsPlus* features offer exam advice based on how students tend to perform in ICT exams. They offer expert advice and guidance from examiners to show students how to achieve better results in their exam. There are three different types of ResultsPlus features used throughout Unit 1:
    - – *Examiner's tip!* These provide examiner advice and guidance to help improve results.
    - – *Watch out!* These warn you about mistakes that examiners frequently see students make, as well as common misconceptions. Make sure that you don't repeat them!
    - – *Maximise your marks* These give advice on how to score the best marks in the ICT exam.
- *Examzone spreads* provide a recap of the chapter's learning outcomes followed by a sample exam question with examiner tips on how to answer the question, the sorts of points that should be included in your answer and common mistakes made by students.

Weblinks

As well as being able to access all of the weblinks via the student CD-ROM (which is part of the Teacher Resource), you can also access them via the Pearson Hotlinks site. Go to http://www.pearsonhotlinks.co.uk/ and enter express code 6145P to see a list of all weblinks referred to in this book.

ResultsPlus
Examiner's tip!

Computers connect to a network in two main ways: using a wired connection or using a wireless connection (WiFi). In the exam, you may be asked to identify which method is most appropriate in a particular scenario. Remember that while WiFi is often more convenient, speeds can be much slower.

ResultsPlus
Watch out!

Correct answers to this question, worth one mark, involve backing up or transferring data to another device. Beware of referring to 'additional storage' as this in the question.

ResultsPlus
Maximise your marks

In the exam you may be asked to recommend the most appropriate digital devices for a given scenario. Satya and Simon want to stay in touch with family and friends as well as taking photographs. A digital phone with a good range of features, including digital camera and ability to communicate using voice, text, photographs and videos would allow them to do everything they want to be able to do on a short trip. You will be asked to **explain** or **discuss** your recommendations but think carefully because your explanation will depend on the scenario.

Unit 1
Living in a Digital World

Overview

This unit helps you to prepare for the exam at the end of Unit 1 – you can use the book to refer to while you work or discuss different issues in class.

The book works alongside digital files that can be saved onto your computer system. You will launch the digital assets such as quizzes, interactive activities and websites from pages that look like these in your book.

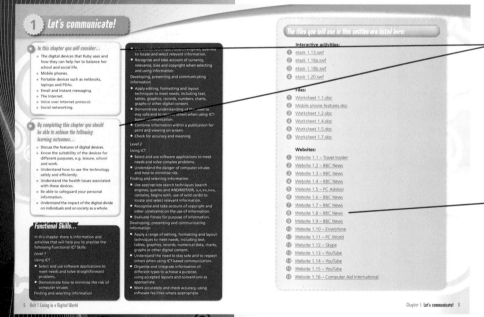

At the beginning of each chapter you will see what you will be learning about and what you should know by the end of the chapter.

The digital assets that you will be using in the chapter will be listed here. You can access them on the computer. When you need to work on a digital asset, you will see this symbol in the book.

e-component

Each chapter has a theme:

1 Let's communicate!

2 On the move

3 Entertain me – what to buy?

4 Smart working

5 Shopping experience!

6 Let's revise! Health and well-being

and a character who needs your help, like Krista.

Examzone

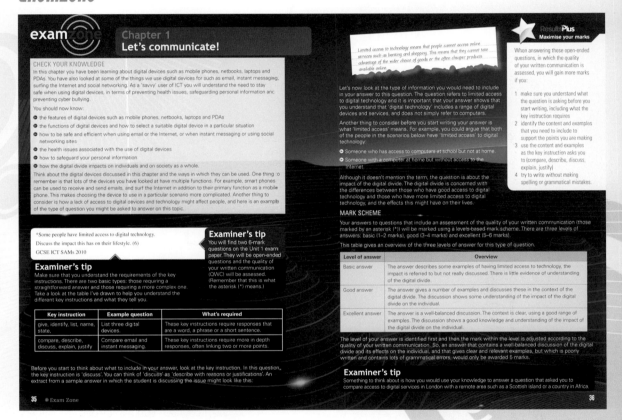

As you go through the book you will see pages like this, which help you to understand how to give the best possible answers in the Unit 1 exam.

ResultsPlus

The ResultsPlus boxes you find throughout Unit 1 contain advice from an examiner on how to get as many marks as you can in the exam. This advice includes tips on understanding what the question is asking and the kind of answer you need to give in order to do well.

1 Let's communicate!

Should I work on the group

Should I do some preparation/research?

Should I go on instant messager?

Should I listen to music?

Should I go out with my friends?

Should I watch TV?

work set by my teacher?

Should I do my homework?

Should I play games?

Should I revise for my exams?

Ruby is a teenage girl who lives at home with her family – they are all big users of technology. She does well at school and is a popular girl, but her social life is affecting her grades. She wants you to help her to make some important decisions about how she can use technology to help benefit her social life and her school life. She knows that the decisions she makes now could affect the rest her life.

Here is a summary of Ruby:

Name: Ruby Jones

Age: 15

Studying: GCSEs

Siblings: 2 (brother Daniel and sister Chloe)

Digital devices: smart phone and netbook

Think about how you use technology to help with your school work and in your social life. Make a list of the devices that you use for each.

1 Let's communicate!

In this chapter you will consider...

- The digital devices that Ruby uses and how they can help her to balance her school and social life.
- Mobile phones.
- Portable devices such as netbooks, laptops and PDAs.
- Email and instant messaging.
- The Internet.
- Voice over Internet protocol.
- Social networking.

By completing this chapter you should be able to achieve the following learning outcomes...

- Discuss the features of digital devices.
- Know the suitability of the devices for different purposes, e.g. leisure, school and work.
- Understand how to use the technology safely and efficiently.
- Understand the health issues associated with these devices.
- Be able to safeguard your personal information.
- Understand the impact of the digital divide on individuals and on society as a whole.

Functional Skills...

In this chapter there is information and activities that will help you to practise the following Functional ICT Skills:

Level 1

Using ICT

- Select and use software applications to meet needs and solve straightforward problems.
- Demonstrate how to minimise the risk of computer viruses.

Finding and selecting information

- Use search techniques (search engines, queries) to locate and select relevant information.
- Recognise and take account of currency, relevance, bias and copyright when selecting and using information.

Developing, presenting and communicating information

- Apply editing, formatting and layout techniques to meet needs, including text, tables, graphics, records, numbers, charts, graphs or other digital content.
- Demonstrate understanding of the need to stay safe and to respect others when using ICT-based communication.
- Combine information within a publication for print and viewing on-screen.
- Check for accuracy and meaning.

Level 2

Using ICT

- Select and use software applications to meet needs and solve complex problems.
- Understand the danger of computer viruses and how to minimise risk.

Finding and selecting information

- Use appropriate search techniques (search engines, queries and AND/NOT/OR, >,<,>=,><=, contains, begins with, use of wild cards) to locate and select relevant information.
- Recognise and take account of copyright and other constraints on the use of information.
- Evaluate fitness for purpose of information.

Developing, presenting and communicating information

- Apply a range of editing, formatting and layout techniques to meet needs, including text, tables, graphics, records, numerical data, charts, graphs or other digital content.
- Understand the need to stay safe and to respect others when using ICT-based communication.
- Organise and integrate information of different types to achieve a purpose, using accepted layouts and conventions as appropriate.
- Work accurately and check accuracy, using software facilities where appropriate.

The files you will use in this section are listed here:

Interactive activities:

1. etask 1.13.swf
2. etask 1.18a.swf
3. etask 1.18b.swf
4. etask 1.20.swf

Files:

1. Worksheet 1.1.doc
2. Mobile phone features.doc
3. Worksheet 1.2.doc
4. Worksheet 1.4.doc
5. Worksheet 1.5.doc
6. Worksheet 1.7.doc

Websites:

1. Website 1.1 – Travel Insider
2. Website 1.2 – BBC News
3. Website 1.3 – BBC News
4. Website 1.4 – BBC News
5. Website 1.5 – PC Advisor
6. Website 1.6 – BBC News
7. Website 1.7 – BBC News
8. Website 1.8 – BBC News
9. Website 1.9 – BBC News
10. Website 1.10 – Envirofone
11. Website 1.11 – PC World
12. Website 1.12 – Skype
13. Website 1.13 – YouTube
14. Website 1.14 – YouTube
15. Website 1.15 – YouTube
16. Website 1.16 – Computer Aid International

What can your phone do?

Learn about

- mobile phones
- features of mobile phones
- ways of connecting mobile phones
- how to select a suitable phone for your needs

Have you ever thought what life would be like on a desert island without technology? Or what life was like 100 years ago? Some of the technologies that affect every aspect of our everyday lives have only been around for a very short time. For example, the boom in mobile phones only started in the 1990s when the technology became cheap enough for most people to afford.

Starter

Do you agree that mobile phones are 'must-have' devices? Discuss this with a partner and think of three reasons for your answer.

Task 1.1

How much do you know about mobile phones? Test your knowledge as a class.

Figure 1.1 Early mobile phones were heavy to carry around and could only make and receive calls. The latest phones are smaller and slimmer and have many functions

Did you know?

Around 80% of British adults own or regularly use a mobile phone according to figures gathered by the Office for National Statistics.

As mobile phones developed, they got lighter. Older mobile phones are now known as 'bricks' because of their size and weight.

A three megapixel camera is as much as you will need to print a picture up to A4 size. Only if you intend to take pictures and enlarge them to poster size will you need a higher-resolution camera.

Mobile phones were originally developed to make and receive calls, but they have now developed into **smart phones**. These can be used for purposes that were never imagined when they were first launched, such as taking pictures or using the Internet. A smart phone is an example of a **multifunctional** device.

> *Smart phone* – a phone offering advanced features, e.g. the ability to send emails, surf the Internet.
>
> *Multifunctional* – having the ability to do many different things using the same device.

Bluetooth   MP3 player   Memory card   USB port   Roaming   Voice recorder

MMS   Alarm   Predictive text

Loudspeaker   Games   Email   Internet

WiFi   3G   Camcorder   Radio

Hands-free device   Network band

Touchscreen   SMS   Calculator

Video calling   GPS   Camera   Memo

Internal memory   Personal organiser

Figure 1.2 Some of the latest features of mobile phones

Task 1.2

Think about the mobile phone you would most like to own. On **Worksheet 1.1** list all the things you think you would use the phone for – sending texts, taking pictures, setting reminders, etc.

When your list is complete, rank the entries in terms of which you think you would use most often, where 1 = most often. Record your ranking in the table on **Worksheet 1.1**.

Discuss your answers in class. Does everyone agree on the features they would use most often or are there big differences of opinion?

Choosing a phone

Even if you know which features you want on your phone, how do you choose between the hundreds available? The following information will help you when deciding between the different phones on offer.

- **Picture resolution** – refers to the quality and detail that can be shown on the screen of the mobile. The higher the resolution, the better the quality of the image displayed on-screen. This is measured in pixels.
- **Camera resolution** – the amount of detail that the camera picks up in one picture. The higher the resolution, the more detail the camera picks up, but this means that the picture files can be very big. The resolution is measured in megapixels (MP).

Be safe/be efficient

When making a phone call, if you do not want the other person to see your number you can withhold it.

For your own security you can have a lock set up on the phone to prevent unauthorised access.

If you register your phone and it gets stolen, you can report it to your network provider. They can block the phone, making it unusable.

SD and SDHC cards – Secure Digital (SD) cards are one type of flash memory card which store up to 2 GB of data. Secure Digital High Capacity (SDHC) cards are another type of flash memory card and they are ideal for video cameras because they can store up to 32 GB of data.

File format – the particular code that a file is stored in. Different software and devices use different formats, which can cause problems if a device cannot decode the information.

Compatible – the ability of a device to communicate and share information with another device.

Bluetooth – allows the exchange of data over short distances from fixed and mobile devices. In order for devices to communicate they must be able to understand the Bluetooth rules (protocols).

WiFi – wireless fidelity. It is similar to Bluetooth in that it is used to exchange data, but the signals can travel further distances.

- **Storage capacity** – the amount of space the phone has in its internal memory to store applications, pictures, sounds, videos, etc. This is measured in gigabytes (GB).
- **Memory card** – a secondary storage device that allows users to store, back up, copy and remove their files. Users can choose an appropriate card size according to what they are using them for. Different devices have different size and shape memory cards. **SD** or **SDHC** cards are commonly used, but there are others. Memory card size is measured in gigabytes (GB), as shown in the table below.

Number of pictures or videos a memory card will store given different capacities

Camera	File size*	Memory card capacity* (number of pictures/ videos stored)			
		2 GB	4 GB	8 GB	16 GB
3 MP	1.01 MB	2,000	4,000	7,238	14,476
5 MP	1.5 MB	1,200	2,500	5,100	10,300
6 MP	1.7 MB	1,100	2,200	4,400	8,900
8 MP	2.3 MB	800	1,650	3,200	6,650
10 MP	2.9 MB	650	1,300	2,600	5,200
Video	5 Mbps (EP)	45	90	180	360

*average file size for a high resolution JPEG

Lexar Media

Music and video player

Music and video players are a standard feature of many phones. The music and video files are stored in different formats, e.g. MP3 and WAV for music and MP4, 3GP, AVI for video. Different phones allow you to play different **file formats** which may or may not be **compatible** with your computer.

Connectivity

To connect to the Internet or share information with other phones, mobile phones need to be able to send and receive signals. As the phone is a 'mobile' device, it needs to be able to connect wirelessly. The most common ways of connecting devices (e.g. phones, routers, computers) to each other are **Bluetooth** and **WiFi**.

If you want to access your online email accounts, your phone needs to support POP3 or IMAP4. POP3 allows you to download your inbox and IMAP4 allows you to view your entire inbox and subfolders. In order to communicate effectively, the devices need to be compatible.

Task 1.3

Your friends want a copy of a photo you took on a day out in London. It is common to send images between phones via an MMS but imagine that this service is down and you cannot use this method. Your task is to send the picture from your phone (A) to all your friends' phones without using MMS. Discuss different ways of getting the picture to each of the phones using only the features specified in the table on the next page.

Feature	Your mobile (A)	Person B's mobile	Person C's mobile	Person D's mobile	Person E's mobile	Person F's mobile
Bluetooth	✔	✔	✗	✗	✗	✔
Memory card	✔	✗	✔	✗	✔	✔
Internet access	✔	✗	✔	✔	✗	✗
Infrared	✗	✔	✔	✗	✗	✗
USB connection	✗	✗	✗	✔	✔	✗

Network band

Mobile phones operate on different frequencies in different countries. To be able to connect with a phone on a different frequency, the phone needs to be able to receive one or more frequencies. A phone can be:

- dual band – picking up 2 frequencies
- tri band – picking up 3 frequencies
- quad band – picking up 4 frequencies.

Having a quad-band phone allows you to use it in five different continents.

Task

 e-component

Look at **Website 1.1** for more details of where you can use phones with different frequencies. You can find further information in the information sheet **Mobile phone features**.

Skills builder 1.1

Use the Internet to find a phone that Ruby could use to help her:

- communicate with and share information with her friends
- organise her school work.

First decide what Ruby will want to use her phone for. Then decide which features she will need to do these things. Then find the phone that best delivers them. You must be able to give reasons for your choices. Discuss your suggestions with the class and decide together on the best phone for Ruby.

Exam question

Many mobile phones have a memory card for extra storage. Give another use for this memory card. (1)

Results Plus
Watch out!

Correct answers to this question, worth one mark, involve backing up or transferring data to another device. Beware of referring to 'additional storage' as this is in the question.

Knowledge check

1. What are the differences between dual-band, tri-band and quad-band phones?
2. Why do mobile phones have features that not everyone uses?
3. What is the advantage of having a memory card slot/feature built into a phone?
4. Name two of the different ways of connecting devices to a mobile phone.

Designing a mobile phone

Learn about

- ways in which people use mobile phones in their everyday lives
- the differences in user interface and designs of phones

Ruby is entering a competition to design a new mobile phone and the deadline is looming, so she would like your help with ideas and suggestions. Mobile phones have a range of uses, and Ruby uses hers both for school work and in her social life.

Figure 1.3 Mobile phones have a range of uses for both school work and social life

Starter

In pairs, create two spider diagrams. One should show all the phone features Ruby might use for school work, and the other should include all the phone features Ruby might use in her social life.

Did you identify all of the ways that Ruby could use a mobile phone? Did you think of any more?

Mobile phone batteries

The battery life of mobile phones is becoming increasingly important as they include more and more features needing increasing amounts of power.

Task 1.5

Ruby finds that her mobile phone battery is lasting longer for some activities than others. Rank these activities in order of energy consumption from those that use the most energy to those that use the least:

- surfing the Internet
- watching Internet TV
- talking to friends
- sending text messages
- taking photos
- using the calculator to keep tabs on her finances
- using the **GPS** when meeting friends.

Mobile phone designs

The design and **user interface** of a device is extremely important to consider. Mobile phone manufacturers have to take into account all of their users and try to meet their needs. This is why there are many different types of phones available.

Global positioning system (GPS) – a navigational system used in many devices which gives current location, directions from current location to specified destination and distance from current location to specified destination using signals from satellites. Assisted GPS (AGPS) is a technology that has been built into mobile phones. When the signal between a mobile phone and satellites is weak (as is the case in some urban areas and enclosed spaces), the signal sent by the mobile phone is diverted to mobile masts which identify the phone's exact location and allow the user to carry on using the feature.

User interface – the way in which a user interacts with a system such as a computer or mobile phone, e.g. keypad, screens, menu and icons.

Task 1.6

With a partner discuss the things that you would need to think about if you were designing a mobile phone. Why is it important to consider the audience for the phone? Share your ideas with the whole class.

There are different phones available for different purposes.

FASHION PHONES

These can be different shapes and have the ability to be customised, e.g. change the fascias. Buttons may be in odd places and may be inconvenient to use. They can be bright colours and highly designed, appealing to the fashion-conscious person.

Features often include high-spec cameras, the ability to store large amounts of data like photos and videos, and speakers that allow music to be played out loud. The batteries are designed to last longer but can be bulky, often making the phone larger.

BUSINESS PHONES

These use a slim, sleek design, usually in black or metallic colours. They have large screens and an integrated, full qwerty keyboard.

Features often include speaker phone, voice-activated dialling, the ability to synchronise it with other devices like netbooks and laptops, large screens to enable work on data files, GPS to get the user to unfamiliar destinations with ease, camera, personal digital assistant (PDA), and 3G compatibility for Internet access – allowing users to carry one device rather than many.

MULTIFUNCTIONAL PHONES

These combine both style and business features, appealing to the mass market rather than a niche. They have the best of both worlds: high-spec features, large amounts of storage, high-speed processing, slim design with touch screens and access to the Internet.

Task 1.7

e-component

All products are designed with an audience in mind. What kind of people do you think fashion, business and multifunctional phones are aimed at? On **Worksheet 1.2** create a profile for the typical user of each phone type. Do you match any of the profiles you have created? Which profile do you think Ruby matches?

Task 1.8

Ruby wants her mobile phone design to be for a new audience. Can you think of a group of people for whom mobile phones don't already cater?

Knowledge check

1 Which features on a mobile phone might cause the battery charge to be used up quickly?

2 Give three advantages of having GPS built into a mobile phone.

3 Give three features on multifunctional phones that could help with work.

4 Give three features on multifunctional phones that could help in your social life.

Mobile phones for everyone?

Learn about
- the impact that age, gender and disability have on the choice of device
- the health, safety and security risks when using phones

Ruby has noticed that her gran finds her mobile phone too fiddly and difficult to use. Ruby realises that the design is not suitable for her gran. Figure 1.4 shows a list of the things Ruby might need to consider if she designed a phone for her gran's age group.

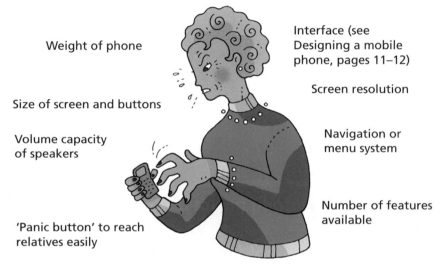

Weight of phone

Interface (see Designing a mobile phone, pages 11–12)

Screen resolution

Size of screen and buttons

Volume capacity of speakers

Navigation or menu system

Number of features available

'Panic button' to reach relatives easily

Figure 1.4 Points to consider when designing a phone aimed at elderly people

Did you know?

People aged 15–34 are more likely to have a mobile phone than any other age group.

Every year, in the UK, 800,000 people have their phones stolen. More than 50% of street crime involves a mobile phone.

Approximately 80,000 unintentional 999 calls are made by mobile phone users in the UK and this number is rising.

Starter

With a partner, think of another group of people who may not be able to use an average mobile phone. How would you adapt the phone for them?

Pros and cons of mobile phones

Ruby's brother, Daniel, is 10 years old. Their parents are undecided about whether he should have a mobile phone. Here are some of their worries:

- Texting too much can lead to **repetitive strain injury (RSI)**.
- Mobile phones have not been around for very long, so scientists are unsure of the risks associated with using them. As a precautionary measure, government health advisers recommend that children under 16 should not use mobile phones regularly.
- Overuse of 'text speak' could have an impact on his ability to spell words correctly.
- Young people can be the victims of bullying and crime if they are targeted for their phone.

Too much texting can lead to RSI

Task

Can you think of any more concerns about a 10-year-old having a mobile phone?

Task 1.10

e-component

Ruby's parents would like you to help them make up their minds by finding out the advantages and disadvantages of using mobile phones.

Have a look at some news reports about mobile phones. There are several articles on this subject for you to look at – see **Websites 1.2– 1.9**.

What advice would you give to Ruby's parents about young people using mobile phones?

Write a review of mobile phones telling them both the positive and the negative aspects. Use some or all of the headings below to help you structure your report.

> Communicating with others; Invasion of privacy; Crime; Peace of mind; Changes to the landscape; Environmental cost; **Etiquette**; Cost

---

Repetitive strain injury (RSI) – damage caused to the muscles, tendons, ligaments, nerves or joints, usually because of repeating the same action.

Etiquette – a set of rules that people try to abide by out of respect for other people around them.

Public domain – materials that are available for anyone to use for any purpose (not subject to laws of copyright).

Be safe/be efficient
Mobile phone etiquette and safety advice

If you have a mobile phone, here are some basic rules that you should try to follow:

✔ Mobile phones can be expensive and are an easy target for thieves. You should activate the lock feature which requires a PIN.

✔ If you take a video or photo of someone on your phone, you should ask for their permission before you upload it to a **public domain**.

✔ Try to avoid using phones in quiet places, e.g. quiet coaches on trains and in libraries.

✔ Recycle your old phone if you can.

✔ As on the Internet, you should avoid viewing content that is unsuitable for your age range.

✔ You should not send malicious messages or make prank calls. This could lead to the police charging you with harassment.

✔ When you are driving a vehicle, it is illegal to talk on the phone without a hands-free kit.

✔ You should activate the keypad lock on your phone to prevent accidental emergency calls being made.

Exam question

Some people find it difficult to use a mobile phone. State two features that can make a phone easier to use. **(2)**

ResultsPlus
Examiner's tip!

In this question you are asked to state **two** features for **two** marks, obviously **one** mark per feature. So it is important to state **two** features. Writing a lot about one feature will still only gain one mark. Answers such as these would gain one mark each:

- being able to set a louder ring tone
- larger keys
- having only basic functions like being able to make and receive calls.

In practice

e-component

Disposing of old mobile phones

When you are ready to replace your mobile phone you should recycle your old one.

Some companies reuse the components. Others refurbish phones and sell them for a cheap price to people in developing countries.

For more information look at **Website 1.10**.

Which kind of computer?

Learn about

- the difference between desktop and portable computers
- how you can make decisions about whether a computer will meet your needs
- the different devices that you can connect to your computer

Ruby has done well in her studies and her parents want to reward her. They have decided to buy her a laptop, as they think it will be a good incentive to continue working hard.

Starter

Carry out a quick survey in class. Do most people prefer laptops or desktop computers, and why? Then complete **Worksheet 1.4**.

Desktop computers are designed for regular use in one location, such as a desk. Ruby has decided she would like a portable computer as it is more flexible.

Types of portable computers

Ruby and her parents are looking at the different types of computer:

- **Laptop** – a **portable computer** designed to fit on the lap (although most people use them on a table or desk). It carries out the same functions as a desktop computer but in a compact version that is light enough to be carried around.
- **Notebook** – similar to a laptop but even more compact. The name comes from its small size, comparing it with the size of a notebook.
- **Netbook** – similar to a notebook but designed mainly for wireless communication via email, messaging and access to the Internet. A netbook is usually cheaper and has a lower **specification** compared to laptops and notebooks. They increasingly have solid state memory.
- **Personal digital assistant (PDA)** – a portable device that is small enough to hold in the palm of a hand. It usually contains an address book, note-making features, telephone and Internet facilities. It allows data to be exchanged with computers.

Did you know?

The size of a terabyte

1 kilobyte (KB) = ½ page of text

1 megabyte (MB) = 500 pages or 1 thick book

1 gigabyte (GB) = 500,000 pages or 1,000 thick books

1 terabyte (TB) = 1,000,000 thick books

Some portable devices have specially designed processors called mobile processors. They use less power and switch off when not being used, therefore producing less heat and saving energy (battery power).

Task 1.11

Would a desktop or a portable computer be most suitable for the following people, and why?

- teacher
- news reporter
- website designer
- doctor (in a GP surgery)
- traffic warden.

Desktop

Laptop

Notebook

Netbook

PDA

Figure 1.5 Ruby can choose from a range of computers

Buying a computer

When buying a computer, you need to consider all of the following features.

PROCESSOR (CPU)

This is the brains of the computer – it does all the calculating. The number of calculations it carries out (processes) is measured in gigahertz (GHz). The higher the processing speed, the faster the computer but the more power it uses. This is an important consideration when buying a portable device.

MEMORY

This usually refers to RAM (Random Access Memory), which is the temporary memory that the computer uses. RAM is used to run the programs that are open on the computer. The higher the RAM, the more programs you can have open at any one time and the faster they will respond. If the power fails, the temporary memory is lost – that's why you lose unsaved work when the computer is switched off. You need to consider what you will be using your computer for, as graphics and videos require more RAM.

HARD DRIVE SIZE

The hard drive is the **primary storage** area of the computer. It is where the software, files and data are kept and where they are retrieved from. The size of the hard drive is measured in bytes – usually in gigabytes. The bigger the hard drive, the more data can be stored.

WIRELESS ENABLED

This allows the device to pick up WiFi signals, enabling you to connect to a **network**, connect devices together and access the Internet without wires. Data exchanged wirelessly is slower than data travelling though a cable. This is because data can be distorted as it travels through the air by other signals and interference travelling though the same air space. This can cause unwanted glitches and freezes in programs.

Sometimes signals may not be able to travel through walls, or certain locations may be out of range. This is an important consideration when using WiFi – the alternative is to use a cabled connection.

USB CONNECTION

USB (Universal Serial Bus) is the most common method of connecting devices to a computer. Because many **peripherals** use this type of connection, it is good if the computer has many USB ports.

SOUND CARD/GRAPHICS CARD

These are devices that fix to the computer's main circuit (the motherboard), allowing computers to play and record sound and display graphics. Different cards will enhance the sound and graphics, so if you use a lot of graphics, videos, music or games, this is an important factor to consider.

OPTICAL DRIVE

The optical drive uses lasers to read data encoded on CDs and DVDs. This allows you to install **software**, listen to music and watch films with ease. Some optical drives also allow CDs/DVDs to be written (burned) – this is useful if you want to transfer information from your device.

Did you know?

A cabled network is more reliable than a wireless network because there is little interference from other household devices.

Solid state drives are becoming more popular as they have no moving parts and are less likely to fail than normal hard drives which have moving parts. They also help conserve battery power.

Desktop computer – a stationary computer, usually consisting of a tower and separate monitor. It is generally more powerful and has a larger storage capacity than a portable computer.

Portable computer – designed to allow the user to use the computer on the move, e.g. laptop, notebook, netbook and PDA.

Specification (spec) – the technical details of a device or system.

Primary storage – built-in storage designed to be directly accessed by the central processing unit (CPU).

Network – devices connected together to allow communication and exchange of data.

Peripherals – external devices connected to a computer, e.g. printer, microphone.

Software – programs that give instructions to a computer and which allow the user to carry out different tasks.

Be safe/be efficient

To conserve (save) power:

- Do not play multimedia like computer games, music or DVDs.
- Reduce screen brightness.
- Change the power options and allow the computer to turn off certain parts when inactive, e.g. turn monitor off after 10 minutes of inactivity.
- Copy files CD/DVDs on to the hard drive and run them from there. This typically consumes less power than an optical drive.
- Turn off WiFi and Bluetooth when you are not using them.
- Disconnect devices that are not being used.
- Use earphones instead of listening though speakers.

Task 1.12

These people use their computers for different things:

a) Person A stores lots of films and music.

b) Person B enjoys playing computer games.

c) Person C likes connecting devices wirelessly.

d) Person D uses powerful programs.

e) Person E produces videos and copies them to a CD.

Which feature(s) would be most important to them? Choose from those shown in Figure 1.6.

Can you think of any more features they might find important?

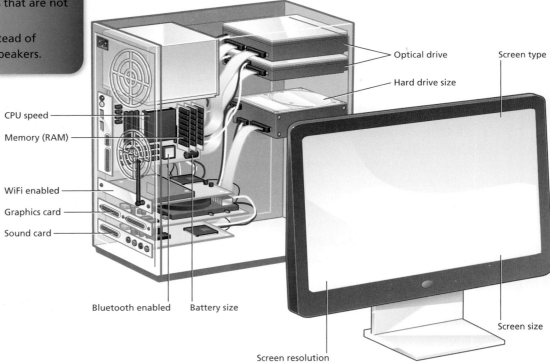

Figure 1.6 Features to consider when choosing a computer

In practice

When buying a computer, desktop, laptop, PDA, netbook or notebook always use a price comparison website to get yourself a good deal. It's also worth paying attention to:

- processor speed – the quicker it is, the faster your device will work
- amount of RAM – the more RAM it has, the more applications it will be able to support
- storage capacity – the more storage you have, the more files you can save
- battery life (of portable device) – how long will the power last?

Peripherals

Ruby has chosen a laptop with the following spec. It is a mid-range one, but she wants to add to it.

Processor	Intel Centrino 2 GHz
Memory	2 GB
Hard drive	150 GB
Wireless	WiFi enabled
Operating system	Windows Vista Home Premium
USB	2 × USB ports

Ruby has bought the following peripherals to go with her laptop: printer, scanner, webcam, microphone, speakers, memory card reader, USB hub, wireless router.

Peripherals can be divided into input, output and storage devices:

- **Input devices** take new information and put it into the computer, ready for the computer to process, e.g. keyboard, mouse, scanner, microphone.
- **Output devices** allow you to view or hear information after it has been processed, e.g. printer, speaker, monitor.
- **Storage devices/media** allow you to store data so that it can be accessed by the computer, e.g. hard drive, CD-R, DVD-R, flash memory cards.

Task 1.13

 e-component

Do **etask 1.13** to check your knowledge of which peripherals are input, output and storage devices.

Task 1.14

e-component

Choose one person from Task 1.11.

Which type of computer would you recommend for this person?

What spec would you recommend for this person?

Use Website 1.11 to recommend a computer and justify your decision.

Technology is always advancing, so something that is top of the range today might be considered bottom of the range in a couple of years' time. When buying a new computer you should try to **future proof** it as much as you can.

Knowledge check

1 Name three portable devices.
2 Give three advantages of portable computers and three disadvantages.
3 Give three advantages of desktop computers and three disadvantages.
4 Peripherals can be split into three categories – name them and describe the difference.

Future proofing – anticipating future developments when you buy something in the hope that it will not go out of date quickly. Future proofing can be expensive, as buying something top of the range will cost more than if you wait a short while.

ResultsPlus
Examiner's tip!

The selection of a computer that meets the needs of a particular user or scenario should be based on three main criteria: cost, weight and functionality, linked to the target context. For a given functionality, the smaller and lighter machines are more expensive. They are also less suitable for use over extended periods at a time.

Socialising on the Internet

Learn about

- how computers can be used for communicating
- the advantages and disadvantages of instant messaging, VoIP and social networking

Ruby is very confident with technology – she can see the benefits of it and uses it to enhance her social life. There are many options available to her for keeping in touch with friends, family and interest groups – look at Figure 1.7 to see the ones Ruby uses.

Figure 1.7 Using the Internet to keep in touch

Real time – the actual time during which something takes place, without noticeable delays.

Emoticon – the use of icons or text to portray mood or facial expression, e.g :) when happy and :(when sad.

VoIP (Voice over Internet Protocol) – this technology is used to make telephone calls via the Internet, usually at a cheaper cost.

3G – third-generation wireless communication allows high-speed wireless data transfer.

Latency – the time delay between the moment something is initiated and the moment it becomes detectable.

Internet service provider (ISP) – a company that provides Internet access to its customers.

Starter

How do you keep in contact with friends and family? List all the different types of technology that you use. Which ways are best for which types of communication?

Instant messaging (IM)

This is a form of real-time communication between two or more people that enables them to have a 'virtual' conversation. IM involves 'talking' to someone in **real time** by typing and receiving messages.

It is popular because it allows:

- quick and easy communication in real time
- people to work collaboratively and discuss their views
- the user to see who is online and decide if they want to engage in a conversation – you are able to set the status so that people know if you are available to talk or busy
- use through certain mobile phones, PDAs and other portable devices.

DISADVANTAGES OF IM

- You need Internet access to use IM.
- If the connection is slow, this could impact on the real-time feature.

- Overuse of IM could result in less face-to-face contact with people.
- People may misunderstand information as it lacks emotion – to combat this, **emoticons** have been invented.
- If you use text language regularly, it could affect your writing skills.
- You may prefer to chat rather than type a message.

VoIP (Voice over Internet Protocol)

This is similar to IM on a computer, but sound rather than text is sent. It is just like making a telephone call.

Ruby's friends were getting large phone bills using their mobiles, so they switched to using **VoIP**. They can use this feature when they have access to the Internet on their computers or in some cases on their mobiles. They can now talk without running up huge phone bills.

To use VoIP through a computer you need a headset or speakers and a microphone, and a webcam if you wish to stream video to the other caller. Mobile phones must have a **3G** or mobile Internet connection. If you are using a landline phone, it needs to be plugged into the Internet router.

Making calls this way is free, even international ones, but some VoIP service providers charge a membership or monthly fee.

Task **1.15**

An example of VoIP is Skype – see **Website 1.12**. Using the website, list the advantages/features of using VoIP.

Figure 1.8 You can get special handsets that plug in to your computer to allow you to use VoIP

DISADVANTAGES OF VOIP

- A slow Internet connection can cause a delay in the sound being received by the callers – this is known as **latency** and may spoil the experience.
- VoIP will only work with an Internet connection. If the **Internet service provider (ISP)** or the VoIP service provider is temporarily unavailable, then calls cannot be made.
- VoIP is designed to be used from anywhere in the world. Users do not have a geographical telephone number, e.g. area code then number. When people dial 999 from a home phone or a mobile, the emergency services can track down the signal, but with VoIP this is not always possible and could be a problem.

Social networking site – an online community where people can communicate and share information.

Link – allows users to navigate around a product. By clicking on a link, the user can 'jump' to a new screen.

Blog – short for 'web log', a shared online journal where people can post diary entries about their personal experiences and hobbies.

Social networking

Instant messaging and VoIP are great for communicating with just a few people, but what if you want to communicate with large numbers of people?

Ruby likes to use **social networking sites**. These websites are specially designed to bring together people who share interests. They also enable users to connect with friends, family and colleagues online. They provide a range of ways for users to interact, such as chat, messaging, email, video, voice, file sharing, blogging and discussion groups. Users can play games and quizzes that allow them to share information with each other.

Social networking is very popular; the websites are used by millions of people all over the world every day. Popular social networking sites include Facebook, MySpace, Bebo and Twitter. Some sites allow users to personalise their own space by adding photos, **links** and blogs, and by adapting the layout to their own individual style.

Figure 1.9 Two of the popular social networking sites

Task 1.16

e-component

Complete **Worksheet 1.5** by deciding whether each statement about social networking is an advantage or a disadvantage. Once you've sorted the advantages and disadvantages on the worksheet, try to think of some more.

Web page with a blog

Ruby has her own web page and a **blog** that she updates daily. She produces video content and uploads this on to her web page, which her friends and other Internet users can see. She has to be careful not to put personal information on the blog.

Task 1.17

Look at the following scenarios and think about what method of Internet communication would be best for each. Justify your choices.

a) Parents on holiday in Australia want to keep in contact with their son at home in the UK.

b) A group of friends are arranging a party for another friend.

c) A young person with a speech impairment wants to keep in contact with friends.

d) Members of an art group want to share pictures/information with each other.

e) A young woman travelling the world wants to write to tell people about her experiences.

f) A group of computer novices want to set up an online computer class.

Did you know?

Social bookmarking

Normal bookmarking can only been seen by you on your computer. But if you sign up to a social bookmarking website, this adds a button on to your web **browser**. When you add a website link this can be seen by other people who have subscribed to your social bookmarking. The use of tags (keywords) allows people to search for websites a lot faster than having to trawl through the whole of the Internet.

Social bookmarking can be used by friends to share their favourite websites or by teachers to share websites with their students. There is a simple explanation of social bookmarking available on **Website 1.13**.

Staying safe on the Internet

Ruby knows how to keep herself safe on the Internet. Her sister, Chloe, has started to use IM, chatrooms and social networking to communicate with her friends.

> *Browser* – a software application for retrieving, presenting and navigating information resources on the World Wide Web.

Task 1.18

e-component

Use **etasks 1.18a** and **1.18b** to test your knowledge of Internet and social networking safety.

Skills builder 1.2

Produce a digital poster for children or young teenagers, highlighting the dangers of communicating online and what they can do to avoid these dangers. Remember to use language and images that are suitable for your audience.

Task 1.19

Discuss with a partner what you would do in the following situations:

a) You have been chatting with another boy/girl and you want to meet up.

b) You are on a social networking site and see a rude picture.

c) You see pictures of someone that you do not get on with on a social networking site. There is an option for you to write something underneath the picture.

d) You notice that one of your friends has not protected their website, giving anyone access to see what is on their profile.

e) Your friend has been chatting to a girl for a while but does not believe she is actually who she says she is.

f) Your friend uses IM and webcam to talk to other friends. There is one person she chats to who never turns on his webcam, making the excuse that it does not work.

Knowledge check

1 What equipment do you need for VoIP?

2 Why is social networking popular?

Learn about

- the advantages and disadvantages of email
- different email protocols
- virtual learning environments and their advantages
- information sources such as user-generated websites, user-generated forums and news websites

Ruby wants to do well in her studies. She does most of her school work on the computer. We are going to look at ways in which the computer improves learning.

Starter

Think of as many ways in which technology can help with learning as you can.

Think of as many reasons why working on a computer may be better than working on paper as you can. What about any disadvantages?

Email

This is a popular method of communication. It involves sending messages over a communications network, such as the Internet, between computers and other devices. Email is a popular way of communicating in school.

Task 1.20

Make a list of the advantages and disadvantages of using email. Check your answers using **etask 1.20** and then add to your list any that you didn't think of yourself.

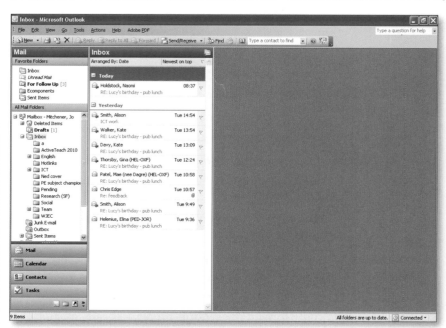

Figure 1.10 Microsoft Outlook inbox

Emails are now commonly accessible using mobile phones, laptops and other devices using wireless dongles which use 3G mobile network. This allows users to connect to the Internet without being close to a wireless router as it uses the mobile network.

Protocols

There are two types of common **protocol** used by email services providers: IMAP4 and POP3.

Task 12

Find out the differences between IMAP4 and POP3. Write a brief description of how each protocol works.

Virtual Learning Environments

There are many ways in which technology can help with education. For example, one tool Ruby uses to help her is the Virtual Learning Environment (VLE) at her school.

BENEFITS OF A VLE

- Teachers can put up detailed information about the lesson.
- Teachers can work collaboratively on courses to make them fun and interesting.
- It can include links so students can look up information in more detail if interested.
- Information and courses can be **personalised** for individual students.
- It can have interactive polls and questionnaires to engage the students.
- It can have notice boards for sharing information.
- Students can access their homework and submit assignments online, saving paper.
- Students can contribute to blogs and give their views and opinions.
- Students can do quizzes and get feedback so they can monitor their progress.
- Students have their own space which they can personalise.
- Email systems can be integrated into the VLE so that students use only one system rather than lots of different ones.
- Parents can access students' data shared by the school, such as attendance rates, homework marks and test results.

Spam – unwanted or junk email sent to lots of recipients at the same time.

Protocol – a set of rules used by computers to communicate with each other across a network. Without protocols, computers would not be able to communicate effectively.

Personalised learning – learning that is tailored towards the individual to allow them to make progress.

In practice

- If you always want the latest information, use RSS feeds. These will give you live updates direct to your desktop.
- Subscribe to podcasts which will download ready for you to watch or listen to.
- Subscribe to blogs and you will be notified when other members add information.
- Use social bookmarking and let others update you with the information you want to know.

The Internet

Ruby also uses the Internet to help with school work. She finds the Internet very useful for finding answers to questions and suggesting a range of websites that she can use to research topics. Here are some different types of websites that she finds useful.

USER-GENERATED WEBSITES

These websites, also know as wikis, are made by people working **collaboratively**. They allow people to add their own content and edit it. A well-known example is Wikipedia. There is a simple explanation of user-generated websites on **Website 1.14**.

Advantages of using wikis:

- They are updated all the time by users, making the information current.
- People from different parts of the world can work together on material.
- Changes can be tracked to see who has made contributions.
- The material is not usually bound by copyright laws.

Disadvantages of using wikis:

- Anyone can add information, so if not managed correctly, information may be inaccurate, biased or untrue.
- An Internet connection is needed for people to work collaboratively.
- Information can become disorganised, and there may be too much information, errors or duplication.

USER FORUMS

A user forum allows users to get together for open discussions. There are both general forums and specialist forums. Forums can be very useful if you have a question you want to post as other users can respond with answers or advice.

NEWS WEBSITES

News websites such as the BBC and Sky News are great sources of information. They allow users to see news as it comes in, using RSS feeds. You can also search the archives for old news that is relevant to what you are studying.

PODCASTING

Personal and On Demand Broadcasting (podcasting) allows users to watch or listen to material at a time that suits them. People can create podcasts and upload them to websites, blogs, social networking sites, etc. for others to subscribe to and download. There is a simple explanation of podcasting on **Website 1.15**.

Be safe/be efficient

Rules for using the Internet

- Do not sit researching on the Internet for too long, as this could cause problems such as stress from **information overload**, and physical problems such as back problems and eye strain.
- Do not always believe what you read or hear on the Internet – information can be biased, exaggerated or simply untrue. Always try to check the information using another source.
- Work on the Internet may be copyright, shown by the © symbol. You must not reproduce copyright protected work without the permission of whoever owns the copyright.
- Do not copy someone else's work and pass it off as your own. This is known as **plagiarism**. Although it is not illegal, it is forbidden by exam boards.

You should always reference information you find on the Internet (give the name of the source) because:

- it shows you have done your research
- it can help demonstrate certain points or support an argument
- it allows others to see where the piece of work has come from
- you can get credit for the work produced rather than being accused of plagiarism.

Collaboratively – working together with other people.

Information overload – having so much information available that the user feels overwhelmed and is unable to take any of it in, possibly leading to stress.

Plagiarism – copying someone else's work and presenting it as your own.

Exam question

The Internet is a useful source of information for studying, work and leisure. An exam question on this topic might be as follows.

John is researching some ICT terms using a wiki. Explain why he would need to be careful when using the information he finds.

Task

Look at the list below and decide if each example is legal or illegal:

a) You copy a music CD bought from a shop and give it to a friend.

b) You copy a music CD bought from a shop and sell it.

c) You buy software intended for one computer and put it on to other computers.

d) You download music and do not pay for it.

e) You make your own picture and add it to your work.

f) You copy images from the Internet and add them to your work.

g) You copy copyright images and put them into your work, including details of the source.

ResultsPlus
Maximise your marks

A weak answer might identify that Wikipedia is a wiki. A grade C answer might explain that a wiki is developed over time by people adding their own contributions and this would mean that some information may not be correct.

A grade A answer might focus on why John needs to be careful when using the information and might include the following: anyone can add information without it being checked; the information may be biased or one-sided; incorrect or outdated information may not have been removed.

Knowledge check

1   What is the difference between POP3 and IMAP4?

2   How is emailing different from instant messaging?

3   Give three things that a VLP can be used for. In your opinion, what are the main benefits to students of VLPs?

4   Describe the advantages of using the Internet to help with school work. Can you think of any disadvantages?

Internet safety

Learn about

- dangers associated with the Internet:
  - > viruses
  - > spyware
  - > cookies
  - > spam
  - > hackers
  - > phishing
  - > identity theft
- ways to protect yourself

There are many problems associated with the use of computers and especially the Internet. Ruby has come across problems herself and has heard about problems that her friends have had too.

Starter

What problems have you had when using the Internet? Produce a list of problems that people in your class have had. Include as much detail or as many specific examples as you can.

Virus – a program designed to cause other programs on a computer to malfunction or stop working altogether.

Fraud – tricking someone for personal gain or to damage them.

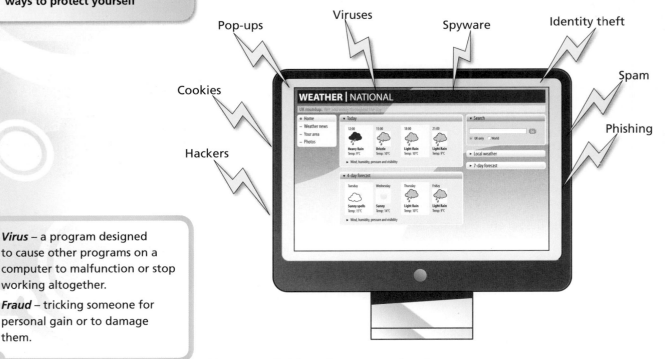

Figure 1.11 Problems that can occur from Internet use

Beware of viruses that can damage your computer

Viruses

Viruses are programs that can infect a computer without the permission or knowledge of the user. They can damage the system's settings and memory, generating error messages and causing the computer to malfunction.

Viruses can get on to your computer through:

- visiting certain websites
- opening emails
- downloading attachments or content from the Internet
- using infected portable storage devices such as memory sticks, CDs, DVDs
- connecting to an infected hard disk.

Task 123

Write a list of guidelines for Ruby to help protect her computer from viruses. You might want to include:

- installing anti-virus software and keeping it updated
- taking care when opening email attachments
- taking care when downloading from the Internet
- scanning CDs, DVDs and memory sticks
- backing up work
- avoiding using pirate copies of CDs and DVDS.

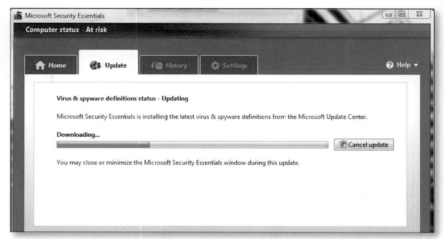

Figure 1.12 Antivirus software needs to be updated regularly so it can deal with the latest viruses

Spyware

Spyware is a computer program which is installed without permission, sometimes through a virus or sometimes as part of the installation of a program. It works by collecting information and sending it back to another source. The information collected could include the websites you have been visiting or what you have been downloading. This information is often used for marketing purposes, but can also be used for illegal purposes such as **fraud**.

Spyware allows someone else to access the information on your computer

Peer-to-peer (P2P) – sharing files among groups of people who are logged on to a file-sharing network.

Hacker – someone who gains unauthorised access to a computer in order to obtain data stored on it.

Identity theft – a crime that involves someone pretending to be another person in order to steal money or obtain other benefits.

Cookies

A cookie is a small file which stores information related to your Internet activity and then reports this back to the website server.

Cookies are used legitimately by website creators to enable websites to be customised for individual users. For example, if you go on to the BBC website, you can customise the homepage, and the next time you visit the site the layout will appear as you have set it.

However, cookies can cause problems such as pop-ups being generated or details like passwords stored which could be used by hackers.

Spam

Spam is all unwanted email such as unsolicited commercial email, unsolicited bulk email and chain letters.

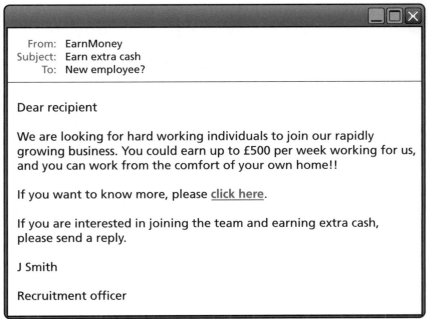

Phishing

Phishing involves sending a link via an email to a website which looks like a genuine website (e.g. a bank website) but is in fact bogus. The recipient may be tricked into following the link and entering details such as bank passwords or personal information on the website. (Phishing is covered in more detail in Avoiding online fraud, pages 131–4.)

Hackers

It is important to keep the information that is stored on your computer secure. Hackers are people who try to get access to your computer without your permission in order to steal information which they could use for malicious or criminal purposes.

Using **peer-to-peer (P2P)** software could increase the risk of **hackers** accessing data stored on your computer.

Identity theft

This takes place when someone collects personal information about you and uses that information for malicious or criminal purposes. In the past, criminals used to rummage though bins to get information, but now people can access Internet social networking sites where people's profiles contain personal information, which could prove valuable to the criminals. **Identity theft** is a growing problem.

e-component

Task 1.24

Complete **Worksheet 1.7** to learn about ways of protecting yourself against the dangers associated with computer and Internet use.

Task 1.25

Ruby wants to install all the protection she needs for her new laptop. What would you recommend that she puts on to her computer to protect its contents? Give reasons for your choices.

Knowledge check

1   Ruby purchased an item online. When she checked her bank statement she noticed that she had been charged for something she did not buy. How could this have happened? What should she do?

2   Ruby has installed free software on her computer. She notices that her computer has slowed down. What steps should Ruby take?

3   Ruby keeps receiving spam mail. What should she do?

The digital divide

Learn about

- economic, educational, social and cultural influences of technology

Throughout this chapter we have been looking at the technology that Ruby has and how she uses it. Ruby is fortunate and has technology available to her, but this is not the case for everyone.

Starter

Think about digital TV, the Internet and 'must-have' gadgets. Do you know people who have them all? Did they tend to get these services and products at the same time?

What factors influence people's decisions to buy into such services or products?

Do you think everyone is able to get these services or products?

What is the digital divide?

This is the gap between people in society who cannot or do not have effective access to digital technology and those who do. Because of the importance of technology in modern life, people who do not have access to it can be disadvantaged in many ways.

A gap exists between people who have access to the latest technology and those who have limited or no access

Did you know?

An average household could make annual savings of £840 simply by doing their shopping online in a broad range of categories, including utility bills, clothing, travel and home entertainment.

Households with access to the Internet are far more likely to use other types of digital equipment, such as digital cameras, MP3 players and mobile phones.

The Oxford Internet survey

1.6 billion people – a quarter of humanity – live without electricity.

Task 1.26

Lack of access is most common in the UK if you:

- have a low income
- live in a rural area
- have weak literacy skills
- have a disability
- are from an ethnic minority
- are elderly.

Can you think of reasons why these groups in society do not have access to the latest technology or may choose not to get the latest technology? Give reasons for your answers.

The implications of the digital divide

The digital divide has economic, educational, social and cultural implications.

ECONOMIC

Economics is to do with money, wealth, jobs, production, distribution and consumption of goods and services.

- People with knowledge of technology and the skills to use it can get better-paid jobs.
- Online banking allows people to use the facilities of a bank in the comfort of their own homes.
- The Internet gives people access to a wider range of products and services.
- The Internet allows people to research products and get cheaper deals for goods and services.
- Less well off people may not be able to afford the initial set up costs of ICT systems resulting in them being unable to access certain services.
- People may feel pressure to purchase equipment and ICT systems that they cannot afford, resulting in debt.
- The Internet has led to a rise in **e-commerce** and **globalisation**.
- Countries with less ICT infrastructure may be unable to make the most of globalisation, and fall further behind at a greater rate.

EDUCATIONAL

This is about learning and the knowledge gained from learning.

- Students who use computers at home or school can become independent learners and excel in education.
- Most schools are moving to personalised learning using VLEs. Without Internet access, young people cannot benefit from this.
- Having access to online educational resources allows students to do better work.
- People can take part in online courses to gain further skills and qualifications, no matter where they are in the world.
- A gap in ICT skills may exclude people from particular jobs.

e-commerce – buying and selling goods electronically, usually over the Internet.

Globalisation – the increasing integration of economies and societies around the world, particularly through international trade.

Access to computers and the Internet gives learners of all ages a real advantage

SOCIAL

This is about human society and the people who live in it.

- People can feel left out if they do not have technological goods and services.
- Not having access to communications such as email, IM and mobile phones can affect people's social interactions.

CULTURAL

This refers to the behaviour, attitudes and lifestyles of a particular social group.

- Many cafés now offer facilities such as the Internet to attract customers.
- Many people carry around MP3/4 players, mobile phones and other digital devices.
- People can watch video on demand and catch up on TV that they have missed.
- More children stay indoors and play on games consoles instead of playing outside.
- Cultural and/or religious influences might dissuade some groups of people from using ICT which could lead to lack of access, lack of education and an inability for countries to participate in globalisation.

Task

Can you add to the above lists? Think about the economical, educational, social and cultural uses of technology.

If people do not have access to the technology needed, how is this likely to affect their ability to participate?

Government initiatives

The government recognises that there are people who do not have up-to-date technology, such as digital TV, computers and the Internet. There are government schemes to help people who cannot afford them.

Task

Using the Internet, research ways the government has tried to help reduce the digital divide. Think about the people affected by the digital divide listed at the beginning of this topic.

Constant change

The fast pace of advances in technology widens the digital divide. Because of the cost of new technology, many people are unable to keep up to date. This also causes issues of compatibility; for example, an old computer may not have the specification needed to run new software or **hardware**.

The digital divide is not just a UK problem, it affects the whole world.

Hardware – the physical parts of a computer system, e.g. the CPU and the devices connected to it.

After just a few years, technology can become virtually useless

There are a number of organisations working to reduce the **e-component** digital divide. Computer Aid International (see **Website 1.16**) encourages companies to donate their old computers rather than throwing them away or recycling them. All data is wiped from the donated computers, which are then refurbished and donated to not-for-profit organisations in the developing world. Reuse of digital devices is better for the environment than recycling them and can also reduce the digital divide.

Knowledge check

What problems might the following people have?

a) Ruby's friend has bought an old second-hand phone.

b) Ruby's gran has an old laptop.

c) Ruby's next door neighbour does not have access to the Internet.

d) A friend of Ruby's dad has recently lost his job and has no computer skills.

Chapter 1
Let's communicate!

CHECK YOUR KNOWLEDGE

In this chapter you have been learning about digital devices such as mobile phones, netbooks, laptops and PDAs. You have also looked at some of the things we use digital devices for such as email, instant messaging, surfing the Internet and social networking. As a 'savvy' user of ICT you will understand the need to stay safe when using digital devices, in terms of preventing health issues, safeguarding personal information and preventing cyber bullying.

You should now know:

- the features of digital devices such as mobile phones, netbooks, laptops and PDAs
- the functions of digital devices and how to select a suitable digital device in a particular situation
- how to be safe and efficient when using email or the Internet, or when instant messaging or using social networking sites
- the health issues associated with the use of digital devices
- how to safeguard your personal information
- how the digital divide impacts on individuals and on society as a whole.

Think about the digital devices discussed in this chapter and the ways in which they can be used. One thing to remember is that lots of the devices you have looked at have multiple functions. For example, smart phones can be used to receive and send emails, and surf the Internet in addition to their primary function as a mobile phone. This makes choosing the device to use in a particular scenario more complicated. Another thing to consider is how a lack of access to digital devices and technology might affect people, and here is an example of the type of question you might be asked to answer on this topic.

*Some people have limited access to digital technology.

Discuss the impact this has on their lifestyle. (6)

GCSE ICT SAMs 2010

Examiner's tip

You will find two 6-mark questions on the Unit 1 exam paper. They will be open-ended questions and the quality of your written communication (QWC) will be assessed. (Remember that this is what the asterisk (*) means.)

Examiner's tip

Make sure that you understand the requirements of the key instructions. There are two basic types: those requiring a straightforward answer and those requiring a more complex one. Take a look at the table I've drawn to help you understand the different key instructions and what they tell you.

Key instruction	Example question	What's required
give, identify, list, name, state,	List three digital devices.	These key instructions require responses that are a word, a phrase or a short sentence.
compare, describe, discuss, explain, justify	Compare email and instant messaging.	These key instructions require more in depth responses, often linking two or more points.

Before you start to think about what to include in your answer, look at the key instruction. In this question, the key instruction is 'discuss'. You can think of 'discuss' as 'describe with reasons or justifications'. An extract from a sample answer in which the student is discussing the issue might look like this:

Limited access to technology means that people cannot access online services such as banking and shopping. This means that they cannot take advantage of the wider choice of goods or the often cheaper products available online.

Let's now look at the type of information you would need to include in your answer to this question. The question refers to limited access to digital technology and it is important that your answer shows that you understand that 'digital technology' includes a range of digital devices and services, and does not simply refer to computers.

Another thing to consider before you start writing your answer is what 'limited access' means. For example, you could argue that both of the people in the scenarios below have 'limited access' to digital technology:

● Someone who has access to computers at school but not at home.
● Someone with a computer at home but without access to the Internet.

Although it doesn't mention the term, the question is about the impact of the digital divide. The digital divide is concerned with the differences between those who have good access to digital technology and those who have more limited access to digital technology, and the effects this might have on their lives.

When answering these open-ended questions, in which the quality of your written communication is assessed, you will gain more marks if you:

1 make sure you understand what the question is asking before you start writing, including what the key instruction requires
2 identify the content and examples that you need to include to support the points you are making
3 use the content and examples as the key instruction asks you to (compare, describe, discuss, explain, justify)
4 try to write without making spelling or grammatical mistakes.

MARK SCHEME

Your answers to questions that include an assessment of the quality of your written communication (those marked by an asterisk (*)) will be marked using a levels-based mark scheme. There are three levels of answers: basic (1–2 marks), good (3–4 marks) and excellent (5–6 marks).

This table gives an overview of the three levels of answer for this type of question.

Level of answer	Overview
Basic answer	The answer describes some examples of having limited access to technology, the impact is referred to but not really discussed. There is little evidence of understanding of the digital divide.
Good answer	The answer gives a number of examples and discusses these in the context of the digital divide. The discussion shows some understanding of the impact of the digital divide on the individual.
Excellent answer	The answer is a well-balanced discussion. The context is clear, using a good range of examples. The discussion shows a good knowledge and understanding of the impact of the digital divide on the individual.

The level of your answer is identified first and then the mark within the level is adjusted according to the quality of your written communication. So, an answer that contains a well-balanced discussion of the digital divide and its effects on the individual, and that gives clear and relevant examples, but which is poorly written and contains lots of grammatical errors, would only be awarded 5 marks.

Examiner's tip

Something to think about is how you would use your knowledge to answer a question that asked you to compare access to digital services in London with a remote area such as a Scottish island or a country in Africa.

2 On the move

In this chapter you will consider...

- Digital cameras and camcorders.
- GPS devices.
- Wireless hotspots.
- Biometric identification.
- Internet-based services.

By completing this chapter you should be able to achieve the following learning outcomes...

- Discuss the uses and features of digital cameras and camcorders.
- Discuss the uses and features of GPS devices.
- Explain how digital images can be stamped with geographical coordinates.
- Explain how the Internet can be used for booking services.
- Explain how to find wireless hotspots.
- Explain how physical characteristics can be used for identification.
- Develop criteria to help you select the correct device or feature.

Functional Skills...

In this chapter there is information and activities that will help you to practise the following Functional ICT Skills:

Level 1
Using ICT
- Select and use software applications to meet needs and solve straightforward problems.
- Work with files, folders and other media to access, organise, store, label and retrieve information.

Finding and selecting information
- Use search techniques (search engines, queries) to locate and select relevant information.
- Recognise and take account of currency, relevance, bias and copyright when selecting and using information.

Developing, presenting and communicating information
- Apply editing, formatting and layout techniques to meet needs, including text, tables, graphics, records, numbers, charts, graphs or other digital content.
- Enter, search, sort and edit records.
- Combine information within a publication for print and for viewing on-screen.

Level 2
Using ICT
- Select and use software applications to meet needs and solve complex problems.
- Manage files, folders and other media storage to enable efficient information retrieval.

Finding and selecting information
- Use appropriate search techniques (search engines, queries and AND/NOT/OR, >,<,>=,><=, contains, begins with, use of wild cards) to locate and select relevant information.
- Recognise and take account of copyright and other constraints on the use of information.

Developing, presenting and communicating information
- Apply a range of editing, formatting and layout techniques to meet needs, including text, tables, graphics, records, numerical data, charts, graphs or other digital content.
- Analyse and draw conclusions from a data set by searching, sorting and editing records.
- Use collaborative tools appropriately.
- Organise and integrate information of different types to achieve a purpose, using accepted layouts and conventions as appropriate.

The files you will use in this section are listed here:

Interactive activities:

1. etask 2.2.swf
2. etask 2.7.swf
3. etask 2.22.swf

Files:

1. Worksheet 2.6.doc
2. Photo1.jpg
3. Photo2.jpg
4. Photo3.jpg
5. Photo4.jpg
6. Photo5.jpg
7. Photo6.jpg
8. Photo7.jpg

Websites:

1. Website 2.1 – InterRail
2. Website 2.2 – UK Passport Information (unofficial passport website)
3. Website 2.3 – Identify and Passport Service (government's official passport website)
4. Website 2.4 – The Cyber Captive Search Engine
5. Website 2.5 – Internet Techies
6. Website 2.6 – Total Hotspots
7. Website 2.7 – Google Docs
8. Website 2.8 – Google Apps
9. Website 2.9 – Simple Spark
10. Website 2.10 – Geocaching
11. Website 2.11 – Daily Telegraph

Planning a trip

Learn about

- search engines
- online encyclopaedias

Satya and Simon have only been on package holidays before, where all the travel and accommodation were included in the price. They are now going to have to make their own arrangements.

OK, what should we do first?

Starter

Make a list of all the arrangements that Satya and Simon will have to make for their holiday. Try to decide which they can do online and which they can only do face to face.

Skills builder 2.1

Write down the keywords that Satya and Simon could enter into a search engine to find out information about InterRail passes.

They have decided that their first task is to find out about InterRailing. They need to know the cost of a rail pass, where they can buy one and if they can use it in Britain.

They have found the InterRail website (see Figure 2.1), which they think might provide them with answers.

Figure 2.1 The InterRail website

More than 60% of leisure travellers now book their holidays online, with only 9% using high street travel agents. The rest book by telephone after carrying out research using the Internet.

23% of people over 55 book three holidays a year online. This group is also likely to book a holiday at the last minute: 28% of people aged over 55 booked their holiday a month or less before departure, compared with 25% of under 24s and 18% of Internet users overall. Can you explain these statistics?

Skills builder 2.2

e-component

Use the InterRail site (**Website 2.1**) and any others you have found to try to help Satya and Simon by answering the following questions:

a) Where can they buy a pass?

b) Can they get a cheap rate because they are 17?

c) How much will a month's pass cost?

d) Can they get on any train in Europe, or do they have to book in advance?

e) What are the rules about using the pass in Britain?

Satya and Simon now have their rail passes and need to book the first stage of their trip. They plan to get the train to Paris and stay there at least three nights before deciding where to go next.

Task 2.1

Use an online journey planner to plan Satya and Simon's rail journey to Paris. How long will it take? Will they need to change trains? Which station will they arrive at in Paris?

They intend to stay in good-quality hostels where there will be lots of other young people.

Skills builder 2.3

Use a search engine to find hostels in Paris. Check out what people who have stayed there have to say. Which one would you recommend to Satya and Simon, and why? Use Google Maps and Google Earth to locate the hostel you have recommended. How far is it from the Eiffel Tower?

Task 2.2

e-component

Satya and Simon have used the Internet to help plan their trip. It has been a great help, but could they use it for all of their preparations? Use **etask 2.2** to help you think about which tasks are best done online and which are best done face to face.

Be safe/be efficient

Before making a booking you should carry out as much research as possible. Customer reviews and traveller blogs are good sources of information.

ResultsPlus
Examiner's tip!

The Internet is a useful source of information for a trip like the one Satya and Simon are planning. Search engines find links related to key criteria. If asked a question related to Internet searches, use the term 'search engine', rather than using a trade name.

Exam questions might ask you to:

- describe what a search engine does

- identify how to limit the number of hits from a search

- make hits as useful as possible to the task.

When searching the Internet, a poorly structured search may result in a very large number of 'hits' (the possible links identified in a search). Make your search more effective by using AND, OR and NOT. Use speech marks to identify whole phrases that must be matched.

Solving a last-minute hitch

Learn about

- the widespread use of the Internet
- biometric identification
- bias and validity
- privacy
- the effective use of search engines, validity of results and searching techniques

The last time Satya and Simon went away they used their child passports, but they have suddenly realised that as they are now 17 they will need adult ones.

Starter

The purpose of a passport is to prove the holder's identity. What does your passport say about you? What other ways of proving someone's identity can you think of?

Finding information about passports

Satya and Simon entered 'passport information' into their search engine and found the URLs shown in Figure 2.2.

Figure 2.2 Screenshot of Google search results when 'passport information' was entered

The second site listed looked official but when they clicked on one of the help links on this site they were told to phone an 0906 premium rate number. Satya told Simon not to phone as she noticed the small print which said that calls cost £1.50 a minute!

e-component

They eventually clicked on the official passport site and found the information they wanted. (To access both the unofficial site and the Home Office's Identity and Passport Service (IPS) site, go to **Websites 2.2 and 2.3**.)

Task 2.3

How could they have immediately recognised that the IPS website was the government's official site and the other wasn't?

Task 2.4

Why was the official passport site only fourth in the list? Why did the other sites, those trying to make money from the advice they give, get to the top of the list? Carry out some research to find out how you can get a URL to the top of the list.

Charging people for 'free information' is big business, and firms which supply premium-rate phone lines to people who then overcharge can be fined. Three premium-rate phone line providers that allowed firms to charge consumers up to £10 for freely available passport advice have been fined £55,000 after the practice was exposed. The providers supplied lines to companies that ran official-looking websites inviting callers to dial a 10p-a-minute 0871 number for recorded information. Customers were then directed to an even more expensive 090 line that cost at least £1.50 a minute. But the same details about passport office locations and opening times are on the Home Office's free website and its 24-hour advice line, which charges just 8p a minute.

Using passports for identification and authentication

When Satya and Simon received their new passports they noticed that the page containing their personal information contained a **microchip**, and accompanying the passport was a letter explaining their new **biometric** passports.

The chip is an RFID (Radio Frequency Identification) chip that stores the user's photograph and all of the personal information printed on the page. RFID chips were introduced to increase security, especially at airports.

At passport control the access code at the foot of the personal details page is scanned. The reader then communicates with the chip and the customs official can view the stored image. The face can also be recognised automatically by biometric software using information such as the distances between eyes, nose, mouth and ears.

A biometric passport

Be safe/be efficient

When you are trying to find official government information about passports, citizens' rights, etc. on the Internet, always carefully check the site's web address. If you don't do this, you may pay lots of money for information that you could get for free!

Microchip – a miniature electronic circuit used to control computers and most other electronic devices.

Biometrics – an automated method of recognising a person based on physical characteristics. Among the features measured are face, fingerprints, hand geometry, iris and voice.

Exam question

ICT innovations are used in a number of different contexts. Biometric systems are used in passports and for computer security because they uniquely identify an individual. This question concerns the use of biometrics instead of a username and password.

Some PC manufacturers include fingerprint scanners on their machines. These are used to log on instead of entering usernames and passwords.

(i) The fingerprint scanner may be bypassed, so that a user can log on using the keyboard. Give two reasons why this facility is needed.

(ii) State two other biometric methods that can be used to log on to a PC.

IGCSE ICT (2007)

Satya and Simon have made a list of how they want to stay in touch while they are away.

- Contact friends and family.
- Take photos.
- Show photos to friends.
- Let them know where the images were taken.

Now they have to decide how to do this.

Starter

Look at Satya and Simon's list. Which digital devices could they take with them to help them stay in contact?

Netbook – a small portable laptop computer designed for wireless communication and access to the Internet.

SD cards – Secure Digital cards are one type of flash memory card which store up to 2 GB of data. Secure Digital High Capacity (SDHC) cards are another type of flash memory card and they are ideal for video cameras because they can store up to 32 GB of data.

Bluetooth – allows the exchange of data over short distances from fixed and mobile devices. In order for devices to communicate, they must be able to understand the Bluetooth rules (protocols).

USB (Universal Serial Bus) – a standard method of connecting devices such as keyboards and printers to a computer.

Flash memory card – used for fast and easily transferable information storage in digital devices such as mobile phones, media players and cameras. Flash memory is known as a solid state storage device, meaning there are no moving parts. Everything is electronic instead of mechanical and so it is ideal for mobile devices.

Sending messages and taking photos/videos

Satya and Simon plan to send messages (verbal and written) and to take and send photos and videos.

Task 2.5

Make a list of the different ways that Satya and Simon could:

a) send messages to tell their friends what they are doing

b) take photos and display them for their friends.

How many different digital devices did you include in your list?

Satya has researched the different ways and created an ideas map, as shown in Figure 2.3. Did you think of all the ways that Satya included in her ideas map?

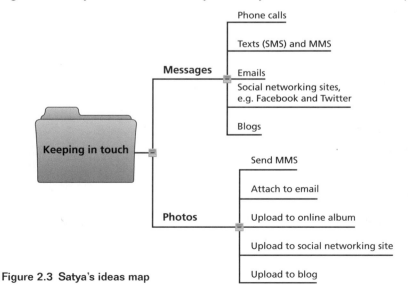

Figure 2.3 Satya's ideas map

Satya and Simon are discussing whether to use their mobile phones to take photos and videos or whether to buy a digital camera or camcorder.

Task 2.6

Carry out research to compare digital cameras/camcorders with mobile phones. Think about:

- **the quality of the images – which has the highest resolution?**
- **close-up and wide-angle images**
- **storage capacity.**

Features of netbooks

They have also been researching laptops to take with them and have discovered a small one called a **netbook**. Here are its features:

- light, robust and easily portable
- small 10-inch monitor
- large keyboard
- WiFi connection for the Internet
- browser software
- solid state hard drives and **SD cards** for data storage
- **USB** connections
- microphone and speakers
- long battery life.

Task 2.7

Use etask 2.7 to identify the features of a netbook that make it suitable for travellers.

Task 2.8

Look at the ways of sending messages and photos/videos shown in Figure 2.3. Which of these could be carried out using a netbook?

Transferring images

If Satya and Simon take a netbook, they will have to transfer photos from their camera or mobile phone using one of these methods: **Bluetooth; USB cable; Flash memory card**.

Task 2.9

Research the three main methods of transferring photos.

a) **Which can be used with standard mobile phones and basic digital cameras?**

b) **Which would provide the fastest transfer speed?**

c) **Which one should Satya and Simon use?**

Skills builder 2.4

How could Satya and Simon alter the images to send a comedy version to their friends? Use a photo of yourself and edit it into an amusing image for your friends.

In practice

Netbooks at being marketed at the education market. The manufacturers claim that there are many advantages to using netbooks in schools.

- They are about the size of a hardcover book, easily fitting into a schoolbag, and would-be thieves are unable to tell if a netbook is in a bag.
- There is space on the desk to use them alongside a textbook.
- They have fast boot-up times, taking just 20 seconds to power on.
- They are relatively inexpensive.
- They are WiFi enabled, and students can remain logged in as they move from room to room.

ResultsPlus
Maximise your marks

In the exam you may be asked to recommend the most appropriate digital devices for a given scenario. Satya and Simon want to stay in touch with family and friends as well as taking photographs. A digital phone with a good range of features, including digital camera and the ability to communicate using voice, text, photographs and videos would allow them to do everything they want to be able to do on a short trip. You will be asked to **explain** or **discuss** your recommendations. Think carefully because your explanation must be related to the scenario.

How can we connect?

Satya and Simon are going to keep in touch with their friends to tell them about their adventures. To do this, they will need to use the Internet.

Starter

Most providers have 'roaming' facilities enabling you to use your mobile phone abroad. Investigate the major networks to find out how much it costs to phone and send texts from Europe.

Did you know?

There are tens of thousands of cyber cafés around the world, with at least one in almost every small community in many countries.

Connecting to the Internet

When Satya and Simon are travelling, how can they connect to the Internet? The Internet is a huge network and there are two main ways that people can connect to it from their computers:

- by cable
- using a wireless connection (see Figure 2.4).

Radio waves

Figure 2.4 A computer with both cable and wireless connections to the Internet

CYBER CAFÉS

A cable connection to a network is always far quicker than a wireless connection, but there won't be many places where Satya and Simon will be able to find a socket to plug in their computer when they are travelling.

They could use a **cyber café**, but they would have to pay.

Cyber café – a café or coffee shop that has a number of personal computers connected to the Internet and available for use by customers. Most charge by the hour or fraction of an hour.

Task 2.10

Look at the Cyber Captive Search Engine on **Website 2.4**. Use it to locate:

a) cyber cafés in the area where you live

b) cyber cafés in Paris for Satya and Simon to use.

Using the Internet in a cyber café

Task 2.11

If Satya and Simon are going to use computers in a cyber café that other people will be using, they will have to take extra security precautions.

Produce a set of instructions for Satya and Simon to follow. Look at **Website 2.5**, which contains a useful article from the Internet Techies website, to get you started.

WiFi ACCESS

Most of the hostels that you found in Paris should offer WiFi access, as this is far easier to do than provide cabled access.

In many towns and cities around the world, there are places where you can use a WiFi connection to the Internet for free. They are mostly located at hotels, restaurants and café chains such as Starbucks and McDonald's. These places are called wireless **hotspots**.

Task

Using Website 2.6, find hotspots in your area.

You can also use this site to find hotspots around the world. Find some hotspots near the main sights in Paris for Satya and Simon.

With free WiFi Internet access, they will be able to keep in contact with their friends.

Task

List the ways that Satya and Simon will be able to use the Internet to keep in contact with their friends to tell them what they are doing and showing them what they have seen.

Online photo albums

Instead of emailing copies of photos to their friends, they have decided to create lots of online photo albums and allow access to the people they want to show each album to. Figure 2.5 shows an example of an image from an album.

Hotspot – a venue that offers a WiFi Internet connection. Many are located in hotels and restaurants and lots of them are free.

Cloud computing – a system in which all computer programs and data is stored on a central server owned by a company (e.g. Google) and accessed virtually.

Web app (web application) – any application that can be accessed using a web browser. The application can be as simple as a message board or guest sign-in page on a website, or as complex as a spreadsheet.

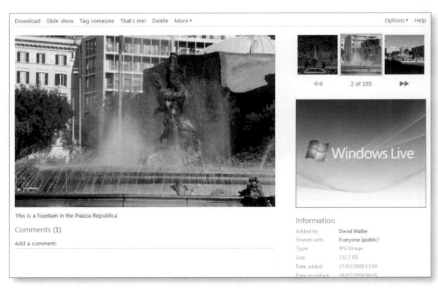

Figure 2.5 An image from an album that Satya and Simon's friend shared with them

Task 2.14

What are the advantages of uploading images to online albums and allowing friends to access them rather than emailing them or placing them on a social networking site?

Uploading and storing images online is safer than simply keeping them on the camera or netbook, where they might get deleted or even stolen.

Cloud computing

Satya and Simon could use **cloud computing**, a system in which computer programs and data are stored centrally. All they would need to access this is a connection to the Internet and an input device. There would be no need to buy and install expensive software or powerful computers and hard disk drives.

Satya and Simon can use cloud computing as they are travelling and use free online software such as Google Docs, which will allow them to create documents and spreadsheets. The documents are also saved online.

Many businesses are using software such as this for financial reasons and also for collaborative working. Have a look at:

- Google Docs for personal use on **Website 2.7**

e-component

- Google Apps for business use on **Website 2.8**.

In practice

e-component

As more people recognise the advantages of cloud computing, giving users the ability to access software on the Internet and share data with anyone, thousands of **web apps** are being produced covering all needs and interests. Many of these are free and can be found through directories such Simple Spark – see **Website 2.9**.

Task 2.15

With your class consider the advantages and disadvantages of cloud computing.

Skills builder 2.5

Investigate features and functions of online photo albums. Upload some of your own photos to an online photo album and set the access rights so that your friends can view and comment on your photos.

Finding the way

Learn about

- the impact of the use of digital devices on the way organisations operate

Satya and Simon are always getting lost, even in their home town! They are worried about finding their way around all of the cities and towns they will be visiting.

Starter

Global positioning systems (GPS) have lots of positive applications for people who find themselves in unfamiliar places. How many can you think of?

GPS sat navs

Their father has offered to lend them his car GPS **sat nav**, like the one shown in Figure 2.6.

However, this model has been created for drivers and is not really suitable for pedestrians. Also, it only has maps for the United Kingdom.

Sat nav – a device, usually used in a car, that gives directions based on information received from a series of satellites.

Convergence – when one device is developed to carry out functions that were originally performed by several different devices.

Metadata – provides information about the content of a digital item, e.g. each digital image from a digital camera has a file attached listing such things as date, time, camera and shutter speed.

Geotag – to attach the exact geographical coordinates of longitude and latitude to a digital image, giving the location of where it was taken.

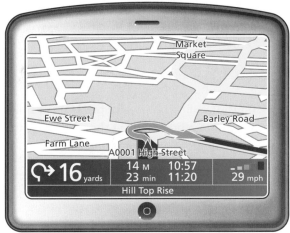

Figure 2.6 A screenshot of a car sat nav, showing roads and route

Task 2.16

Investigate how GPS works with a sat nav to aid navigation.

Task 2.17

Carry out some research to find a suitable sat nav for Satya and Simon to use to find their way on foot around European cities.

Convergence

One of the features of modern digital devices is **convergence**, where one device is developed to carry out functions that were originally performed by other devices. An excellent example is the mobile phone. Its primary function is to make voice calls, but it can also be used for other things such as taking photos, listening to music, watching videos and surfing the Internet. Now more mobiles are appearing on the market with GPS facilities.

Task 2.18

Carry out research to find a mobile phone with GPS capabilities.

MORE CONVERGENCE

Satya and Simon have just received a link from a friend travelling in Italy. The link is to an online photo album and, using GPS technology, the images have the exact geographical coordinates of where the photograph was taken. When you take a digital image, lots of information such as date, time, camera type, speed and exposure are stored in the file. This information is called **metadata** – see Figure 2.7. If you have a camera with GPS, it also stores the exact location coordinates.

Figure 2.7 The metadata linked to a photo in an online album

When they double-clicked on the GPS latitude, Google Maps opened showing exactly where the picture was taken – see Figure 2.8.

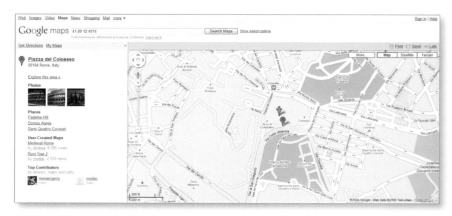

Figure 2.8 The location of the photo shown in Google Maps

They could also copy and paste the coordinates into Google Earth for more virtual sightseeing, as shown in Figure 2.9.

Figure 2.9 Using the coordinates will allow you to see the exact location of the photo in Google Earth

Task

Satya and Simon think it would be great if they could include this facility in all of their photos. Carry out some research to see if you can find them a camera with GPS.

GPS tracking

Businesses have been making use of GPS to increase their efficiency. For firms that have lots of delivery vans, knowing where each one is at any given time can be a problem. If each van is fitted with a GPS system and a modem, then its location can be constantly sent via the mobile phone network to the firm's computer system.

Task 2.20

With your class, investigate the advantages and disadvantages to a delivery firm of using GPS tracking devices.

Skills builder 2.6

As GPS systems are becoming cheaper and are found in an ever-increasing number of digital devices, people have invented a new game called **geocaching**.

- Using **Website 2.10**, carry out some research on geocaching.
- Find out if there are any geocaches in your area.
- Create a digital map of an area with hotspots to highlight and give information on local geocaches.

Privacy issues

Although most people think of advances in technology as something positive, it is important to remember that sometimes technological developments can lead to new issues. For example, the development of GPS tracking devices allowed one mother to track her son's whereabouts on his gap year. She insisted that he carry a credit card sized tracker at all times while travelling in Australia, Thailand and South Africa. She was then able to log on to a website and find out his exact location. While this is an amusing story, it raises questions about whether the son's privacy was violated by his mother with the help of this tracking device. Go to **Website 2.11** to read more about this story.

Exam question

GPS is widely used by motorists and by walkers and this is the type of question you might be asked about it in the exam.

Many mobile phones now have GPS as a feature.

State two uses of GPS on a mobile phone. (2)

GCSE ICT SAM (2010)

ResultsPlus

Watch out!

Note that this question relates to the uses of GPS rather than how it works. Most of the questions on your exam paper will be about how something is used or how it impacts on our lives. Make sure you read the question carefully. If your answer goes into great detail about how GPS on mobile phones works, you won't get any marks. You must give two uses of GPS on a mobile phone as the question asks. Possible answers include: helping you find your way to a specified location; giving the distance to a specified location; giving the location of key services like railway stations.

What digital devices should we take?

Learn about

- how to select suitable digital devices/features to meet particular needs

Satya and Simon are arguing again. This time it's about what devices they should take with them. Here is their list of the things they want to do.

- Take photos.
- Share photos with their friends and family.
- Make voice calls.
- Make hostel bookings over the Internet.
- Send emails.
- Upload photos to an online album.
- Write a blog.
- Update social networking sites.

Starter

Read the list of things that Satya and Simon want to be able to do while they are on holiday. What digital devices do they need?

Simon likes new gadgets and is keen to buy a new smart phone, but Satya prefers to take a digital camera and a netbook.

Did you know?

£3.5 billion worth of goods have been stolen from British holiday makers abroad in the past five years.

Thieves are most likely to go for electrical goods: the top five are iPods, mobile phones, digital cameras and camcorders.

Task 2.21

e-component

Carry out research into the new smart phones and netbooks. Fill in the table at the top of the next page to indicate which features they possess and which functions they can carry out. (A downloadable version of the table is available for you to complete on **Worksheet 2.6**.) For some of them a simple tick or cross will be enough, but for others you may have to write a short explanation, as shown for 'voice messages'.

Features and functions of smart phones and netbooks

	Smart phone	Netbook
Voice messages	✔	✔ – if VoIP software has been installed
SMS – Short Message Service used for text messages		
MMS – Multimedia Message Service		
Video calls		
Digital camera		
Record video		
Mobile TV		
Mobile radio		
GPS with sat nav		
Bluetooth		
WiFi		
Access the Internet		
Send and receive emails		
Social networking		
Music player		
Video player		
Touch screen		
Qwerty keyboard		
Applications, e.g. calculator, word processor, spreadsheet		
Calendar		
Contact list		
Games software		
Data storage		

Task 2.22

Complete **etask 2.22** to help Satya and Simon decide which devices to take.

Skills builder 2.7

Satya and Simon have selected seven of their favourite photos of Paris and named them Photo1 to Photo7.

Use these photos to create a digital photobook which will scroll through the images or allow the viewer to pause the display. It should have buttons to move to the next or previous image.

Knowledge check

Check your knowledge of this chapter with the Chapter 2 quiz.

ResultsPlus
Examiner's tip

In this section you have learned about the digital devices that Satya and Simon might take on holiday.

You may be asked to identify the devices that would be best in a particular scenario. The key is to consider what the person needs the device for and in what context they will be using it. When you recommend a device you will normally need to justify your decision. Things to consider are:

- Weight
- Cost
- Battery life
- Robustness
- Ease of use
- Functionality (the features it has).

What features make the device you've chosen the best solution? If weight is an issue, as it is when travelling, a netbook with a small screen would probably be a better choice than a high specification laptop with a large screen.

CHECK YOUR KNOWLEDGE

In this chapter you have been learning about the digital devices and services that you might use when planning a trip. These digital devices, including digital cameras, camcorders and GPS devices can now be added to the list of devices you were introduced to in Chapter 1 (mobile phones, laptops, netbooks and PDAs). The digital services used by travellers include wireless hotspots, which allow travellers to connect to the Internet when they're out and about, and biometric identification, which is used in passports.

You should now know:

- the features of digital cameras and camcorders, and how and when they are used
- the features of GPS devices and how they are used
- how digital images can be stamped with geographical coordinates
- how the Internet can be used for booking services
- how to find wireless hotspots
- how physical characteristics can be used for identification
- how to develop criteria to help you select the correct device or feature.

Think about the ways in which Satya and Simon intend to use digital devices. A key idea that has been developed in this chapter is that of the multifunctional device, which is sometimes referred to as convergence. This is a particularly important consideration in the functionality of mobile phones. Many modern mobile phones can, in addition to being used for basic functions such as making calls and sending text message, be used:

- to take photos
- as an MP3 player
- to record and play videos
- to surf the Internet
- to send and receive emails
- as GPS devices
- as simple games consoles.

They are truly mobile multifunctional digital devices.

As well as considering the digital devices that Satya and Simon might use on their trip, you've also looked at various ways of them keeping in touch with friends and family while they are away. One of the options they were considering was social networking sites. Here are some examples of the types of question you might be asked to answer about social networking in the exam.

Manjit is opening a social networking account. She wants it to be secure.

(a) The account requires a password.
Which one of these passwords is the most secure? (1)

A   Seahorse ☐

B   C-hor4se ☐

C   Chor4se ☐

D   C-horse ☐

ICT GCSE SAMs 2010

Examiner's tip
Unless you really don't know the answer to a multiple-choice question you should try to work out the answer using the knowledge you have. I'll show you how to do this on the next page.

This is a multiple-choice question. There will be a number of multiple-choice questions on the Unit 1 exam paper but they won't all be in one section.

When answering multiple-choice questions it is important to think carefully about the alternative answers you are offered. In this case, the question is testing whether you can apply the rules about how to create strong passwords. Using a strong password when creating a social networking account is important as strong passwords are a lot more secure.

The characters that can be used in a password are:

- Lower case letters
- Upper case letters
- Numerals
- Punctuation or other symbols.

The strength of a password is defined by the number of different types of character being used.

- Seahorse contains two types of character
- C-hor4se contains all types of character
- Chor4se contains three types of character
- C-horse contains three types of character.

By taking what you know and applying it to the question, you can work out that C-hor4se is the most secure password because it contains both upper and lower case letters, as well as a numeral and a punctuation symbol.

Now let's look at the next part of this question.

(b) Manjit will use the social networking site to share photographs with friends.

    (i) One way in which she can control who can view her photographs is by setting access rights. State one other way in which she could do this. (1)

Adapted from GCSE ICT SAMs 2010

This question gives one possible answer and asks you to provide another one. This approach is used to help you as giving one possible answer clarifies the question. In this case, 'setting access rights' makes it clear that the question is about controlling access.

Other ways in which Manjit could control who can view her photos include:

- using privacy settings
- creating guest accounts.

If you included one of these in your answer you would receive the mark.

Here is the next part of the question.

    (ii) Some of Manjit's friends exchange personal details with people they meet online.

    Give two reasons why this might not be a good thing to do. (2)

GCSE ICT SAMs 2010

Examiner's tip

Make sure you read questions carefully. It is easy to misread questions, particularly when the question includes a 'not', like this one.

The question asks you to give two reasons and the question is worth two marks. This should make it clear to you what is required. Possible reasons why it is not a good thing to exchange personal details with people you meet online include:

- puts you at greater risk of identity theft
- results in a loss of personal privacy
- could lead to cyberbullying.

3 Entertain me – what to buy?

Do you need a complete multimedia experience? Relax in the multimedia pod

e-component

For £50,000 you can buy the new Ovei home cinema and game pod designed by the Formula 1 motor racing team, McLaren Applied Technologies. With flat screens, touch control, media servers and games consoles of your choice, you can relax in air-conditioned luxury. But it is too small for real-time socialising, so you'll only be able to mix with virtual friends. Read more about this on **Website 3.1**.

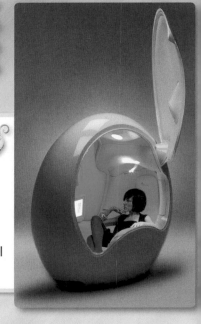

Or is this the end of the games console?

e-component

As more people have fast broadband connections, experts have been predicting the rise of cloud computing, where all of our computer programs and data will be stored on a central server owned by a company such as Google and accessed virtually. This will be ideal for streaming gaming. All of the processing will be done on an external server, thousands of miles away. The player can then log into the server, so they will not need an expensive games console or computer, just a connection to the Internet and an input device. They will be able to play any game, not just the ones for the console they have bought, and interact with other players in MMOs (massively multiplayer online). Read more about this on **Website 3.2** and decide whether you think this could mean the end of the games console.

What about using your brain?

e-component

The Emotiv EPOC headset is the first Brain Computer Interface (BCI) device for the gaming market, and its designers claim to have already mastered its use in thought-controlled games. Soon, you could be required only to 'think' to operate a video game. Read more about this on **Website 3.4**.

Or is virtual reality the future?
Hands-free gaming

Meet the Cocoon. The motion-tracking cameras and wrap-around visuals could make for an incredibly realistic gaming experience, where you use your whole body to fight off enemies who approach from all directions. Instead of using a joystick or mouse to navigate the screens, motion-tracking cameras will follow the movement of your arms, legs and face, and a motion-sensitive platform will detect if you're walking or jumping. Display, sound and interaction all combine to create a fully immersive digital experience. Imagine having a Cocoon in your home, connected to the Internet. Its unique interface means that rather than inputting commands with a keyboard or moving a cursor with a mouse, you can simply reach out and 'grab' information from all around you. You can find out more about the Cocoon on **Website 3.3**.

Or what about actually feeling the game?

The Virtual Cocoon, a virtual reality headset, can electronically stimulate all five senses so that the wearer can experience a virtual environment that they cannot distinguish from the real world. They will actually be able to live in a game world – and feel the pain when they're 'killed' by one of the monsters! You can find out more on **Website 3.5**.

What do you think?

Have a look at the websites mentioned on these pages. Then make your predictions about the future of multimedia and gaming. Will consoles become even more sophisticated with better graphics? Is the future with online service providers? Will we be playing in a virtual world?

In this chapter you will meet Jamie, who is 16 and keen on the latest music, games and films which he watches with friends each week. He would now like to access digital content through online entertainment services.

3 Entertain me – what to buy?

In this chapter you will consider...

- Games consoles.
- Media players.
- Digital TV.
- Internet service providers.
- Internet-based services.
- Copyright.
- Privacy, cyber crime and staying safe on the Internet.

Functional Skills...

In this chapter there is information and activities that will help you to practise the following Functional ICT Skills:

Level 1

Using ICT

- Use ICT to plan and organise work.
- Select and use software applications to meet needs and solve straightforward problems.
- Demonstrate how to create, use and maintain secure passwords.
- Demonstrate how to minimise the risk of computer viruses.

Finding and selecting information

- Use search techniques (search engines, queries) to locate and select relevant information.
- Recognise and take account of currency, relevance, bias and copyright when selecting and using information.

Developing, presenting and communicating information

- Apply editing, formatting and layout techniques to meet needs, including text, tables, graphics, records, numbers, charts, graphs or other digital content.
- Process numerical data.
- Display numerical data in a graphical format.
- Enter, search, sort and edit records.
- Demonstrate understanding of the need to stay safe and to respect others when using ICT-based communication.
- Combine information within a publication for print and for viewing on screen.

- Check for accuracy and meaning.
- Evaluate own use of ICT tools at each stage of a task and at the task's completion.

Level 2

Using ICT

- Use ICT to plan and analyse complex or multi-step tasks and activities and to make decisions about suitable approaches.
- Select and use software applications to meet needs and solve complex problems.
- Select and use a range of interface features and system facilities effectively to meet needs.
- Understand the danger of computer viruses and how to minimise risk.

Finding and selecting information

- Use appropriate search techniques (search engines, queries and AND/NOT/OR, >,<,>=,><=, contains, begins with, use of wild cards) to locate and select relevant information.
- Recognise and take account of copyright and other constraints on the use of information.
- Evaluate fitness for purpose of information.

Developing, presenting and communicating information

- Apply a range of editing, formatting and layout techniques to meet needs, including text, tables, graphics, records, numerical data, charts, graphs or other digital content.
- Process and analyse numerical data.
- Display numerical data in appropriate graphical format.
- Analyse and draw conclusions from a data set by searching, sorting and editing records.
- Understand the need to stay safe and to respect others when using ICT-based communication.
- Organise and integrate information of different types to achieve a purpose, using accepted layouts and conventions as appropriate.
- Work accurately and check accuracy, using software facilities where appropriate.
- Evaluate the selection, use and effectiveness of ICT tools and facilities used to present information at each stage of a task and at the task's completion.

By completing this chapter you should be able to achieve the following learning outcomes...

- Discuss the uses and features of games consoles, media players and digital TVs.
- Discuss suitability of games consoles and media players for different personal uses.
- Develop criteria to help you select an appropriate device.
- Describe the services provided by Internet service providers (ISPs).
- Develop criteria for selecting an ISP.
- Explain your legal responsibilities when downloading entertainment content.
- Explain how to maintain your security when using online services.
- Explain how you may be affected by cyber crime and how to stay safe.

The files you will use in this section are listed here:

Interactive activities:

1. etask 3.1.swf
2. etask 3.8.swf
3. eknowledge check 3.6.swf
4. etask 3.19.swf

Files:

1. Laptops 3.1.mdb **or** Laptops 3.1.accdb
2. Worksheet 3.2.doc

Websites:

1. Website 3.1 – TechRadar
2. Website 3.2 – BBC News
3. Website 3.3 – The Hottest Gadgets
4. Website 3.4 – CNN
5. Website 3.5 – h+ Magazine
6. Website 3.6 – IT Schools Africa
7. Website 3.7 – Xbox
8. Website 3.8 – engadget
9. Website 3.9 – PlayStation 3
10. Website 3.10 – BBC News
11. Website 3.11 – Blog entry (Xbox)
12. Website 3.12 – BT Broadband Availability Checker
13. Website 3.13 – Speedtest.net
14. Website 3.14 – About.com: Wireless/Networking
15. Website 3.15 – Relativity: Business Technology Solutions
16. Website 3.16 – BBC News
17. Website 3.17 – BBC News
18. Website 3.18 – What Is My IP
19. Website 3.19 – BBC Webwise
20. Website 3.20 – Get Safe Online
21. Website 3.21 – Microsoft
22. Website 3.22 – Microsoft
23. Website 3.23 – BBC News
24. Website 3.24 – Daily Telegraph
25. Website 3.25 – NHS
26. Website 3.26 – Guardian
27. Website 3.27 – Guardian
28. Website 3.28 – Microsoft
29. Website 3.29 – Thinkuknow

Setting up a multimedia system

Learn about

● choosing the best method to view films, listen to music and play games

Jamie has worked all summer and has saved up enough money to kit himself out with a system that he can use for his favourite pastimes, which are watching films, listening to music and playing computer games.

Starter

Make a list of all the devices that you can think of that Jamie could use to watch films, listen to music and play games.

There is currently an Internet connection in the house. There is no phone line in Jamie's bedroom, but he already has a laptop and a DVD player connected to a TV. Before he buys anything, he needs to do some research into what is available.

The list of devices available is large and growing all the time, so how does Jamie choose?

First, he needs to ask himself two questions:

● What does he need the system to do? (What is its purpose?)

● Who is going to be using the system, and are they familiar with using digital devices?

Here are Jamie's replies:

I want to be able to watch the latest films in high definition (HD) that I've found on the Internet, are available on satellite or cable or on optical disk.

I want to listen to my music that I've downloaded as MP3 files.

I want to play online games with my friends. All of us are really into computers, so I want to buy the most up-to-date stuff.

Skills builder 3.1

Jot down the key words that you would enter into a search engine to research the devices available to Jamie. How can you refine your search to get more useful results?

The devices that Jamie would like to have

From the list that you made in the Starter activity, you will have realised there are many devices available: media players, desktop PCs, laptops, **HDTV**, games console, Blu-ray, DVD, MP3 player, etc.

As Jamie does not have unlimited funds, he has decided to use a laptop as the basis of his multimedia system and connect it to a HDTV to watch the films. As Jamie's laptop is a few years old, he has decided to buy a new one.

Choosing a laptop

Jamie needs to consider the following when deciding which laptop to buy:

- **features** – a list of what a device includes, e.g. LCD flat screen, DVD-RW (re-writer), webcam, touch sensitive screen
- **functions** – a list of what the device's features can do, e.g. connect to a network, play **high-definition** films, access the Internet, play sound at hi-fi quality. Most of the digital devices that people buy have far more functions than they need or use
- **hard disk drive (HDD) size** – multimedia like video, images, graphics and MP3 audio files need lots of storage capacity
- **performance** – processor speed, e.g. 1.66 GHz, and size of RAM (random access memory), e.g. 4 GB
- **connectivity** – the range of peripheral equipment the computer can connect to through its interfaces such as USB, **HDMI**, WiFi, Bluetooth
- **future proofing** – Jamie does not want to buy something that will be out of date and unusable very quickly
- **upgradability** – the games Jamie wants to play may need a faster processor or he may need a larger hard disk drive; he needs to be able to upgrade easily as it would be too expensive to keep buying new computers
- **support** – Jamie may need help with setting up and using his devices, or they may break down and need repairing. He should check with friends, in magazines and on the Internet which suppliers offer the best support.

For more information on features to consider when buying a computer, see Which kind of computer?, pages 15–18.

HDTV – high-definition TV.

High definition (HD) – the picture on a TV screen is made of lines of pixels. In a conventional TV there are 625 lines, which are refreshed 25 times per second. HD has either 720 or 1080 lines, so it produces a clearer, sharper picture.

HDMI (high-definition multimedia interface) – required for connecting devices to show high-definition video.

Jamie has narrowed down his choice to three laptops. To help him compare their features and functions, he has put the information into the table below.

	Laptop 1	Laptop 2	Laptop 3
Display	15-inch widescreen	16-inch widescreen	17-inch widescreen
Processor	1.6 GHz	1.8 GHz	2.8 GHz
Memory	1 GB	3 GB	8 GB
Hard disk drive	120 GB	200 GB	1 **TB**
Optical drive	DVD-RW	Blu-ray disk read only DVD-RW	Blu-ray combo read and write
Wireless enabled	No	Yes	Yes
Card reader	No	Yes	Yes
USB ports	2	4	8
Web cam	No	Yes	Yes
HDMI port	No	Yes	Yes
Support	1 year return to base	2 years return to base	2 years onsite
Price	£300	£450	£1,200

TB – terabyte or 1000 gigabytes.

Task 3.1

Complete **etask 3.1** to make some decisions about the laptops that Jamie has found.

Task 3.2

Jamie will be able to use media player software on his laptop to listen to the MP3 music files he has downloaded. He could, however, buy a portable media player such as an iPod, Microsoft Zune or one of the many others on the market.

Carry out research to answer the following questions:

- What are the advantages of buying a media player like the ones mentioned above?
- What other media could he access as well as MP3 files?
- What other devices could he use to listen to his music?

Jamie's responsibilities

Jamie will now have to dispose of his old equipment carefully, as his laptop, DVD player and television all contain materials that can harm the environment and are classed as hazardous waste. He can either take them to a waste disposal site or he could give them to an organisation which recycles computer equipment by donating them to other users.

Jamie's recycled computer could be used by a child in Africa

Be safe/be efficient

Before he disposes of his old laptop, Jamie must ensure that he deletes any files stored on the hard drive that might contain private or personal information about him, such as his name or his password.

He must also uninstall any software packages that he plans to re-install on his new computer, so as not to breach the licensing agreement.

The most effective way for Jamie to do this is to reformat the hard disk drive.

Task 3.3

e-component

Have a look at IT Schools Africa on **Website 3.6**, and create a digital factfile highlighting the environmental and social advantages of recycling.

Skills builder 3.2

e-component

When Jamie was researching laptops, he created a database of ones he thought might be suitable. Use the database **Laptops 3.1** to carry out the following tasks:

- Find all the laptops that have a Blu-ray drive and an interface that allows films to be viewed in high definition through an HDTV. Sort the results by price, with the most expensive first.
- Search for laptops in the price range £400 to £750. Sort the results by price, with the cheapest first.
- Add three new records to the database.
- Produce a report for Jamie showing all the laptops that have a processor speed of 1.8GHz or more, are wireless enabled and have at least four USB ports.

Exam question

You will be asked to identify suitable digital systems to be used in particular contexts. This is an example of a question about a method of input.

Mark wants a 'hands-free' games console.

Give **two** ways in which a game can be controlled hands free. (2)

(GCSE ICT SAM)

ResultsPlus
Examiner's tip!

Names of particular games consoles will not be awarded marks here. The question is looking for 'hands-free' methods of input **to a game**. This is a developing area so an interest in new controllers or new games will be helpful.

Ideas that would be accepted are: balance board, voice activation, thought generation, pressure pad, breaking a light beam.

Which games console?

Jamie's friends enjoy playing on their games consoles

Did you know?

In 2008, Britons spent about £4 billion on computer games and consoles: more than we spent on buying music and going to the cinema combined.

British homes contain approximately 21.4 million consoles and hand-held game devices and gamers have bought in excess of 335 million games in the past 10 years.

According to new research, 40% of Britons are gamers and 60% of them are over 20 years of age. Women are the largest group of gamers in the over-35 category.

'Meet the secret gamers' in *The Sunday Times*, 15 November 2009

Lots of Jamie's friends have games consoles such as the Xbox 360 and PlayStation®3. They are all enthusiastic about their particular console and tell Jamie that he should get one.

Starter

Carry out a quick survey in your group. Calculate the percentage of people who own a games console. Which brand is the most popular?

Using criteria similar to those he used to select a laptop, Jamie has decided to investigate games consoles. He wants to be able to play interactive games online with his friends but without spending more money than he needs to.

You can see the checklist Jamie has prepared to help him compare the Xbox 360 and PlayStation®3 on **Worksheet 3.2**. **e-component**

Task 3.4   **e-component**

Carry out some research for Jamie and complete **Worksheet 3.2** by writing 'yes' or 'no' in the checklist to show whether the games consoles have the features listed. Which of the games consoles would you recommend? Have a look at **Websites 3.7–3.9** to get you started.

Task 3.5

Jamie wants to play online games with his friends. Find out if he can play online with friends who do not have the same type of games console as he has. He needs your advice.

Console versus laptop

Before he finally decides what to buy, Jamie has been carrying out some more research. He is especially keen to play online multi-player, role-playing games but has found out that he can only play them using a computer.

He has made a list of advantages and disadvantages of gaming using a console and gaming using a laptop.

Disadvantages	
Console	Laptop
If one component breaks, the whole unit has to be replaced	More expensive
Can only be used for one purpose	Need some technical knowledge to set up
Can't play against people with a different type of console	Difficult to play on the couch especially if using a mouse and keyboard

Advantages	
Console	**Laptop**
Cheaper	More multi-player games available through the Internet, e.g. Mud, World of Warfare
Compact – all-in-one unit	Can edit games and modify maps
Simple – start to play straight out of the box	Monitors have better resolution than HDTVs
Multi-player games through the Internet	Easy to upgrade
Play on the couch, don't have to sit at a desk	Can play games online against people who have different brand of computer

Task 3.6

Would you buy a laptop or a games console? Give reasons for your decision, using Jamie's table to help you.

More options!

Jamie decided to buy a laptop for playing games and watching films. Since then he has played some games on his friend's Nintendo Wii. He really enjoyed the game play and he loves using the balance board to go snowboarding and the controller to play tennis.

HANDS-FREE GAMING

e-component

Jamie has also heard about true hands-free games consoles that are being developed. Have a look at two articles about these on **Websites 3.10** and **3.11**.

Task 3.7

Investigate the technology of hands-free games consoles. How can they sense movement? The latest consoles can even detect facial expressions. How do they do this?

Hands-free consoles might be the future of computer games

Connecting to the Internet

Learn about

- the functions/features and strengths/weaknesses of services provided by Internet service providers (ISPs), including:
  - ⟩ Internet access
  - ⟩ email
  - ⟩ web hosting
  - ⟩ storage
- criteria for selecting an appropriate ISP, such as:
  - ⟩ cost
  - ⟩ bandwidth
  - ⟩ the effect of bandwidth on speed and volume of data transfer
  - ⟩ download restrictions
  - ⟩ support

Jamie is now the proud owner of a WiFi-enabled laptop and a HDTV. He has been watching films in high definition supplied on **Blu-ray** disks, but now he wants to download them from the Internet and play online games. He will therefore need to investigate how to connect to the Internet.

Starter

The latest government statistics show that about 70% of households in the UK have an Internet connection. Almost 60% of these are broadband. Make a list of all the advantages to a household of having a fast Internet connection.

National Statistics Omnibus Survey, 28 August 2009

Broadband

If Jamie is to **download** films and play online games, he will need a **broadband** connection with a large **bandwidth**.

Task

Before Jamie can select an Internet service provider (ISP), he will need to know what all of the jargon means. Use **etask 3.8** to test your knowledge of the terms used when talking about Internet connections.

The fastest broadband is supplied by fibre-optic cables. Unfortunately, Jamie does not live in an area served by a cable company such as Virgin Media, so he will have to rely on providers that use the copper cables used for telephone services.

ADSL

Broadband over copper telephone lines uses Asymmetric Digital Subscriber Line (ADSL) technology. It allows much faster transmission speeds by using frequencies that are not used for voice calls.

With ADSL the volume of data flow is greater in one direction than the other, so download speeds are usually much faster than **upload** ones.

The ISP supplies an ADSL modem that translates the high-frequency broadband signals carried on your phone line into data signals that your computer can understand. A cable connects your computer to the modem.

Unfortunately, not all telephone exchanges are equipped for broadband, so Jamie uses an ADSL checker website to find out if the telephone exchange covering his area is equipped for broadband. He is pleased to find that it is.

Task 3.9

e-component

Use the BT Broadband Availability Checker on **Website 3.12** to find out if your local telephone exchange is equipped for broadband.

Figure 3.1 Examples of ISPs

Blu-ray – a disk that enables the recording, rewriting and playback of high-definition video and the storing of large amounts of data. It has more than five times the storage capacity of traditional DVDs and can hold up to 25 GB on a single-layer disk and 50 GB on a dual-layer disk.

Download – transfer of a file, e.g. a video, from a central computer to your computer.

Broadband – a high-speed connection to the Internet.

Bandwidth – the amount of data that can fit through an Internet connecton. You can compare it to a ten-lane motorway which can fit more cars on it than a four-lane motorway. Bandwidth is measured in bits per second (bps). This indicates the number of bits of information that can fit down the line in one second. Kb or Kbps means thousands of bits per second; Mb or Mbps means millions of bits per second.

Upload – transfer a file from your computer to a central computer, e.g. your ISP.

Did you know?

BT is planning to create a national fibre-optic network, with speeds of 40–60 Mb available to the first areas by 2011.

Choosing an ISP

There are lots of different ISPs. So which one should Jamie choose? He will have to consider the following:

- **Cost** – most ISPs have a monthly charge and they can vary widely for the same level of service. Jamie will also have to check if there is a set-up cost and if a free wireless router is provided.
- **Speed** – this is usually given in Mb or megabits per second (do not confuse this with MB or megabytes used for file sizes). However, actual speeds are usually less than the 'ideal' given as lots of other people are using the same cables. The speeds given are for downloading data and the speed for uploading will be much less.
- **Download limits** – some ISPs impose a limit on the amount of data that you can download in a month and will charge you if you go beyond this. Jamie will have to consider this if he is downloading lots of films.
- **Email and web space** – the ISP should provide you with several email addresses and also an area on their server to create your own web pages.
- **Storage** – many ISPs allow server space for storing emails, files and even photographs that can be shared with other users.
- **Security** – when you have a broadband connection your computer is vulnerable to hackers from around the world, as the connection is always on. The ISP should provide you with a firewall and also some anti-spam software.
- **Parental control** – some ISPs provide software to filter out undesirable websites so that parents can restrict access.
- **Reliability and customer service** – lots of users complain about their ISPs, especially about speed and poor customer service. Common complaints are: slow response in answering queries, having to phone expensive helplines for support, too slow in fixing problems, too much downtime when you cannot access the Internet. The best way to find out about reliability is to ask friends about their experiences, look in magazines and check on forums and user sites.

Firewall – a system designed to prevent unauthorised access to your computer when connected to a network such as the Internet.

Spyware – software that can be installed on your computer without your knowledge, which collects information about your logins and passwords and sends details to another computer on the Internet.

Be safe/be efficient

When you are setting up an Internet connection, you should ensure that you protect your computer from attacks by other Internet users. It is essential to have a **firewall** and software to prevent **spyware** being installed on your computer without your knowledge.

There are many Internet sites, such as **Website 3.13**, that let you check the speed of your broadband connection. In general, if your bandwidth result is roughly 85% of the rated connection speed for your modem or device, you are receiving acceptable throughput, although shared connections may affect this. However, since Internet performance can be erratic and you cannot expect to get nominal bandwidth every time you test, you should test several times, and at different times of the day, to get the most accurate rating.

Please hold the line...

Users regularly complain about downtime, when they cannot access the Internet, and then have to call an expensive helpline for support

Results Plus
Examiner's tip!

Connecting to the Internet from a home network involves the use of a router. Many routers support the use of wireless and cabled connections. When you use a wireless enabled device you can often 'see' a number of wireless connections.

The obvious answer to this starter-type question is WiFi. The more technical version is wireless Ethernet. You were asked to state the answer so no further discussion or explanation is required.

Exam question

Here is what might be a 'starter' question on the topic of connecting devices to a router.

State **one** wireless technology that can be used to connect digital devices to the router.   (1)

(GCSE ICT SAM)

How to create a home network

Learn about

- equipment needed to create a home network
- factors affecting speed and volume of data transfer and the impact of the number of users
- commonly used communication networks (Ethernet, wireless Ethernet)

Using the criteria in the previous section, Jamie's family has subscribed to an ISP.

Starter

There is one broadband connection in Jamie's house. What problems do you think this might cause for him and his family?

Local area networks

Jamie has carried out some research and has discovered that the family needs to set up a local area network, or LAN. This will connect all the computers in the house so that everyone will be able to share the same Internet connection.

He is enthusiastic about the idea and is finding out about the advantages of networking so he can convince his family.

Task 3.10

Carry out some research to help Jamie convince his family that networking is the way to go. Make a list of at least five advantages for the family of home networking. To get you started, have a look at **Websites 3.14** and **3.15**.

How can everyone in Jamie's family use the Internet at the same time?

Did you know?

It's the combination of bandwidth and latency that determines performance of a network connection. Bandwidth measures the capacity of a connection and is expressed in bits per second. (The more bits per second that can be transferred, the greater the capacity.) Latency measures the speed of the connection and is expressed in milliseconds. (The less time it takes, the greater the speed of the connection.)

Jamie has now convinced his family that they need a network. The next questions he needs to answer are: 'What type of network?' and 'How do we set it up?'

Types of networks

Jamie has discovered three different methods the family could use to create a home network.

The first two are Ethernet networks. Ethernet (sometimes called IEEE 802.3) is a set of software and hardware rules or protocols for linking computers together to form a LAN. It was first developed in 1973 and has been modified and improved many times. Ethernet defines the ways in which computers 'talk' to each other, but they can be connected together in two ways: cable and wireless.

The third method is known as Powerline.

ETHERNET CABLE

Ethernet cable is the original method for connecting computers. Modern cable is often referred to as Cat5 or Cat5e – these are the standards that show it is a high-quality cable. The cable is connected to the computers' network interface cards (NICs) by plugs like those that connect telephones. Most computers and laptops now have NICs already installed.

Ethernet cards provide the following transmission speeds:

- basic – up to 10 Mb (10 megabits per second)
- fast – up to 100 Mb
- Gigabit – 1000 Mb (1 billion bits per second).

The speed depends on the type of network cards installed on the computers.

WIRELESS (WiFi)

Wireless networks allow computers to communicate by radio or microwaves if they have wireless network cards installed.

The speeds of transmission vary, depending on the types of cards, from 11 Mb to 54 Mb, but these are maximum speeds and are usually never reached.

Wireless transmission can be affected by household appliances such as microwave ovens and cordless phones, and even walls and ceilings. WiFi performance is distance-sensitive, so speeds drop the further a computer is from the transmitter. It is also greatly affected by the number of devices using the wireless LAN.

Whichever method they use, Jamie's family will need a router to connect to the ADSL or cable modem. The router connects all of the computers to the modem.

The ISP has issued the family with an **IP address** that can be used externally on the Internet, but the computers will each need an internal IP address so that they can communicate with each other and the router inside the house. The router (see Figure 3.2) assigns each computer with an internal IP address, so it 'knows' where to send the web pages they are each looking at.

Most routers on sale have both wireless and cable connections, so it is possible to have a mixed cable/wireless network.

POWERLINE

Jamie found another method for creating a home network, called Powerline, which uses the existing mains power circuits in the house for data transmission. As most houses have plug sockets in every room, no new wiring is needed.

Task 3.11

Find out the types of network cards installed in your school computers and the transmission speeds possible on the network.

> *IP (Internet Protocol) address* – the personal address of your computer (just like your home address), so that servers know where to send the information you have requested.

Task 3.12

As a class, discuss the advantages and disadvantages of ethernet cable and wireless networks.

Figure 3.2 A wireless router used to connect all the computers in a network to the modem

Skills builder 3.3

Carry out research and produce a fact sheet for Jamie's parents outlining the network options available to them, i.e. wired, wireless and Powerline, and recommending the solution that best meets their needs.

Check your fact sheet to make sure it is fit for audience and purpose.

Which type of network?

Jamie and his family have been looking through all of the options and now have to decide which type of network to install.

Did you know?

In August 2007 it was estimated that 63% of homes in the UK had a home network used mainly for sharing a broadband connection.

Parks Associates, April 2008

Starter

What type of network do you use at school: cable, wireless, or mixed? If it is wireless, are there any areas where it is difficult to connect?

Figure 3.3 Jamie's family decides to use a mixed network

Task 3.13

Which type of network should the family choose?

Explain why a cable network would be better for Jamie when playing games. Make sure you include the terms 'bandwidth' and 'latency'.

Why might Jamie's parents prefer not to have a cable network?

Jamie's family has decided on a compromise. Jamie can use cable, as it will be better for gaming, while the rest of the family will use WiFi access. The ADSL modem and router will be in Jamie's bedroom so that he can connect using a cable, as shown in Figure 3.3.

Security

Wireless networks are less secure than cable ones. When you try to connect to your own wireless network you can probably see all of the others in the street – see Figure 3.4.

Figure 3.4 **All the wireless networks are listed in the dialog box**

Likewise, others will be able to see your network and, if it is not secure, they will be able to use your Internet connection for playing games and downloading files. Some Internet sites have lists of so-called 'hot spots' where there are unsecured networks in homes and offices, where you can get free Internet access.

The most important thing is to change the default password on the router. Most of them come with 'admin' as the default one. It is then easy for anyone to connect to it and change the settings.

You should also set up some form of **encryption** which scrambles the data on your network and only official computers with the correct encryption key can read it.

The commonest type is WEP (Wired Equivalent Protection), which uses 64- or 128-bit encryption, but the more secure WAP-PSK (Wireless Application Protocol – Pre-Shared Key) and WAP2 are becoming more widely used.

Skills builder 3.4
Produce a guide for Jamie's parents outlining the measures they should take to prevent unauthorised access to their home network, to minimise the risk of viruses and to protect files stored on their home network.

Knowledge check

Carry out **eknowledge check 3.6** to test your knowledge of networks.

Exam question

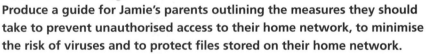

The bandwidth and latency of the Internet connection are both important factors when playing online games.

Explain why both are important.   (3)

(GCSE ICT SAM)

Downloads and on-demand services

Jamie is keen to start getting music and films online, but his parents are concerned as they don't want him to do anything illegal.

Starter

Have you ever downloaded a music track illegally? Did you know what you were doing? Were you aware of the potential consequences?

How can I tell if this download is legal?

Task 3.14

e-component

Look at two articles on the possible consequences of illegal downloading on **Websites 3.16** and **3.17**.

Jamie will have to be very careful that he only uses sites where he can get legal music and film downloads.

Skills builder 3.5

Carry out a survey to find out about your class mates' use of music downloads. What type of downloads do they use? How many music files do they download? Are these downloads legal or illegal? Use graphs to display your findings.

Downloading

These are the things that Jamie should look out for when he is downloading:

● **Avoid peer-to-peer (P2P)** file-sharing sites. They infringe the **copyright** of the people who produced the music and films.
● **Avoid free sites.** All reputable legal sites will have a charge, either a yearly subscription or a charge for each file you download.
● **Check the download conditions in the small print.** Often you can only watch the film on the computer on which it was downloaded and cannot copy it on to a DVD. Some even contain **Digital Rights Management (DRM)** software to prevent you from doing this.
● **Use reputable websites** such as media producers (e.g. record companies, the musicians themselves and studios such as Warner Bros) or companies like iTunes.
● **Check the reliability of the different sites** through forums and blogs.

If Jamie only uses legal sites, he will ensure that he receives good quality files and there will be no risk from viruses and spyware.

Did you know?

It has been estimated that almost 50% of the jobs in the music and film industries could be threatened by illegal downloads.

BBC dot.life

Seven million people in Britain are using illegal downloads.

Mail Online

Task 3.15

Find five legal download sites that Jamie could use, and explain why they are suitable.

Video streaming

Jamie has also been looking at sites that offer video **streaming**. The user needs a player, which is a special program that uncompresses the data. Using streaming technology, Jamie can watch live television and listen to radio stations from around the world on his computer.

Jamie has also found sites offering 'on-demand' streaming – an example is shown in Figure 3.5. This means that he can listen to music or watch films whenever he wants, and he can pause or rewind them. Many of these sites have been created by television companies and are free, but some have a small charge.

Figure 3.5 BBC iPlayer is an example of on-demand viewing

Copyright – gives the creator of an original work exclusive rights regarding that work for a certain period of time, including its publication, distribution and adaptation.

Digital Rights Management (DRM) – allows the copyright holder or the owner of the media control over the number of viewings, plays and copies, and even which devices the media can be played or viewed on. If you download a film from iTunes, you cannot burn it on to a DVD because of the DRM encoded in the film.

Streaming – content is sent in compressed form over the Internet and displayed by the viewer in real time. When streaming video, a web user does not have to wait to download a file to play it. Instead, the media is sent in a continuous stream of data and is played as it arrives on a special player.

Restrictions

Jamie downloaded a film on to his laptop, but before it played he had to obtain a licence. He decided to burn it on to a DVD for one of his friends, but he found that he was unable to do this. He cannot copy the downloaded film because if he gives it to someone else, he is distributing the film, and only the owner of the copyright is allowed do this.

Task 3.16

Illegal copying and downloading of films and games damages the industry. As a class, analyse arguments about how and why this is the case.

Task 3.17

Some professional bands are using 'viral marketing' to promote their music. What is viral marketing? Summarise how it works and give three examples of successful viral marketing campaigns.

ResultsPlus
Watch out!

Make sure you understand the difference between watching TV and films on demand, and downloading them. There are many more options available to people today. It is possible to:

- Download a podcast and listen to it later using an MP3 player.
- Listen to or watch a programme online.
- Watch TV on a mobile phone.

What precautions should I take?

Learn about

- privacy – methods of collecting information (overtly, covertly)
- cyber crime – what data is collected (personal, non-personal, usage, transactional)

In practice

When you log on to the Internet your ISP gives you an IP address (see How to create a home network, pages 73–74) so that servers know where to send the information you have requested.

You can find *e-component* your IP address using the Windows control panel or websites such as What Is My IP? – see **Website 3.18**.

Some criminal users are continually looking for IP addresses where there is no protection (just as some criminals check out areas where houses may be left empty with the windows open or the keys left under a plant pot). They can then easily get into the computer and steal files, install viruses or spyware.

Before Jamie started using the Internet, he installed anti-virus and firewall software provided by his ISP and thought he was fully protected.

COME IN AND TAKE WHAT YOU WANT!!

Starter

Make a list of all the programs that you already know about that can be harmful to your computer or your security when you are online. This type of software is called **malware**.

Jamie has noticed that his computer is running more slowly and the 'home page', which he sees when he first opens his browser, has changed to a different site. He keeps getting pop-up adverts opening in new windows and has unwanted toolbars in his browser.

What is wrong with Jamie's computer?

Jamie has been using his computer without adequate protection. It looks as if he has installed some spyware without realising it. He probably did this when he installed free or peer-to-peer sharing software. As this spyware runs, it is slowing down his computer. (To find out more on spyware, see Avoiding online fraud, pages 131–4.)

Task 3.18

 e-component

Carry out some research into spyware. Find out what it is and why it is a potential threat. Look at **Websites 3.19** and **3.20** to get you started.

Spyware collects information without Jamie knowing about it, and this is called covert data collection.

Task 3.19

e-component

Use **etask 3.19** to check out what you know about protecting your computer.

How else can information be collected about Jamie?

After Jamie bought and downloaded a racing game from a particular supplier, he has been getting messages and adverts from similar suppliers. This is probably through the use of **cookies**.

Cookies allow websites to remember you when you next log in and to suggest game or film titles that you might be interested in. They can also store quiz scores and if you have voted, for example for your favourite game or film.

Some sites, however, allow marketing companies to send cookies to your computer. These third-party cookies allow the marketing company to find out information about you, such as your email address and the types of game or film you like. They can then sell this information to other suppliers.

Jamie has also knowingly given many of the firms information about himself. This is called overt data collection as he knows about it, but this data can also be sold to other companies. If they do this, they should ask Jamie's permission first.

Figure 3.6 Jamie's questions about the collection of covert data

Task 3.20

e-component

Jamie is worried about companies covertly collecting information about him. Look at his questions in Figure 3.6. Use **Websites 3.21** and **3.22** to help you answer them.

Exam question

A website Gia visits creates a cookie on her computer.

(i) State what a cookie does. (1)

(ii) Give one benefit of the cookie to Gia. (1)

(GCSE ICT SAM)

ResultsPlus
Examiner's tip!

Cookies are used in transactional websites.

A typical answer to (i) would include the fact that a cookie stores a user's browsing history, which means that the website can build up a profile of Gia.

One benefit to Gia (asked for in (ii)) is that a cookie can save her having to type in her password every time she visits the website. You should be aware, though, that this can be a security risk if someone else uses her computer.

What are the dangers?

Learn about

- the risks of being online
  - › addiction
  - › damage to health
  - › predators

Jamie's parents are worried that he is spending too much time playing games. They are concerned that he might become addicted.

Starter

Carry out a survey in your group to find the average time each person spends playing computer games each day. Are there any differences between the amount of time spent by males and females?

Symptoms of computer addiction

Jamie could be becoming addicted if he has these symptons:

- He spends nearly all of his free time playing games or watching films.
- When he is sad or upset or has a problem, he escapes into a computer game.
- He is not keeping up with his homework and his grades are falling.
- He lies to his family about how much time he spends on his computer.
- He would rather play games than spend time with family and friends.
- He has given up other hobbies and interests.
- He is irritated and agitated when he is not playing games.

Jamie's parents are also worried that constant game playing could lead to other health issues, such as those shown in Figure 3.7.

Did you know?

MMORPGs (Massively Multiplayer Online Role-Playing Games) are a huge business.

One of the most popular, World of Warcraft, has over 11 million paying subscribers. Some players around the world can earn a living from developing characters and selling them and treasure they have accumulated to other users for real money!

In 2009, Broadway Lodge in Weston-super-Mare became the first addiction clinic in the UK to welcome gaming addicts.

Guardian

Eye strain

Overuse injuries of the hand, such as repetitive strain injury – especially thumbs

Muscle and joint problems

Lack of exercise might lead to obesity

Figure 3.7 Some of the health effects of spending too much time on the computer

Task 3.21

What are your thoughts on the questions below? Carry out some research using Websites 3.23–3.27 and create a presentation of your findings.

- Is computer game playing always bad for your health and well-being?
- Can playing games be good for people?
- Can they help us to keep fit?
- Are they good for our brains?
- Do they help us to remember?
- Can they help children to learn?

Task 3.22

With your class, analyse views on the advantages and disadvantages of playing computer games.

Meeting people online

Jamie's parents are concerned that as he sees less of his 'real' and more of his 'virtual' friends, he may come to trust them more than he should (see also Is the Internet safe?, pages 149–50).

Skills builder 3.6

You have been asked to create a section of the school website, aimed at parents, giving them advice on how they can ensure that their children stay safe and healthy when they are playing games and communicating online.

- Create a structure chart showing how the pages will be linked.
- Use a storyboard to design each page.
- Design the navigation.
- Gather and prepare the content.
- Use suitable software to create the web pages.
- Test that they work as intended.
- Ask a test user for feedback and make any changes necessary.
- Evaluate the web pages and suggest ways in which they could be improved.

Have a look at Websites 3.28 and 3.29 to get you started.

Knowledge check

Check your knowledge of this chapter with the Chapter 3 quiz.

Exam question

'Nintendo thumb' is one form of repetitive strain injury (RSI) associated with playing video games.

State two things Mark can do to avoid RSI when playing games. **(2)**

(GCSE ICT SAM)

Be safe/be efficient

What should Jamie beware of?

- **Identity theft** – criminals may try to find out personal details that they can then use to commit fraud.
- **Predators** – paedophiles who make friends with young people online and then try to meet them in the 'real' world. A United Nations report estimated that there may be up to 750,000 online at any one time. Unicef also estimates that there are more than four million websites featuring minors, including those of children aged under two years.

APF 'Some 750,000 paedophiles prowling Internet: UN', 16 September 2009

ResultsPlus
Watch out!

Read questions carefully and be 'savvy' about the answers. 'State' signals that you should give short statements in your answer. Be careful that you don't give two general answers. The answers must relate to playing computer games.

Correct answers include: taking regular breaks, using ergonomically designed equipment, doing hand or finger exercises.

Be careful not to give two similar answers. For example, if your answer says do hand exercises and do finger exercises, you will not be awarded two marks.

exam zone

Chapter 3
Entertain me – what to buy?

CHECK YOUR KNOWLEDGE

In this chapter you have been learning about the digital devices that are used to play games and download music and films. While many mobile phones provide limited games facilities, some music and video capability and even mobile TV, dedicated devices provide greater functionality and an enhanced experience.

These dedicated devices include games consoles, media players and digital TV in addition to the more unusual examples given at the start of the chapter.

You have also learned about issues that are particularly important when using the Internet to play games, download music and video or access Internet services. The issues we have looked at include choosing a suitable Internet service provider, copyright and privacy, cyber crime and staying safe.

You should now know:

- the uses and features of games consoles, media players and digital TV
- the criteria to use when selecting an appropriate device for a particular task
- the services provided by Internet service providers (ISPs)
- your legal responsibilities when downloading entertainment content
- ways of maintaining your security when using online services
- how you may be affected by cyber crime and how to stay safe.

Much of the content of this chapter has been about playing games on digital devices and the best type of digital device to choose in particular circumstances. Choosing the best type of digital device is also a key concern when downloading music and films. The key things to think about when selecting which devices to use or to buy are:

1. the quality of the experience
2. the cost of the device
3. whether the device can be used for other activities.

If you want a digital device that will allow you to play computer games what is the best option?

- Use a website that streams games.
- Buy a laptop with a large screen and a large amount of memory.

- Buy a games console.
- Buy a mobile phone with games functionality.

The answer to the question, 'What is the best option?' is that there isn't one best option. The answer depends on:

- where you want to play
- whether you want to play with other people and where those people are
- what you can afford
- where you live (broadband speed may be critical)
- whether you have to share the devices with the rest of your family (access to HDTV may be limited).

Examiner's tip

When answering an exam question, the reason why you have made a particular choice is as important as the choice itself. You must be able to explain why you have made a decision in light of the circumstances that have been described to you.

WHAT TYPES OF QUESTIONS MIGHT BE ASKED?

You may be asked about the choice of digital device in a given situation, or about the advantages and disadvantages of using a games console, rather than a laptop or a PC.

Alternatively, you may be asked about communications.

Mark plays online video games with people all over the world.

(i) Explain one benefit of using a network cable rather than a wireless connection for online gaming. (2)

GCSE ICT SAMs 2010

ResultsPlus
Maximise your marks

When asked questions about Internet connections, always avoid giving answers such as 'It's faster' or 'It's cheaper' without qualifying the statement. In the table below, I show you the difference between answers that would gain no marks, basic answers worth 1 mark and extended answers worth 2 marks. You would only need one of the extended answers to gain full marks to the question above.

Not worth a mark	Basic answer worth 1 mark	Extended answer worth 2 marks
Reliable.	A network cable is more reliable than using wireless.	A network cable is more reliable than using wireless *because there is less risk of signals from other household devices interfering with the playing of the game.*
Range.	The operation of the network using cable is not affected by the distance of the user from the router or whether house walls are in the way.	The operation of the network using cable is not affected by the distance of the user from the router or whether house walls are in the way. *This means that Mark can play games online in his bedroom or in any other room in the house, providing that there is a cabled network point there.*
Speed.	Use of cable means that the connection will be faster.	Use of cable means that the connection will be faster *because the speed of a wireless connection depends on the number of people/devices using the wireless connection in the house.*

You may also be asked a question about the dangers of spending a lot of time playing computer games. The question may be related to:

● Addiction to video/computer games
● Health issues related to lack of exercise or social interaction
● Not doing well at school
● Meeting inappropriate 'friends'.

4 Smart working

How can I market and sell my

How am I going to make my millions?

How do I provide a personalised service for my customers?

How do I work safely?

Which software should I use?

products to a wider audience?

How can technology help me work collaboratively with colleagues?

How can I store and back up my data safely?

Kyle left school after finishing his A levels and decided to set up his own business. He receives help and support from an old school friend, Zara. His business idea was to create games and applications for mobile phones. The business has been very successful and it is continuing to grow. Zara now lives in America but she and Kyle still work together. Kyle's ambition is to become a millionaire selling his games and applications to the growing number of people using mobile phone applications.

Setting up a new business can be an exciting prospect. What sort of business would you set up and why?

4 Smart working

In this chapter you will consider...

- Health and safety considerations when working with computers.
- The benefits and drawbacks of mobile broadband.
- Ways of working collaboratively.
- Software buying and hosting.
- Backing up data.
- Looking after customers.
- General business advice.

By completing this chapter you should be able to achieve the following learning outcomes...

- Understand health and safety issues connected with using a computer.
- Understand ways in which mobile broadband can benefit a business.
- Understand the different ways of working collaboratively with people.
- Understand ways of safeguarding your personal information and that of customers.
- Be able to create strong passwords.
- Understand the need for backing up.
- Understand how businesses use the Internet and how this affects us.

Functional Skills...

In this chapter there is information and activities that will help you to practise the following Functional ICT Skills:

Level 1

Using ICT

- Select and use software applications to meet needs and solve straightforward problems.

Developing, presenting and communicating information

- Apply editing, formatting and layout techniques to meet needs, including text, tables, graphics, records, numbers, charts, graphs or other digital content.
- Combine information within a publication for print and viewing on-screen.

Level 2

Using ICT

- Use ICT to plan and analyse complex or multi-step tasks and activities and to make decisions about suitable approaches.

Developing, presenting and communicating information

- Apply a range of editing, formatting and layout techniques to meet needs, including text, tables, graphics, records, numerical data, charts, graphs or other digital content.
- Use collaborative tools appropriately.
- Organise and integrate information of different types to achieve a purpose, using accepted layouts and conventions as appropriate.

The files you will use in this section are listed here:

Interactive activities:

1. etask 4.12.swf

Files:

1. Software types 4.4.doc

Websites:

1. Website 4.1 – Mobile broadband
2. Website 4.2 – Top 10 broadband providers
3. Website 4.3 – Times Online
4. Website 4.4 – mindmeister
5. Website 4.5 – Office Live Workspace
6. Website 4.6 – cnet
7. Website 4.7 – OpenOffice.org
8. Website 4.8 – Amazon
9. Website 4.9 – BBC
10. Website 4.10 – Directgov
11. Website 4.11 – NHS Direct
12. Website 4.12 – Just Like Sugar
13. Website 4.13 – Fabric Land
14. Website 4.14 – Yvette's
15. Website 4.15 – Barnard Castle Life
16. Website 4.16 – Google AdWords
17. Website 4.17 – YouTube
18. Website 4.18 – BlogStorm

Creating a safe workspace

Learn about
- health and safety issues associated with computer use
- ways of avoiding health problems related to computer use

Kyle understands that when working with computers safety comes first. He knows that while employers legally have to follow the Health and Safety Act 1974, he doesn't have to because he works from home. However he understands that, as someone who is self-employed, he needs to look after his own health and well-being.

Starter

List the health and safety issues related to using computers that you came across in Chapter 3. Suggest ways in which these could be avoided.

In Chapter 3, we looked at some of the problems that can result from using a computer (see What are the dangers?, pages 81–2). Here we will look at these in more detail and at ways to reduce these problems.

Computer-related health problems

Here are some computer-related health problems:

- **Back pain** can be caused by sitting incorrectly for a long time.
- **Eye strain** can be caused by staring at the screen for too long.
- **Repetitive strain injury (RSI)** is a result of doing the same thing again and again (e.g. typing or moving a mouse) – it causes stiffness, pain and numbness, usually in the joints of the arm, wrist or hand.
- **Stress** is often a feeling of not being able to cope, for example because of too much work, poor relationships with colleagues and a lack of support from employers.

… and some ways to avoid them:

- **Breaks** – people working at a computer must have frequent breaks to help prevent health problems. Computer users are advised to take 30-second micro-breaks every 10 minutes. You should try to do the following: look away from the screen, stretch, change your position frequently, move your feet, lift your arms and adjust your hips.
- **Training** – employers need to train their staff on how to use work stations correctly, to help prevent injury. It is a legal requirement for employers to display a health and safety poster produced by the **HSE**. The poster tells workers what they and their employers need to do in simple terms, using numbered lists of basic points.
- **Eye care** – employers have to pay for regular eye-sight tests for anyone who needs prescription glasses in order to use the computer. If the employee needs glasses to correct their eye sight, then the employer has to make a contribution to the glasses.

Did you know?

In 2008, 34 million work days were lost (1.4 days per worker) due to work-related illness and injuries.

Health and Safety Executive

ERGONOMICS

People come in many shapes and sizes, so it is important to have equipment that caters for these differences. Ergonomics is the science of designing equipment, so that it reduces the user's fatigue (tiredness), discomfort and injury. Ergonomics is used to design objects in the workplace, such as keyboards and chairs, to provide safety and comfort for the worker.

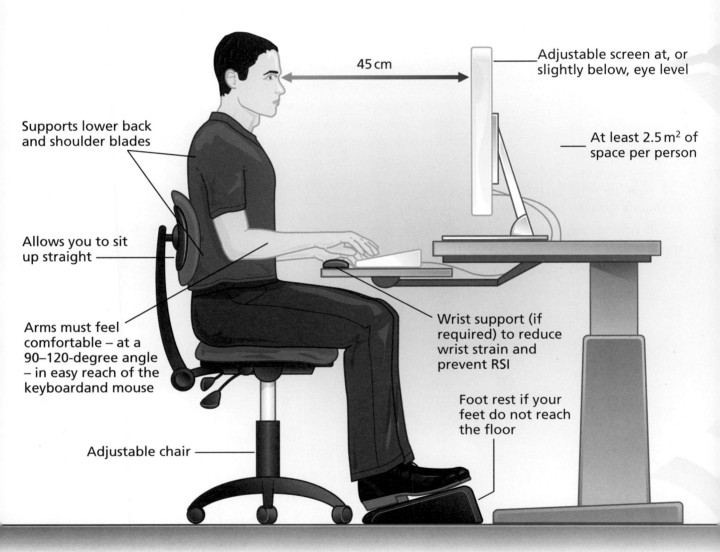

Figure 4.1 A well-designed work station is important to avoid fatigue and injury in the workplace

Other safety considerations

- Electrical sockets must not be overloaded with too much equipment, as this could be a fire hazard.
- When working at home it's easy to leave things lying around so it's a good idea to have a dedicated storage space to keep things out of the way.
- It is important to clean workspaces regularly, as bacteria and viruses can live on surfaces.
- Food and drink are best consumed away from the computer. Spills over electrical equipment can cause an electric shock, short circuit or even a fire.
- Electrical equipment emits heat so a room can get too hot. A well-ventilated room keeps the air flowing.
- Have the right safety equipment, including smoke detectors and fire extinguishers, and make sure you know how to use them, e.g. using the wrong type of fire extinguisher could make the fire worse.

Did you know?

Keyboards can have more bacteria then a toilet seat!

People tend to cough, sneeze and eat at their desks, and sometimes return from the toilet without washing their hands. Bacteria then transfers from their hands to the keyboard. This can be prevented by cleaning the keyboard and work area regularly.

Task 4.1

Read the following statements. Explain what might be wrong in each case and what you would recommend:

- Person A has neck ache.
- Person B is stressed by the large number of emails he is receiving.
- Person C's knees are hurting.
- Person D squints at the computer screen.
- Person E does not know how to use the equipment on her desk.
- Person F suffers from constant back pain.
- Person G gets hot and sweaty in the office.

Sitting in front of a computer for long periods may affect your health – ensure you are seated correctly and take regular breaks

Task 4.2

Create a digital poster for Kyle, highlighting computer-related health problems and how they can be prevented.

Knowledge check

1. What are the health problems commonly associated with computer use?
2. What does ergonomics mean?
3. When sitting at a work station what should you consider to maintain a comfortable posture?

ResultsPlus
Examiner's tip!

Creating a safe workspace involves consideration of health and safety issues. Make sure you understand the health problems that may result from using digital devices, and how these problems can be avoided.

Don't just think about computers. Mobile phones, games consoles and other devices can also cause health problems. In general, good lighting, ergonomic design and taking regular breaks are the most important ways of avoiding health problems.

Any time, anywhere

Learn about
- mobile broadband
- the advantages and disadvantages of mobile broadband
- factors affecting the broadband signal

Kyle has home broadband but would like to be able to use the Internet on the move so he is considering getting mobile broadband.

Starter

 e-component

Go to **Website 4.1** to see a short video on mobile broadband. What are the advantages of being able to use the Internet when you're on the move?

Mobile broadband allows devices such as smart phones, laptops and netbooks to connect to a high speed Internet connection over a wide geographical area, without the need for wires. Mobile broadband relies on the 3G network, the same technology used by 3G mobile phones.

Unlike those who use a WiFi connection to the Internet and have to find hotspots when out and about, users who have mobile broadband are able to access the Internet virtually anywhere there is a 3G mobile phone signal. Many modern mobile phones have the technology that allows them to pick up 3G signals built in, whereas other devices, such as laptops, require a **dongle** in order to be able to pick up 3G signals.

Here are just some of the reasons why Kyle would like mobile broadband.

- Kyle wants to be able to contact Zara wherever he is. When he has ideas for new games and applications, he wants to be able to share them with Zara straight away.
- Kyle often has meetings with his clients when he is out of his office. Having access to the Internet during these meetings is invaluable.
- Kyle wants to be as productive as possible and he finds the idea of being able to send emails on the move, without having to find WiFi hotspots, very appealing.

Dongle – a small piece of hardware that connects to a computer and has uses including data storage and picking up Bluetooth and 3G signals. A dongle may be portable like a USB pen.

Did you know?

Mobile broadband users can boost their speeds at no extra cost by using specially designed browsers such as Opera Turbo. Browsers such as Opera Turbo use advanced compression technology to speed up data transfer and to reduce the amount of data that needs to be downloaded.

Task 4.3

 **e-component**

Look at the top ten providers of mobile broadband on **Website 4.2** and see what they offer customers.

Be safe/be efficient

A mobile broadband dongle is a small device that can easily be lost or stolen. Anyone could simply plug your dongle into their own computer and download as much as they want to, leaving you to foot the bill. If you lose your dongle or if it is stolen, make sure you notify the mobile broadband provider so that they can block the service.

Kyle knows that mobile broadband could benefit his business but before he signs up to a contract he needs to consider both the advantages and disadvantages of mobile broadband.

Advantages

- Kyle wouldn't have to be restricted to working at home as he should be able to pick up the 3G signal in most locations, though the signal will be better in populated areas.
- It would allow Kyle to work much more flexibly as he would no longer be restricted to working in areas with WiFi connections when he's out of the house.
- With mobile broadband on his mobile phone and laptop, Kyle would be able to make the most of his time when travelling to meet clients.
- He won't need a landline or cable to access the Internet, which will save him money.
- Mobile broadband is more secure than a WiFi connection as all the data is encrypted.
- Mobile broadband can act as a backup if the home broadband goes down.
- Kyle can use mobile broadband to use VoIP technology to call Zara instead of having to pay for expensive international calls.
- The dongle does not require an additional power source, as a router does.
- The ability to work anywhere means that Kyle could save costs by minimising his office space.

Disadvantages

- Kyle may not be able to get a consistent 3G signal everywhere and in some places there may be no 3G reception at all.
- Most providers limit the amount users can upload and download. If Kyle goes over this limit, he will have to pay more.
- If Kyle accesses the Internet while he's abroad, he will incur roaming charges which can be quite expensive.
- Being able to access the Internet any time and anywhere means that Kyle may not know when to stop working, which could put him under pressure and cause stress.

Task 4.4

Consider the following scenarios and decide whether or not mobile broadband is a good option. Give reasons for your answers.

a) **A woman selling handmade cards from home.**

b) **Students living in temporary accommodation.**

c) **A business woman who travels to other countries regularly as part of her job.**

d) **A family on holiday on a remote island.**

e) **A family living in a very built up city.**

f) **A teenager who likes playing online games.**

Having considered the advantages and disadvantages of mobile broadband, Kyle has decided to invest in a mobile broadband dongle. However, he is going to keep his home broadband for the moment as it is cheaper and offers higher speeds. In the future, he plans to rely solely on mobile broadband.

Privacy issues

e-component

The advances in mobile broadband, and the resulting increase in popularity, has lead to the development of new mobile phone applications. You can read about one of these, and the possible privacy issues, on **Website 4.3**.

In practice

Before you sign up to a mobile broadband contract, check the 3G coverage in your area. You should also research the different contracts available before committing, as different mobile broadband providers offer different levels of service. If the 3G signal has to travel a long distance from the provider's mobile phone mast to reach you, the signal weakens and, as a result, you may not get the strength or speeds quoted by the provider. It is also important to consider the fact that tall buildings and building walls can also affect the signal you receive. As you have limited download capacity with mobile broadband, switch to WiFi wherever it's available.

Knowledge check

1 What are the advantages and disadvantages of mobile broadband?

2 What do you need to get the 3G signal on your laptop?

3 What factors could limit the 3G signal your device receives?

Collaborative working

Learn about

- advantages of working collaboratively
- different ways of working collaboratively:
  - ⟩ video conferencing
  - ⟩ VoIP
  - ⟩ online workspaces
  - ⟩ wikis
  - ⟩ online forums

Collaborative – working together to achieve common goals.

Multitask – to perform more than one task at the same time.

Remotely – from a different location.

Wiki – a type of website that encourages collaboration by allowing users to add, edit and remove content.

Online forum – an online message board where people can share their ideas and views.

Teleworking – working from home but staying in touch with others with the help of technology.

There are many more ways of working collaboratively than most people think. Go to **Website 4.4** and look at the spider diagram of technologies that allow collaboration. Are there more than you thought?

Kyle and Zara work collaboratively despite living in different countries. When Zara first moved to America, Kyle worried that the distance between them would be a big issue. Thanks to technology, they have found that this is not the case. Kyle and Zara have different strengths and they are good working partners.

Starter

Make a list of the ways in which you can work with other people thanks to technology.

Advantages of working collaboratively

Kyle and Zara have found that working collaboratively has a number of advantages. It allows them to:

- work simultaneously on the same projects
- get their work done in less time
- share their ideas and be more creative
- produce better products for their customers
- help each other when they come across issues.

One of the most important things collaborative working allows them to do is to maintain a good working relationship.

Different ways of working collaboratively

Kyle and Zara are able to work collaboratively because high speed Internet connections are available in both the UK and America. Without a high speed Internet connection, the type of collaboration they have come to rely on would not be possible. Here are just some of the ways of working collaboratively.

VIDEO CONFERENCING

Kyle and Zara use video conferencing to communicate with each other more effectively. It allows them to show each other designs and prototypes rather than just talking about them. Video conferencing was easy to set up. All they needed was a webcam to capture the video, a microphone to capture the sound and video conferencing software to allow them to send good quality picture and sound without any noticeable latency.

VoIP

Another technology Kyle and Zara use is Voice over Internet Protocol. It allows them to make calls much more cheaply than using a landline, so they talk more often. Both of them have 3G mobile phones so it is easy for them to use VoIP when they're out and about. When working from home, they can use their computers to make VoIP calls. They often use a hands free kit which allows them to **multitask** during the phone call.

ONLINE WORKSPACES

Kyle and Zara use online workspaces, which allow them to save work and access it **remotely**, share files, and work on many projects at the same time. When they have lots of work on they employ other people to help them out and give them access to their online workspaces. To read more about the advantages of online workspaces, go to **Website 4.5**.

Kyle knows that because he occasionally allows other people to access his online workspace, he needs to be careful to protect the information he keeps on it.

PASSWORD PROTECTION

Kyle asks everyone he allows to access his online workspace to create a strong password to prevent unauthorised access. A strong password should:

- be at least eight characters long
- include a mixture of upper and lower case letters, numbers and punctuation marks, e.g. ! " £ $ % ^ & * ( ) ? > <

Kyle tells the people who work for him not to use names or words in their password because these are easier to guess, and that they should never write their passwords down or share them with anyone. He asks them to change their password frequently as well.

Kyle can use these passwords to prevent people from accessing information that he wants to protect. One way he can do this is to install software that will link files to each user's username and password, which means that individual users only see certain files when they log in.

Did you know?

There are four levels of access rights:

- Read
- Read and write
- Read, write and amend
- Read, write, amend and delete (full access).

Typically, an online workspace would have one administrator who has full access rights. All other users would have limited rights.

Task

What problems could be created by giving everyone full access rights to a network?

WIKIS AND ONLINE FORUMS

Kyle and Zara use **wikis** to get feedback from their customers. (For a recap on how wikis work, go to **Website 1.14**.) Customers from around the world contribute to the wiki, and Kyle and Zara use this feedback to improve the products they create. **Online forums** allow Kyle and Zara to keep in touch with others in their industry and keep up to date on recent developments.

Teleworking

Improved broadband and collaborative tools allow people to **telework** more easily. These are some of the benefits of teleworking Kyle and Zara have enjoyed, as well as some of the disadvantages.

Advantages of teleworking	Disadvantages of teleworking
Costs savings – they work from home instead of having to rent office space	*Less social contact* – communicating through devices means they don't meet many people
Increased productivity – they don't have to waste time travelling to and from work (which is also better for the environment)	*Distractions* – family members, TV and noisy neighbours can all stop them concentrating from the task in hand
Flexible hours – they can work when they are most productive, and set their own schedules	*Boundaries* – it's not easy to switch off and stop working which could lead to stress

Skills builder 4.1

Kyle and Zara want to launch their latest game. As a class organise a launch event using only a wiki to communicate your ideas to each other. You need to agree on a launch name, date, location and what will make the event successful.

Was this an easy task? What does it tell you about working collaboratively?

Knowledge check

1 What is an online workspace?
2 What are the different levels of access you can give to people working on online projects?
3 What are the advantages and disadvantages of teleworking for self-employed people?

Learn about

- different types of software
- generic and specialist software
- hosted software (software as a service – SaaS)
- locally installed software
- open source software
- licensing issues

Kyle uses many different software tools in his work, including specialist games authoring and programming applications. Most of the software packages he uses are installed on the desktop PC in his home office, which means he can't use them when he's out and about. With this in mind he's keen to explore the potential of web hosted applications as an alternative.

Starter

What are the advantages of using an online application such as Google docs? Can you think of any drawbacks?

Types of software

Task 4.6

Many individuals and businesses are switching from using locally installed software to web hosted alternatives such as Google Apps. Would Kyle be advised to do the same? Investigate what is on offer and produce a briefing sheet for Kyle explaining what is available and outlining the advantages and disadvantages.

To what extent does web hosted software such as Google Apps pose a threat to established software producers such as Microsoft and Adobe? How do you think these companies can respond?

Hot desking – sharing desks or workstations between workers, as a way of saving space and resources.

Figure 4.2 Google offers a comprehensive web hosted software solution for businesses

When you buy software, you must accept the terms and conditions of the software licence before you can use it.

Software licensing normally makes it illegal for users to:

- copy software to sell or distribute
- adapt software, changing the way it works.

Users need to buy an appropriate licence for how they intend to use the software:

- **Multi-user licence** – the software can be installed on a fixed number of machines.
- **Licence by use** – similar to a multi-user licence. Software can be installed on many machines but only used by a fixed number of people at any one time. This is useful for businesses that use **hot desking**.
- **Site licence** – where software can be used on all computers on one site, e.g. a school or business, although there may be a limit on the number of machines on which the software can be installed on one site.

Kyle uses two types of application software for his business:

- **general-purpose (generic) software** – this is often referred to as off-the-shelf software, and includes standard applications such as word processing, spreadsheets, desktop publishing and presentation software
- **specialist software** – this is software that can be customised by the company or organisation using it, e.g. a stock control system for a supermarket or a database system for a school. Kyle uses specialist games development software. Specialist software is more expensive than general-purpose software.

Buying and upgrading software

Kyle has three options for buying and upgrading his software.

LOCALLY INSTALLED SOFTWARE

He can buy the software in one go (either from a shop or by downloading it) and save it on to his own computer system. He will pay a one-off fee and he will own the software, so he can use it for as long as he wants.

LEASING THE SOFTWARE

He can lease (rent) the software from a company, save it on to his computer and pay for it each month instead of all in one go.

SOFTWARE AS A SERVICE

He can use a system called software as a service (SaaS) where he pays for software as he uses it – similar to 'pay as you go' on mobile phones. The software stays on the system of the company selling it (this is called hosted software). Sometimes the software can be saved on to Kyle's computer, but it will stop working once the period that has been paid for comes to an end.

Kyle often uses specialist software to design games

 **Did you know?** e-component

Each year, more than 55 million boxes of software go to landfills and incinerators, and people throw away millions of music CDs.

Worldwatch Institute

You can try out new trials and download new software from sites such as **Website 4.6**.

ADVANTAGES AND DISADVANTAGES

Kyle has drawn up a table to help him decide which method to choose. You can see his list on **Software types 4.4**.

Task

With your class, check your understanding of the differences between the three types of software.

Skills builder 4.2

Working in a team of three use Google docs to produce a presentation for Kyle and Zara demonstrating how the software's collaborative working tools could help them to work together on a project despite being several thousand miles apart.

Task 4.8

Use the Internet to find two examples of each of the three types of software:

- locally installed software
- leased software
- software as a service (SaaS).

Be safe/be efficient

Using software illegally or copying software is against the law. You will be breaking the Copyright, Designs and Patents Act and could be prosecuted.

Counterfeiters can make copies of software look like the real thing, so always buy software from a reputable source.

Be careful when downloading software for free as it could contain viruses, bugs, spyware, etc. (see What precautions should I take?, pages 79–80). If you do download free software, make sure it is from a reputable source.

Open source software

Kyle does not have to pay for software at all if he does not want to. **Open source software** is available to download free of charge. It is available freely because the 'source code' is created by anybody who is able to and not by a single company.

A well-known example of open source software is OpenOffice.org, a suite of office applications for word processing, spreadsheets, presentations and creating databases – see Figure 4.3.

Here are some advantages identified by OpenOffice.org for its software:

- No licensing fees.
- You can distribute and copy the software as much as you wish, in accordance with either of the Open Source licences.
- File compatibility – OpenOffice.org allows you to open and save files in many common formats, including Microsoft Office, HTML, XML, WordPerfect and Lotus 123.
- Upgrades, fixes and modifications are created by the 'user community' as and when they see the need.

e-component

You can find out more about OpenOffice.org by going to **Website 4.7**.

Open source software – software that is available to download free of charge, e.g. OpenOffice.org, which is a suite of applications.

Task 4.9

Some of the advantages of using open source software are listed above. Make a list of possible disadvantages of using open source software.

Figure 4.3 An OpenOffice.org application being run

Knowledge check

1 What are the advantages of locally installed software?
2 What are the advantages of software as a service (SaaS)?
3 How can you legally use software for free?
4 What is the purpose of a software licence?

Exam question

Explain the term 'open source software'.

ResultsPlus
Maximise your marks

If you are asked to **Explain**, you need linked points for full marks. Both the answers below would achieve top marks:

Possible answer 1: Open source software code is in the public domain which means that anyone can use it.

Possible answer 2: Open source software code is in the public domain so that the software can be developed collaboratively.

Storing and backing up data

Learn about
- different storage media/devices
- issues with storing data online
- backing up data
- disaster recovery
- Data Protection Act 1998

Kyle and Zara spend a lot of time and effort working on computer games they hope to sell. They need to make sure their files are stored securely and that they have a backup just in case disaster strikes.

Starter

With a partner, write a list of reasons why it is important to back up data on a computer.

Did you know?

Data loss is very common: 66% of Internet users have suffered from serious data loss.

Kabooza Global Backup Survey

What is data?

All of the information saved on a computer is known as **data**. Data can be very valuable, sometimes more valuable than the computer itself – for example, all the applications that Kyle has produced are worth a lot of money. Companies have to think very carefully about where to store their data.

Where can data be stored?

Kyle's data includes games and applications, customer details, and documents he produces to run his business. The data is stored on the computer and then Kyle makes another copy – called a **backup** – for safekeeping.

Work stored on a computer is referred to as **primary storage**. When stored in other places, it is known as **secondary storage**.

Task 4.10

Name each data storage device illustrated above. When and for what purpose would you use each one?

OTHER STORAGE DEVICES

You might have heard of floppy disks and zip disks – these are now obsolete because of their poor performance and low storage capacity.

ONLINE DATA STORAGE

Data can be stored online by a host company, as shown in Figure 4.4. To use this service, Kyle needs to set up an account with an online data storage company. He can then select options depending on the needs of his business. He can back up data by sending it to the online data storage company through an Internet connection, and he will be able to access the data whenever he wants.

This is a form of **outsourcing**. Data should be encrypted when being uploaded or downloaded to make it secure.

Figure 4.4 Data from many different companies can be stored at one online data centre

Data – symbols, characters, images and numbers are all types of data. When data is processed and acquires meaning it becomes information. Computers process data to produce information.

Backup – a copy of data that is made in case the original data is lost or damaged. The backup can be used to restore the original data.

Primary storage – built-in storage designed to be directly accessed by the CPU.

Secondary storage – storing data on another device, such as a CD or USB pen.

Outsourcing – using an external service provider to carry out a business function.

Task 4.11

Look at Figure 4.4. When and for what purpose would you use online data storage?

Advantages and disadvantages of online storage

Advantages	Disadvantages
• No need to purchase a device – money can be spent on other things. • Data can be accessed anywhere in the world with an Internet connection. • Data will be protected if there is damage to the site where the original data is held. • Hosting companies are data storage experts, so data will normally be better protected than by a home protection system or onsite storage. • No need to employ someone to be responsible for data backup. • Data backup can be done at quieter times, so that it does not affect the running of the business.	• Less control of the data if it is held by a third party. • Access to data relies on an Internet connection. • Download/upload speeds can be affected by the Internet connection. • The hosting company may host data from lots of different companies, which might encourage hackers to target the host company. • May not be advisable for sensitive data, as there are strict rules on storing personal data (see Data Protection Act 1998 overleaf).

Task 4.12

e-component

Use **etask 4.12** to check your understanding of the advantages and disadvantages of online data storage.

Task 4.13

Choose the most suitable media for storing data in the following situations. Explain the reasons for your choice.

a) Friends sharing songs between themselves.

b) A TV series downloaded on to a computer without a CD/DVD drive.

c) Photos to distribute.

d) All the work produced by a large company in a day.

e) Transferring photos from a digital camera to a computer.

f) A small company of four employees backing up data.

g) A designer accessing work on holiday.

h) A school's daily backup of students' work.

Why back up?

When storing any kind of information, a business needs to protect the data in case of:

- data being stolen
- data becoming corrupt and unreadable
- human error – data accidentally deleted or written over
- natural or manmade disasters, e.g. fire, flood, lightening.

Any of the storage methods listed can be used to back up data.

PROTECTING DATA IN CASE OF DISASTER

It is a good idea for Kyle to have a **disaster recovery** plan so that he can carry on with his business if there is a disaster – see Figure 4.5. Ways to protect data in the event of a disaster include:

- backing up data
- using **RAID** technology
- fitting surge protectors to protect against power surges to the electronic equipment
- using an uninterruptible power supply (UPS) in case there is a power cut
- taking fire precautions such as installing alarms and fire extinguishers
- running anti-virus software and a firewall to stop unauthorised access to the system
- training staff to deal with problems.

Data Protection Act 1998

All companies must abide by the Data Protection Act 1998 when storing personal data about customers. Let's look at what they have to do to keep personal data safe and out of the wrong hands:

- Register with the Information Commissioner's Office.
- Obtain customers' permission before giving our their data to other companies – remember to read the small print on forms and tick those boxes that say you do not want your information passed on.
- Remove customers' personal data when the company no longer needs it.
- Have good security measures in place to prevent data being lost or stolen.

Disaster recovery – the policies and procedures that a company or organisation has in place so it can carry on with normal business after a disaster, such as a major ICT failure, a fire, etc.

RAID (redundant array of inexpensive disks) – a hard disk drive where data is written on to lots of disks at the same time. If one disk gets damaged, data can be accessed from another disk.

Figure 4.5 These are the crucial things that Kyle needs to consider because if he loses all his data, the business will not be able to operate

 4.14

Recommend the method of data storage and backup that you think is best for Kyle. You will need to think about the following:

- Kyle's applications and games do not require large amounts of storage space.
- He often accesses his data on the move.

How often do you think Kyle should back up his data? Give reasons for your answers.

 4.15

Put together a plan of action for Kyle's business in case of a disaster. Think about:

- how often backups should be made
- where backups should be kept
- who is in charge of backing up
- how easily the backup data can be accessed after the disaster
- where the business will be run from in case of a disaster.

Knowledge check

1. Why have floppy disks and zip disks become obsolete?
2. Give some advantages of storing data online.
3. Which law do you need to consider when storing personal information about customers?
4. Explain three ways in which a company can prevent data being lost.

Communicating with customers

Learn about

- different forms of online communication with customers, including:
  › email
  › instant messaging (IM)
  › online help
  › blogs
  › video conferencing
  › VoIP
- the benefits to customer relations

Kyle knows that the key to good customer relations is providing excellent customer service. He uses a range of different methods to communicate with the customers of his online business venture.

Starter

If you had a problem with an online company, how would you contact it? Are there other ways of making contact?

Kyle has to consider which methods are best for him and his business. He is thinking about:

- email
- instant messaging (IM)
- online help
- blogs
- video conferencing
- VoIP.

In Chapter 1 we looked at many of these communication methods for socialising and doing school work. Now we will be looking at how they can be used by a business – see Figure 4.6.

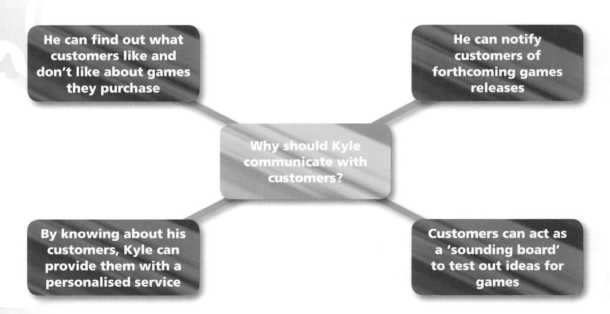

He can find out what customers like and don't like about games they purchase

He can notify customers of forthcoming games releases

Why should Kyle communicate with customers?

By knowing about his customers, Kyle can provide them with a personalised service

Customers can act as a 'sounding board' to test out ideas for games

Figure 4.6 The importance of customer communication

Email

Kyle has an email link on his website which customers can use to send enquiries.

Figure 4.7 The Zen Internet website offers a choice of ways of contacting the company, including an email link

Task 4.16

Reputable companies always give an email address on their website so customers can contact them. Suggest advantages and disadvantages of email contact for customers. What are the pros and cons for the company?

Instant messaging (IM)

Kyle could have a link on his website to launch a chat facility, so that customers can discuss products with him or a member of his team. He could also give a help email address, which customers can add to their IM.

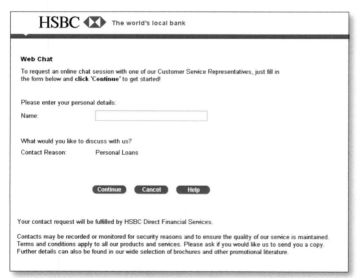

Figure 4.8 The HSBC website offers a live chat feature for customers wishing to find out more about loans

Another similar feature allows the customer to enter a question, and the computer then responds with an appropriate answer. This gives the impression that you are talking to a real person, but it is a computer-generated conversation – see Figure 4.9 on page 107.

Task 117

Copy and complete the table below with the advantages and disadvantages of instant messaging, both for the customer and the business. You could also have a look at Socialising on the Internet, pages 19–20, but remember that you are thinking about a business here.

Socialising on the Internet, pages 19–20

Advantages	Disadvantages
Reassures customers that they can speak to someone at any time.	Kyle's company is very small, so he is unable to staff the system 24 hours a day. He will need to use **presence awareness**.

Presence awareness – a common IM feature that gives you a quick view of the people who are logged on at that time.

Figure 4.9 IKEA's Ask Anna feature allows you to type in a question and the computer will give an answer based on key words you have entered

Blogs

Kyle has a blog where he gives updates on what he is currently working on. This is a great way for a business to show that it cares about its customers and their ideas. It is also a way to receive useful suggestions from customers on how to improve products or services.

On the negative side, some customers could post malicious entries, which might damage the business. Blogs need to be updated regularly or customers might get the impression that the company is slow to react.

Video conferencing

Kyle sometimes uses video conferencing to take part in a conversation with customers; for example, where customers are based in a different country or are interested in making a large purchase. It allows them to talk 'face to face' and gives Kyle the opportunity to show projects that he is working on.

Video conferencing allows Kyle to see the people he is talking to

VoIP

VoIP allows Kyle to keep in touch with customers by speaking rather than using text on a screen. It is a convenient way of communicating clearly and effectively.

Task 4.18

With your class, consider the advantages and the disadvantages of VoIP and video conferencing.

Task 4.19

Imagine you want to buy something online and need to communicate with a customer service representative. Which method of communication would you prefer? Give reasons for your choice.

Knowledge check

1 What are the advantages for a business of using email to communicate with customers?
2 What are the disadvantages of using IM?
3 What hardware do you need for VoIP?

Running a business online

Learn about

- how the Internet has affected the business world
- the advantages of running a business online
- advertising online, including:
  - > search engines
  - > content networks
  - > viral marketing

Kyle's business operates solely online. In this section we will look at the effect of the Internet on businesses, including the advantages of running a business online and advertising online.

Starter

What is your favourite television advert? What is your favourite online advert? What makes them stand out?

Website

Kyle's website is the main way that he advertises and sells his products.

Companies like Amazon.co.uk sell solely online, whereas some companies sell both on the high street and on the Internet.

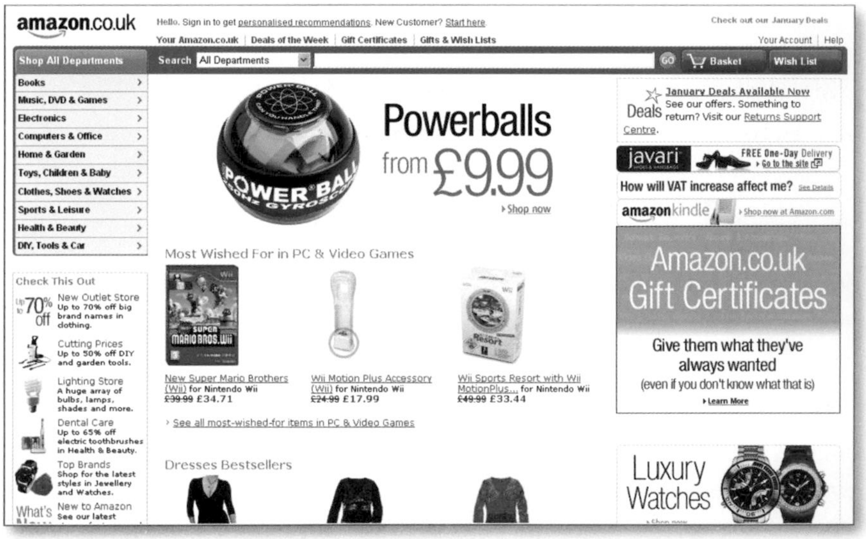

Figure 4.10 Amazon.co.uk sells a wide range of products through its website
© 2010 Amazon.com Inc. and its affiliates. All rights reserved.

Task 4.20

Why do you think more and more companies are using the Internet to advertise and sell? What are the advantages of online selling to a business?

Amazon.co.uk is the world's largest Internet retailer (see Figure 4.10). Have at look at **Website 4.8**. How do you think it got to that position?

Benefits of the Internet to an industry and individual businesses

Benefits to industry	Benefits to businesses
• Companies can market products on their website.	• Minimal start-up time and investment.
• It allows the business to have a large consumer base.	• Lower **overheads** as an Internet business can be set up at home.
• It is an inexpensive way to reach new markets and interact with customers.	• Search engines help direct customers to a business's website.
• Businesses can operate 24 hours a day, 7 days a week, 365 days a year.	• Automated order and payment processes.
• Marketing can be global as there are no restrictions.	• The business can be located wherever it likes.
• It leads to globalisation.	• Once the business is up and running, multiple businesses can be set up from the same base.
• Reduces the number of cars and car miles, and saves paper.	

Task 4.2

e-component

Have a look at **Websites 4.8–4.15**, which are designed for the public.

How does each site cater for the mass market? How effectively does it achieve this? Comment on:

- layout
- colour schemes
- links
- use of media, pictures, sounds and videos
- options available
- general usability.

> *Overheads* – the ongoing expenses of operating a business, e.g. rent, fuel bills, salaries.

Internet advertising

Companies choose to advertise their products and services in different ways. Kyle advertises solely online because Internet advertising:

- can be targeted – search engines monitor what customers enter in the search bar, allowing advertising to be tailored around the most frequently used keywords
- is much cheaper than traditional methods
- reaches a wider range of consumers
- reaches consumers much faster than traditional methods.

A company that advertises online has to compete against millions of other websites, so it is important that its website stands out from the crowd.

Advertising with a search engine

Kyle also pays to advertise with a search engine. Adverts normally appear at the top or along the side of the page, as shown by the red boxes in Figure 4.11.

Figure 4.11 Google ads appear at the top and side of the page

> ### In practice
>
> Customers can be put off using websites by:
>
> - poor design
> - pages with many graphics and slow load times
> - too many images or too much information
> - confusing navigation
> - pop-up windows (advertising and marketing should be designed to encourage customers)
> - outdated information and dead links
> - low-speed Internet connections.

When using this method, Kyle has to set up keywords so that his website will appear in the search engine's results.

KEYWORDS

These must be specific and relate directly to the page. Single words can be used, but sequences of words work better. Here are some simple rules for choosing keywords:

- Include variations, e.g. singular and plural versions of each keyword. Use a thesaurus to find synonyms. Product codes and serial numbers help too.
- Avoid using too many keywords. Only use words that are relevant. Keywords that are too general will not necessarily reach potential customers.
- When creating the advert, it is important to get your message across. Remember, advertising space costs money.
- The headline should contain one or more of the keywords, as it is normally a direct link to the website.
- The body text should contain a brief description of the product or service. Include just the key details.
- The URL should take the user straight to the product or service that is advertised rather than to the home page. If customers cannot find what they are looking for, they may leave the site.

Task **4.22**   *e-component*

Write a search engine advert for one of Kyle's mobile phone applications or games (invent the details). You will find some useful information about advertising in Website 4.16.

Content networks

Being part of a content network enables an advert to be displayed on a huge number of sites other than just in a search engine. For example, the Google content network is a collection of hundreds of thousands of websites on which businesses, large and small, can choose to display their adverts. They range from high-profile websites like Sky News, to small speciality sites such as blogs, social networking sites and discussion forums.

Within this network, Kyle will be sure to find some sites that are relevant to his business and are likely to attract customers who are interested in his products and services. A content network can therefore have a major impact on the success of a business's marketing campaigns.

Viral marketing

Viral marketing campaigns can generate brand awareness. They use entertaining content, which users are encouraged to pass on to other sites or users, and can be very successful – see Figure 4.12.

Figure 4.12 **The Cadbury's Gorilla advert is an example of successful viral marketing, as users sent links to the video clip to their friends**

Figure 4.13 Rowntree's Randoms

Viral adverts can be anything that prompts people to spread the message. They range from short video clips to text messages and online vouchers. Viral adverts aim to get people talking about the brand, which saves the company having to invest large amounts of money on marketing.

In order to advertise Rowntree's Randoms (see the product logo in Figure 4.13) Rowntree's produced a number of short video clips. Go to **Website 4.17** to watch one of these video clips. How might this get people talking about Rowntree's Randoms?

e-component

Skills builder 4.3

e-component

Adverts do not need to be complicated to be remembered. Create a 30-second advert in multimedia software for a mobile phone application or game.

Have a look at the viral ads on Website 4.18, and read about how they worked.

Knowledge check

1   What are the benefits of the Internet to businesses?

2   Which costs can be reduced by running a business from home?

3   What is viral marketing? How does it work?

ResultsPlus
Watch out!

This chapter focuses on businesses but you should think about your own interactions with online businesses and services as well. You may be asked about the impact on customers of using online sites of all kinds. You should consider both the advantages and the disadvantages for customers.

When answering exam questions about advantages and disadvantages of online systems, make sure that you answer in context. The advantages and disadvantages won't be the same in all situations.

Another thing to be careful of is giving general answers. It is possible to buy cheap train tickets online, however, it is possible to get similar discounts over the phone so you need to explain why the online booking system is more popular.

What about banking? How will the introduction of cash cards change our online behaviour?

CHECK YOUR KNOWLEDGE

In this chapter you have been learning about how ICT is used in the working environment. One of the changes in our society brought about by the widespread availability and use of digital devices is where and how people work. Many people now choose to work from home: they stay in touch with colleagues and customers using mobile phones and PDAs; they collaborate with people in other towns and countries and on different continents. The global marketplace is a reality.

These new ways of working have provided momentum for developments in digital technology and how it is used. Communication is vital when people are working in different places and on the move. For many people, the ability to access, send and receive emails on mobile phones is becoming more important, and as a result, this technology is developing rapidly. We can now send emails from planes and use wireless connections on trains, in hotels and while having a coffee in a coffee shop, although the increased availability of unsecured wireless connections has led to some security issues.

Many people find it hard to be parted from their laptops and take them everywhere and, as a result, the weight of the device and battery life have become important concerns. Netbooks have been developed to cater for people who want a lightweight portable device and some of the more expensive laptops available are very lightweight.

You should now know:

- the features of the devices needed for the workplace
- how to use the technology safely and efficiently
- the ways of safeguarding your personal information and that of customers
- how to create strong passwords
- why it is essential to back up data and how this can be done
- how businesses use the Internet and how this impacts you.

WHAT TYPES OF QUESTION MIGHT BE ASKED?

In the exam you might be asked questions on any of the topics below.

The digital devices used for work must be fit for purpose and in many cases these are the same digital devices as those used in the home. Take the availability of email on mobile phones. There are two ways of receiving email on a mobile phone, IMAP and POP.

> Describe how IMAP differs from POP. (2)
>
> Adapted from GCSE ICT SAMs 2010

Examiner's tip

To answer this question you need to understand that IMAP 'pushes' the email to the mobile phone as soon as it is received on the host server. On the other hand, POP requires the user to access email over the Internet.

Many users are happy to read their emails periodically so a phone that uses the POP method would be acceptable. However, business users may need to access their email more immediately so IMAP would be more appropriate for them. They may be willing to pay more for a mobile phone that uses IMAP.

Safeguarding information is important to everyone but businesses have a legal responsibility to safeguard information they hold about their customers. One of the principles of the Data Protection Act 1998 is about keeping information safe. The use of passwords and controlling levels of access are important here. On a more individual level, you should remember to use strong passwords and to control access levels when using social networking sites as well.

Examiner's tip

Make sure that you make the best use of your knowledge. If you understand something in one context you should be able to transfer that knowledge to a different context. The principles of what makes a strong password, for example, apply in a whole range of contexts, though how a password is used might depend on the particular context.

Take as an example the access key that is used on a secure wireless network. This is normally a long string of characters entered by users the first time they use a device to access the wireless network and then stored securely on the device thereafter. The access key is much longer than the passwords we use all the time. We normally limit the length of passwords so that we can remember them but this isn't important when it comes to the access key. Despite the difference in length, all passwords should contain four different character types in order to make them strong.

Backing up data should be an essential part of the use of digital devices. Your school network will be backed up using an identified procedure. Some systems use mirror images of storage to ensure that there is no danger of losing the data. Others take hourly, daily or weekly copies of data. Have you ever lost work when a USB drive failed? Do you back up your work regularly? Imagine what would happen if an online business lost all of its customer data.

You have also been learning about the different ways of obtaining and paying for software. It is important that you understand about copyright when thinking about software. It can take many years to develop a piece of software and the cost of single copies or licences for software help to pay for that time and to fund further developments.

There is a type of software available now that is called Open Source Software and there is also free online software. You may be asked to consider how these developments impact on commercial software producers.

> The availability of free applications software is a threat to commercial software producers, such as Microsoft™.
> Explain two ways in which commercial software producers can respond to this threat. (4)
> GCSE ICT SAMs 2010

This is an interesting type of question. What you have to do is explain two ways of responding to the threat. You need to think in terms of what commercial software producers should do and why this will help them keep their customers, as in the table below.

What commercial software producers should do	Why this will help them keep their customers
They can provide more facilities within the software and make the software easier to use.	Customers will find their software more appealing.
Do deals with hardware producers to package software with hardware. OR Provide technical support and training materials with the software.	The additional resources will make the software more appealing than the free alternatives that offer no extras.
Enforce copyright laws to stop 'similar' products being offered for free.	Customers won't have as many free versions available to them.

Examiner's tip

Make sure that you do not repeat yourself or give very similar answers. Providing technical support and providing training materials are too similar in this example to be awarded separate marks.

5 Shopping experience!

Where can I find new furniture?

How can I pay online?

How do I set up an online account?

Is it safe to buy online?

Is it safe to use a credit card online?

What if I don't like the things I have bought online?

What can online businesses do with my personal information?

Krista will be starting university in three weeks. Her parents have given her some money as a gift for passing her A levels and Krista has decided to use it to buy a few things for her university room to make it into a place where she can sit and chat with the new friends she makes. She has a limited amount of money so will need to manage her finances very carefully and look for bargains.

Krista has a laptop with access to the Internet, so she intends to research and buy as much as she can online.

Carry out some research to see if you can find Krista a site where she can create a budget and manage her finances online. As she doesn't want to use any of the money given to her, it must be free.

5 Shopping experience!

In this chapter you will consider...

- Buying goods and services online.
- Setting up online accounts.
- Online identification and authentication.
- Staying safe and preventing fraud.
- Data protection.

By completing this chapter you should be able to achieve the following learning outcomes...

- Know the advantages and disadvantages of shopping online.
- Know why you have to give certain information when creating online accounts.
- Be able to create strong passwords.
- Be able to identify safe payment sites.
- Know why companies sell goods online.
- Know how your personal data is used for advertising.
- Know how online shopping has affected us.

Functional Skills...

In this chapter there is information and activities that will help you to practise the following Functional ICT Skills:

Level 1

Using ICT

- Use ICT to plan and organise work.
- Select and use software applications to meet needs and solve straightforward problems.

Developing, presenting and communicating information

- Apply editing, formatting and layout techniques to meet needs, including text, tables, graphics, records, numbers, charts, graphs or other digital content.
- Combine information within a publication for print and for viewing on-screen.
- Check for accuracy and meaning.

Level 2

Using ICT

- Use ICT to plan and analyse complex or multi-step tasks and activities and to make decisions about suitable approaches.
- Select and use software applications to meet needs and solve complex problems.

Developing, presenting and communicating information

- Apply a range of editing, formatting and layout techniques to meet needs, including text, tables, graphics, records, numerical data, charts, graphs or other digital content.
- Use collaborative tools appropriately.
- Organise and integrate information of different types to achieve a purpose, using accepted layouts and conventions as appropriate.
- Work accurately and check accuracy, using software facilities where appropriate.

The files you will use in this section are listed here:

Interactive activities:

1. estarter 5.2.swf
2. estarter 5.6.swf
3. etask 5.19.swf

Files:

1. Worksheet 5.10.doc

Websites:

1. Website 5.1 – Kelkoo
2. Website 5.2 – Online Safe Shopping
3. Website 5.3 – PriceRunner
4. Website 5.4 – Microsoft
5. Website 5.5 – ShopDev
6. Website 5.6 – WWF Carbon Footprint Calculator
7. Website 5.7 – Get Safe Online
8. Website 5.8 – Be Card Smart Online
9. Website 5.9 – Times Online
10. Website 5.10 – Times Online
11. Website 5.11 – Guardian
12. Website 5.12 – BBC News
13. Website 5.13 – Guardian
14. Website 5.14 – BBC News
15. Website 5.15 – Information Commissioner's Office

Is shopping online a good thing?

Learn about

- advantages and disadvantages of shopping online
- how and why organisations sell and advertise online
- the impact that buying goods and services online has on lifestyles

Krista wants to start buying things for her university room, but is it better to buy them online or in the high street? What are the advantages and disadvantages of shopping online?

Starter

List all of the items that your family has bought online during the last three months. Are there any websites that your family uses regularly when buying items online? How did you find them? Were they recommended by a friend? Are they always reliable? Have you ever had problems with any of them?

Task 5.1

With your class, investigate the differences and similarities between shopping on the high street and shopping online.

Task 5.2

Here is a list of items that Krista wants to buy:

- iPod speakers
- flatscreen TV
- rug
- desk lamp.

Read through the advantages and disadvantages of online shopping. Then decide whether Krista should shop online or visit the high street for each of the items. Give reasons for your answers.

Advantages of shopping online

- **Availability** – you can shop all day every day, even on Christmas Day. Online stores are always open.
- **Selection available** – there is a far greater choice online than on the high street or in a shopping mall. You are not restricted to what you can find in your local area because you can browse in every suitable online shop across the world.
- **Compare prices** – you can easily find the best price for the item you want to buy by using price comparison websites that search lots of online vendors for you and display their prices – see **Website 5.1** for an example.
- **Convenience** – for some people, physically travelling to the shops is difficult, so being able to shop from home and have an item delivered is a great advantage.

Disadvantages of shopping online

- **Delivery** – all of the items you buy have to be delivered regardless of their size, so you have to pay for the delivery and wait for it to arrive. Sometimes the delivery charge can be more than the product you are buying.

- **Try before buying** – you cannot see or try the products (except in photos) before you buy; for products such as clothing, this is not ideal because if items do not fit, you have the added issue of returning them. Some sites have tried to resolve this by using virtual models, which can be customised to match your face and body shape, as shown in Figure 5.1. You can then try the clothes you want to buy on the model.

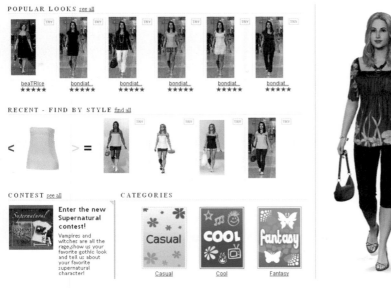

Figure 5.1 **My Virtual Model provides a virtual model to try out clothes**

How to...

... decide on the trustworthiness of a website.

There are a few quick checks you can do.

- Does it have a secure or encrypted website address – one that begins with https rather than http?

- Is there a padlock icon in the address bar?

- Is it owned by a company or an organisation that you know well?

- Does it have a postal address and a landline phone number?

Be suspicious if:

- The offers on the website seem too good to be true.

- You are asked for unnecessary personal information.

- You are asked to provide a credit card number without proof that the transaction is secure.

- **Viewing on-screen** – you might be disappointed by the item delivered. Images and presentations online can sometimes give a different impression of a product.

- **Payment method** – the only way many online shops can take payment for goods is using a credit or debit card and, without either, online shopping is out of reach. Although some sites allow payment through 'third-party payment processors' such as Paypal, or gift vouchers, most accept only credit or debit cards. However, some people with access to such cards prefer not to shop online, worrying about handing over personal details on a computer.

- **Digital access** – not everybody has access to the Internet or the computer skills to be able to shop online.

Online shopping has opened up many more avenues of choice, but nothing can replace the enjoyment for many people of meeting with friends and family and interacting with 'real' people in the shops they visit.

Task 5.3

Have a look at the list of disadvantages of shopping online on page 120. Which do you think might actually be an advantage for a person with disabilities?

Task 5.4

Search the Internet to find a site that Krista could use to compare the prices of televisions.

Recommend a trustworthy site to her.

Online customer rights

When shopping online, as long as you are buying from a UK-based seller or supplier, you will have the same rights as if you were shopping on the high street, and you can return items just as you would to a shop.

One major advantage that UK online shoppers have over 'real-world' buyers is a statutory 'cooling-off' period of seven days. When you purchase an item in a shop, by law, you can only expect a refund if the goods are faulty. If you simply change your mind or decide you do not like the colour, you have no right to a refund, although many shops do allow customers to return goods if they are still unused and fit to be resold. However, you can cancel an online transaction and receive a refund any time within the first seven working days for any reason... or no reason at all.

Be safe/be efficient

e-component

Make use of websites that investigate different online sellers and list the ones that they have found to be safe and secure – see **Website 5.2** for an example.

You can make sure that you're buying from a reliable shop that is known for such things as prompt delivery and good after-sales service by looking at sites that display customer comments and ratings of the different vendors – see **Website 5.3** for an example.

Task 5.5

Make a list of high street shops that you know also have online shops, and then make a list of online shops that do not have outlets in the high street. What conclusions can you draw about the types of shops that are not in the high street?

Discuss why you think some high street shops think it is important to have an online store but why some online stores are not present in the high street – here are some things to think about: staff, costs, customers, type of product being sold, size of business.

Some high street retailers also have an online store

Did you know?

There were computerised shopping systems before the Internet.

In the late 1970s and 1980s people could buy a limited range of goods using Videotext on their TVs. In 1992 the first Internet bookstore opened, and in 1994 you could bank online and order a pizza from Pizza Hut.

Task 5.6

With your class, think about how the availability of goods online has affected our lifestyle and behaviour.

Exam question

This is a common type of question asked about shopping online.

Gia wants to buy a new pair of shoes. She decides to shop online.

(i) Give two advantages of shopping online for shoes rather than buying them from a shop. **(2)**

(ii) Give one disadvantage of buying shoes online. **(1)**

GCSE ICT SAM

ResultsPlus
Examiner's tip!

Make sure you put your answer in context. The advantages and disadvantages of buying shoes online will be different to those of buying food online.

Do not use standard answers like it's 'cheaper', 'more convenient' or 'faster' without explaining **why** this is the case.

Setting up an online account

Learn about

- the use of usernames and passwords and other security measures (challenge tests, security questions) when accessing online systems

When Krista wants to buy goods online, especially from auction sites, she has to set up accounts which ask for personal information. She is unsure why she has to enter all of this information and what the companies might do with it.

I'd love to buy this lamp, but I'll have to register first.

Starter

What information would you reasonably expect to give if you were opening an account at an online shop? List the items.

Internet forms

Figure 5.2 shows part of a sample form that Krista has had to complete to create an account.

Tell us about yourself - All fields are required

ⓘ Your privacy is important to us. eBay does not rent or sell your personal information to third parties without your consent. To learn more, read our privacy policy. Your address will be used for posting your purchase or receiving payment from buyers.

* Indicates required field

First name *

Last name *

Street address *

Town / City *

County *
-- Select County --

Post code *

Country or Region *
United Kingdom

Primary telephone number *
( )
Example: (020) 12345678.
Required in case we need to contact you about your account

Email address *

Re-enter email address *

Figure 5.2 An Internet form

REQUIRED FIELDS

The items of information she has to enter are called 'fields' as she is entering them into a database like the ones you have created in your ICT lessons.

Task

All of the fields shown have an asterisk (*).

a) Why do they have an asterisk?

b) What will happen if Krista does not fill them in?

c) Can you create these types of fields in the database software that you use at school?

COMBO BOXES

Two of the fields – for 'county' and 'country' – have drop-down or combo boxes, where Krista can select an item, as shown in Figure 5.3.

Validation – the process of checking that the data entered is reasonable or one of the expected options, e.g. that a person's age has not been entered as 200.

Verification – the process of checking that the data entered is accurate. The data could be valid but still inaccurate, e.g. someone could enter their age as 81 when they are actually 18.

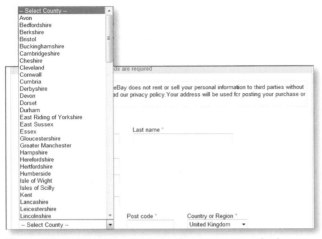

Figure 5.3 A drop-down box, also known as a combo box

This makes it quicker for the user to enter the data, ensures that it is not misspelt and that only valid data is entered, such as a county that actually exists. This way of entering data is a form of **validation**.

Task 5.8

Suggest three more fields where the information could be selected from a list or combo box.

VERIFICATION

At the bottom of the form, Krista has to enter her email address twice. This is a method of **verification** – checking that she entered it correctly the first time. If the two do not match, then she will have to enter her address again.

At the bottom of the form, Krista has to set a password for her account – see Figure 5.4. As she did for her email address, she also has to verify the password. This is very important – if she mistyped the first password, she would never be able to log into her account!

Figure 5.4 Creating a password

Task 5.9

Discuss the following with a partner:

a) **What will happen if Krista forgets her password?**

b) **What will she be asked to do, and how will the online company remind her what it is?**

Secret answer

Krista is asked to supply a 'secret answer' to a question that can be used to identify or verify her – see Figure 5.5.

Figure 5.5 Supplying a secret answer to help protect online security

Captcha tests

At the bottom of the form is a 'challenge test' or 'captcha test', as shown in Figure 5.6. A captcha test is used to prevent automated software from filling in the form. It is assumed that at present there is no software that can read the letters displayed and enter them into the field. Captcha tests can be used to protect systems vulnerable to email spam.

Sometimes even a human finds the letters difficult to read, so they can request a new sequence of letters or even ask for an audio test.

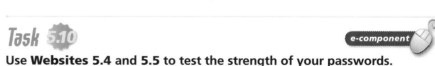

Figure 5.6 Captcha test

How should Krista choose her password?

Krista should create a strong password that will be very difficult to guess. A weak password is often a simple name or something to do with you such as your birth date, telephone number or address. A strong password should be a combination of letters, numbers and punctuation marks and should be at least eight characters in length.

Task 5.10

e-component

Use **Websites 5.4** and **5.5** to test the strength of your passwords.

Activating the account

The online retailer that Krista is using has one more security check. To ensure that the email address she entered is a valid address or has not been used by someone else, the company sends a confirmation email asking her to confirm her details and activate the account – see Figure 5.7. Krista has to select 'Confirm Now' and enter the confirmation code shown.

Figure 5.7 Email to activate the online account

Remember my password

Many online accounts ask if you want the site to remember your password. This is called 'auto-complete', as shown in Figure 5.8. Microsoft Windows has the ability to keep track of your user names and passwords as you visit different websites. With more and more websites asking you to create a user name and password, it is tempting to allow Windows to remember your passwords.

Figure 5.8 Password 'auto-complete'

Task

Discuss the following with a partner:

a) **What should Krista do? Should she allow the computer to remember her passwords?**

b) **Why might it be dangerous to do this?**

c) **How could people find out these passwords?**

Is it safe to pay online?

Learn about

- payment systems
- banking and other financial services
- security and privacy issues that arise when information is transmitted and stored digitally
- security risks and how to minimise them by use of:
  > encryption
  > authentication
  > digital certificates

When Krista buys things for her room, she is often asked to pay with her credit or debit card. She is concerned that this may not be secure and is looking at other ways to pay.

Starter

Carry out a quick poll in your group to find out:

- how many people have used bank cards to pay for goods online
- how many people have had their card used fraudulently.

There are four methods that can be used to pay for goods, as shown in Figure 5.9.

Did you know?

It has been estimated that, by 2011, 32 million UK consumers will be shopping online.

The value of goods they buy online in 2011 will add up to almost £52 billion.

Forrester Research

Figure 5.9 How to pay for goods

Credit or debit card

Krista has a bank account and she could use her **debit card** to pay for the goods or she could use her **credit card**. If she uses a credit card or debit card, she will be asked to fill in a form like the one shown in Figure 5.10.

Task 5.12

Using Figure 5.10, make a list of the details of your card that you are asked to enter when you pay online.

What item do you not have to enter which you would when you buy in person in a shop?

PropertyBLiSS.com

Make a Payment

VISA MasterCard AMERICAN EXPRESS

You are paying :	PropertyBliss.com
Amount :	Lm 1.00
Cardholder's Name :	
Credit Card Number :	
CCV Code :	These are the **last 3 digits** of the code printed on the **reverse side** of your card
Expiry Date :	Month Year

Cancel   Make Payment

Figure 5.10 Payment form using a credit or debit card

CREDIT CARD VALIDATION CODE

The CCV (credit card validation) code is also referred to as the security number or code, and is on the back of the card, as shown in Figure 5.11. It is not embossed on the card and, as it is not included in the black magnetic stripe at the back of the card, it cannot be copied by a dishonest merchant with a card reader. It therefore adds a level of security to card transactions.

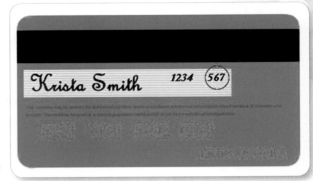

FURTHER CHECKS

When Krista's bank issued her with a Visa card, it asked her if she wanted to sign up for the Verified by Visa scheme.

Figure 5.11 Security code on the back of the card

 Task 5.13

Find out about the Verified by Visa scheme. What is it and how does it work? Why should Krista sign up for it?

SECURE SITES

You can tell if a site is secure when you make a payment if:

- the URL changes from 'http' to 'https' (the 's' stands for secure), and
- a padlock symbol is displayed, as shown in Figure 5.12.

Figure 5.12 How to spot a secure website

The padlock indicates that the website owners have been investigated and found to be trustworthy by the organisations that issue security certificates. If you click on the padlock, you can view the certificate. An example of a certificate is shown in Figure 5.13.

Figure 5.13 The certificate issued to an online retailer

The website uses an encryption system called **SSL (Secure Sockets Layer)** to encrypt the data.

 Task 5.14

Find out about SSL encryption. What is it and how does it work?

> *Credit card* – a plastic card, issued by banks, building societies, retail stores and other businesses, which enables a person to buy goods and services without the need for cash. The holder agrees to pay back the money borrowed at a later date, sometimes with interest.
>
> *Debit card* – similar to a credit card, but the money is taken directly from the holder's bank account.
>
> *SSL (Secure Socket Layer)* – a method of encrypting data to provide security for communications being sent over networks such as the Internet. TLS (Transport Layer Security) is a later version of SSL.

Be safe/be efficient

Before you send your personal or financial information, you should always check that the site is secure and your data is being protected. This is usually done using encryption techniques that encode information into a form that only the official receiver can understand. All hackers would see is a jumble of characters.

Online banking

Krista is still unsure about using her credit and debit cards for paying for goods online. She does not want to give out her personal and card details more than is necessary and is keen to investigate other methods of paying.

If Krista signs up for **online banking**, she will be able to pay some of the bills directly from her account. All she will have to do is complete a form like the one shown in Figure 5.14 on her bank's website.

Figure 5.14 An Internet banking form to transfer money to another account

Task 5.15

Discuss with a partner what the security advantages to Krista would be if she could pay all of her bills in this way.

Online banking has many other advantages, including:

- Krista can manage her finances more efficiently as she will be able to see how much money she has in her account each day.
- She will be able to access her account 24 hours a day, 7 days a week.
- She will be able to make payments directly without having to use cheques or her debit card.
- If she has more than one account, she will be able to transfer money between them to get the best interest rate.
- She will not need paper statements sent to her as she can check them online, so it is a 'greener' method.

Task 5.16

Draw up a list of the benefits and drawbacks of banking online.

Third-party payment processors

Internet commerce has given rise to a variety of **third-party payment processors**, such as PayPal, which allow users to set up online accounts.

A user opens an account and transfers money into it, either by direct debit or by using their credit or debit card. When they buy goods that support the online payment processor, they can transfer money from their online account.

Task 5.17

Carry out a quick survey in your group to see how many people have a third-party processing account.

Task 5.18

What would be the advantages to Krista of opening a third-party payment account and then using it to pay for things she buys online? Write down your answer and compare it with a partner's.

Gift vouchers

Most stores that sell gift vouchers and cards allow them to be spent online, so Krista would be able to use any that she gets for Christmas and birthday presents. She could also buy some herself if she does not want to give out her details online.

Task 5.19

e-component

Complete etask 5.19 to test your knowledge of payment methods.

Online shopping and the environment

People are increasingly concerned about the amount of greenhouse gases they are producing. This is usually measured as the amount of carbon dioxide (CO_2) someone produces and is called their 'carbon footprint'. You can work out the amount of CO_2 you produce for most activities – for travel to school, cooking school lunch, etc.

Task 5.20

e-component

Go to Website 5.6 and calculate your carbon footprint.

It's good news for online shoppers, as most research indicates that online shopping can reduce their carbon footprints.

Skills builder 5.1

Design and create a digital advert to promote online shopping.

Avoiding online fraud

Learn about

- security and privacy issues that arise when information is transmitted and stored digitally
- hacking and identity theft
- security risks and how to reduce them

Krista is concerned about giving her personal and financial details online. She has read lots of articles about online fraud and is worried about sending her card number and security code to people she has never met.

So is Krista right to be concerned? Is using her credit card online less secure than using it in a shop or restaurant?

Starter

Carry out a quick poll of your group to see if people think using debit and credit cards in shops is safer than using them online.

Defrauding money

Stealing other people's money by fraud has occurred throughout history, and criminals have learned new tricks to defraud people using their card details.

- Before the use of 'chip and **PIN**' cards, criminals could use lost or stolen cards by copying the signature on the back when they were buying goods.
- Criminals can make a copy of your card – this is called 'skimming'. Skimming can occur at retail outlets – particularly bars, restaurants and petrol stations – where a corrupt employee puts your card through a card reader without your knowledge. It electronically copies the data from the card's magnetic stripe.
- Sometimes skimming takes place at cash machines, where a criminal has fitted a skimming device. A small camera can record the PIN number you typed in.
- Some criminals, called 'bin raiders', collect old receipts to find out your card details.

PIN (Personal Identification Number) – a type of password applied to a credit or debit card.

Trojan – a program that appears legitimate but which performs some harmful activity when it is run. It may be used to locate password information, or make the system more vulnerable to future entry, or simply destroy programs or data on the hard disk. A trojan is similar to a virus, except that it does not replicate itself. It stays in the computer doing its damage or allowing somebody from a remote site to take control of the computer. Trojans often sneak in attached to a free game.

Phishing – a form of Internet fraud that aims to steal valuable information such as credit card details, usernames and passwords.

Criminals can steal personal details about you and your family from your rubbish – make sure you shred receipts and bank statements before binning or recycling them

Task 5.2

Write a report for Krista explaining why she should never let her card out of her sight when she is paying for goods in a shop or garage.

'CARD NOT PRESENT' FRAUD

When you buy goods online or on the telephone using a card, you cannot enter your PIN number – the card is not present at the place of purchase. You therefore have to give out lots of the card's details, including the security code. With more people buying this way, 'Card not present' (CNP) fraud is now the most common type of fraud in the UK. The criminals do not need a card or even your PIN; all they need are your personal details and the security code on the back of the card.

How can criminals get hold of personal details?

COMPUTER VIRUSES

The most common way is for hackers to install software called **trojans** to spy on your computer. They can record all of your key presses and send the information to criminals, who can find out your credit card details such as card number, expiry date, security code and password when you enter them. Some trojans even take pictures of the screen on sites that require you to use the mouse instead of the keyboard.

Trojans may be included in emails – in the email itself or as an attachment. Your computer can also be infected if you visit a malicious website, or through a glitch in the computer software that allows the trojan to infect the computer directly from the Internet.

Task 5.2

How can Krista prevent trojans and spyware? Make a list of the steps she should take. Have a look at Websites 5.7 and 5.8 to get you started.

In practice

According to a study in the USA, 14% of **phishing** emails are successful, allowing identity thieves access to the personal information of their victims. In the study, traceable 'phishing' emails were sent to potential victims, featuring a link to eBay. While the link in the test indeed took them to eBay (as they were not actually 'phishing'), notification data was recorded when the link was clicked.

University of Indiana, School of Informatics

PHISHING

This is when fraudsters spam the Internet with an email claiming to be from a reputable financial institution (bank or building society) or e-commerce site – see Figure 5.15. Phishing can also be done via text messages.

The email or text message tries to make you click on a link and update your personal profile or carry out a transaction. The link takes you to a fake website designed to look like the real thing. Any personal or financial information that you enter will be sent directly to the scammer.

Sometimes the criminals have most of your details except the security code on the back of the card, which cannot be read by a card reader. They can try to make their emails look more official by giving the details that they already have, such as card number and name and address and just ask for the security code.

There is a huge market for the information obtained.

Criminals use phishing emails to obtain personal and financial details from their victims – never respond to a phishing email or click on the link it contains

Task 5.23

Have a look at a newspaper article on online fraud on **Website 5.9**. As a class, see if you can spot the features of phishing emails.

Task 5.24

Complete **etask 5.24** to check your knowledge of online security and fraud.

ResultsPlus
Watch out!

To answer a question on online fraud you need to understand the threats and how to avoid them. Online fraud is likely to occur when criminals get hold of and use:

- your bank account details
- details of any other accounts you have (e.g. email)
- your username and password for a particular website.

In the exam, students often see a key word in the question, such as **fraud**, and write everything they know about it. Be careful though because this may not be what is required. Read every question on the exam paper carefully and then make sure you answer the question that's been set.

Attachments – sometimes you will be asked to open programs or documents sent with the email. These attachments may contain spyware or take you automatically to an online form.

Impersonal – in a phishing attempt you are not addressed personally, whereas you are in a legitimate email from your bank, for example.

Careless use of language – spelling errors and a careless writing style are often signs of phishing.

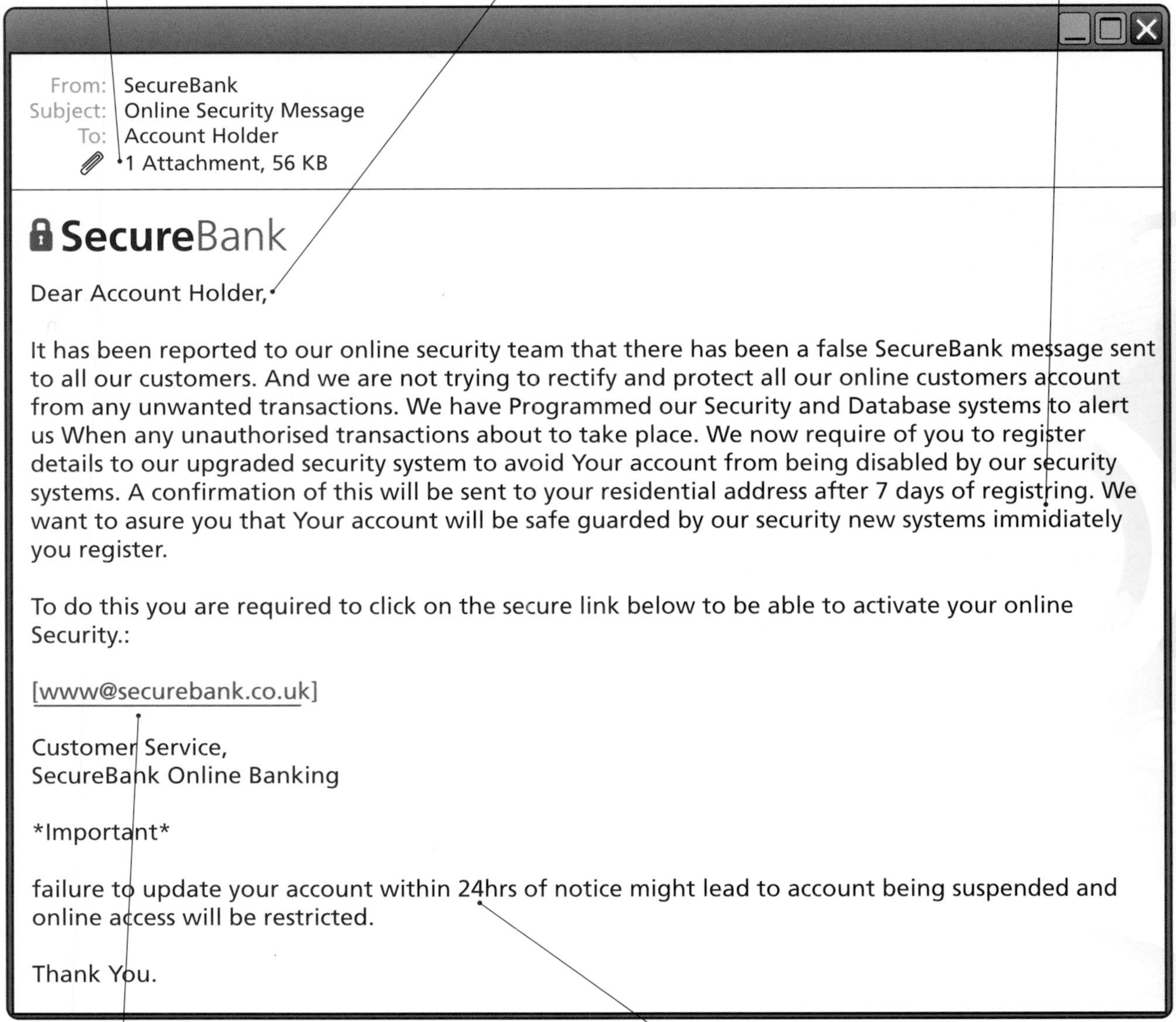

From: SecureBank
Subject: Online Security Message
To: Account Holder
📎 1 Attachment, 56 KB

🔒 SecureBank

Dear Account Holder,

It has been reported to our online security team that there has been a false SecureBank message sent to all our customers. And we are not trying to rectify and protect all our online customers account from any unwanted transactions. We have Programmed our Security and Database systems to alert us When any unauthorised transactions about to take place. We now require of you to register details to our upgraded security system to avoid Your account from being disabled by our security systems. A confirmation of this will be sent to your residential address after 7 days of registring. We want to asure you that Your account will be safe guarded by our security new systems immidiately you register.

To do this you are required to click on the secure link below to be able to activate your online Security.:

[www@securebank.co.uk]

Customer Service,
SecureBank Online Banking

Important

failure to update your account within 24hrs of notice might lead to account being suspended and online access will be restricted.

Thank You.

False links – look closely at the structure of the link you are asked to follow: for example, instead of 'http://www.bank.com', it might be 'http://wwwbank.com', or the link will contain elements which mean nothing to a browser, such as @ or a space.

Urgency – phishing attempts usually ask you to respond quickly. The fraudsters say that you will miss out on a special offer, or that your account will expire if you do not respond quickly.

Figure 5.15 How to recognise a phishing email

Is my data safe?

Learn about
- consumer protection
- legislation relating to the use of ICT, including data protection

Krista has freely given her personal details to online retailers. Many government departments such as HM Revenue and Customs and the DVLA, which issues driving and vehicle licences, store data about the population electronically.

Starter

Who keeps your personal details in computer files? Make a list of all of the companies and organisations that store details of you in this way, such as your school.

In practice

The European Commission has launched proceedings against the UK, claiming that the country is not sufficiently complying with European data protection laws. They began in April 2009 following complaints that BT was using technology that allowed it to monitor its customers' surfing habits and then use targeted advertising, all without the customers' knowledge. EU e-privacy and personal data protection rules state that EU countries have to ensure the confidentiality of communications by prohibiting the interception and surveillance of such communications without the user's consent.

Personal data

e-component

Krista is concerned that her personal data might not be secure or confidential. She has been reading news items about companies selling personal data – have a look at **Websites 5.10–5.12**.

The sites Krista visits and what she buys online are important information for marketing companies because they can be sold to third parties. Some firms even offer courses on how to make money out of personal data. One course even advises on how to dodge questions that we might ask.

As well as being concerned about her data being sold, Krista has also read news articles about government departments actually losing data in the street.

Task 5.25

Mobile phone companies can sell information about your online activity.

a) Who buys this information?

b) Why do they want it?

c) Do you think that it is an invasion of your privacy?

Task 5.26

e-component

Carry out Internet research to find examples of data loss or theft over the last two years. Have a look at **Websites 5.13** and **5.14** to get you started.

Data protection

Ever since computers were first used by businesses and governments to store personal data, people have been concerned about security and privacy as electronic data is far easier to misuse than paper-based data.

Task 5.27

List five ways that electronic data is easier to misuse than when it was all stored on paper.

Data Protection Act 1998

This Act sets out the responsibilities of people who store data and the rights of the data subjects. There are eight Data Protection Principles. These can be found on **Worksheet 5.10**, together with the rights of the data subject.

To find out more about the Data Protection Act, have a look at **Website 5.15**.

e-component

Task 5.28

Carry out some Internet research to find out how much different organisations would charge you to look at the personal data they hold about you.

Privacy policy

Reputable firms will have their privacy policy in a prominent place and tell you what you are signing up for.

Figure 5.16 shows an example from the Amazon.co.uk website – it even tells the user about the cookies it uses.

Figure 5.16 Amazon.co.uk's privacy notice

Skills builder 5.2

Work with a partner to research methods of protecting data stored on a portable memory device such as a pen drive. What levels of protection are there and what technology do they use? Work collaboratively with your partner to summarise your findings and to create a front-of-class presentation.

Knowledge check

Do the Chapter 5 quiz to check your knowledge of this chapter.

CHECK YOUR KNOWLEDGE

In this chapter you have been learning about buying goods online, how to make purchases safely and securely, and how companies use the information that they collect about you to increase their sales.

You should now know:

- the advantages and disadvantages of shopping online
- why you have to give certain information when creating online accounts
- how to create strong passwords
- how to identify safe payment sites
- why companies sell goods online
- how your personal data is used for advertising
- how online shopping has affected our lifestyles and behaviour.

Think about each of the points above in turn.

Using what you have learned in this chapter, let us compare online shopping with mail order shopping. Here's an example of the type of question you might get on this topic in your exam.

'Sporting Books' is a mail order company that sells books by post.

A website www.sportingbooks.co.uk has been created to allow an online ordering service.

(a) Identify **three** advantages to the **customers** of being able to order books online rather than using the mail order system. (3)
(b) Identify **three** advantages to the **company** of being able to receive orders online rather than via the mail order system. (3)

Some customers are concerned about using credit cards to pay online.

(c) Give **two** concerns the customers may have about using credit cards. For each concern identify **one** action the company can take to reduce customers' concerns. (4)

(Adapted from June 2009)

Examiner's tip

Be careful to read this type of question carefully. It is easy to mix up customer and company and to give the correct answer to the wrong question. If you are asked for three advantages and there are three marks available, you should be careful to give three **different** advantages. An in-depth discussion of one advantage will still only gain one mark.

Let's now look at the type of information you would need to include in your answer. Part (a) of the question asks you for the advantages for customers of online ordering compared to using the mail order system. To enable you to think of the advantages, you first need to know the differences between online ordering and the mail order system. The table below gives a summary of the differences (though note that some small companies work slightly differently).

	Ordering	Payment
Online	Use the Internet to order, normally using a 'shopping basket' and 'checkout'	Pay using a credit or debit card (or another way of transferring funds electronically)
Mail order	Complete a paper order form and post this to the company or telephone the company to give them the information verbally	Write credit or debit card details on the order form or give them to the person taking your order on the telephone

Listing the differences between the two systems should allow you to identify the advantages for companies that you need to give when answering part (b) of the question. Part (c) needs you to have an understanding of using online accounts and how they are made secure.

Now let's look at some specific points that you might make as part of your answer to the question. There are also some tips on how to avoid common mistakes made by students in the past.

	What the examiner is looking for	Common mistakes made by students
(a)	**Three** different advantages to the **customer** of **ordering online**. These should be in comparison with using the mail order system. You could include the following: ● Being able to order 24/7. ● Receiving confirmation of your order immediately. ● Being able to compare similar items. ● Being able to see how other customers have 'rated' items.	● Not giving three advantages. ● Giving advantages that refer to another part of the process, such as payment. ● Giving advantages like not needing to go to the shops which apply in both cases. ● Giving advantages to the **company** rather than to the **customer**.
(b)	Again, the examiner is looking for **three** different advantages but this time to the **company** of **receiving orders online**, in comparison with mail order. You could include the following: ● Able to receive orders 24/7. ● Likely to make fewer errors. ● Orders go directly into computer system – no need to input data. ● Company can access a wider customer base.	● Not giving three advantages. ● Giving advantages not related to the receipt of orders. ● Giving answers such as saving costs or it being cheaper for company without justification.
(c)	The examiner is looking for two concerns that customers might have about using credit or debit cards with an action that might be taken by the company in each case. This is a more general question and will relate to more than paying for goods online. <table><tr><th>Concern</th><th>Action</th></tr><tr><td>Identity theft</td><td>Spyware detector used</td></tr><tr><td>Hacking</td><td>Firewall</td></tr><tr><td>Fraud / misuse of credit card</td><td>Encryption</td></tr></table>	● The problems should relate to the use of a credit or debit card online. Be careful not to give answers that refer to more general security issues as some students have in the past. ● Questions that require 'paired answers' (so in this case two concerns and two actions to ease concerns) often cause problems. To get the second mark, the action suggested must match the concern given.

Make sure you have read through the table above carefully and that you understand each of the points made. If there are any gaps in your learning, look back through the chapter and find the information you need.

Some issues to think about…

1 What kinds of goods are not suitable for online shopping? Give reasons why.
2 This chapter has detailed many aspects of security. Remember that these security issues don't just apply to online shopping. So, for example, you should be able to take your knowledge of passwords and apply it to other situations where passwords are used.
3 Think about the personal information that the company collects when a customer interacts with its website. What might a company use this information for?

6 Let's revise!
Health and well-being

Robotic legs help people walk again

A robotic suit helps paralysed people to stand, walk and climb stairs.

Life phone for older people

The Life phone is aimed at older people who want an easy-to-use mobile phone that just makes and receives calls and text messages. With its large buttons and screen, the phone also has an emergency button which, when pressed, will call a pre-programmed number for help.

Schools use Wii to help pupils get fit

Secondary school pupils who regularly miss PE lessons are being encouraged to get fit by using Nintendo Wii consoles.

Remote control operates household appliances

A remote control, which enables paralysed people to operate everyday household appliances, means they no longer need to rely on others.

Computer game can improve your maths

Pupils, using a specially designed computer game at the start of class each day, found their maths scores had improved by the end of the experiment. Researchers found that pupils' concentration and behaviour had improved too.

ICT keeps families in touch

Mobile phones and the Internet are helping families to keep in touch and socialise together.

Flat-screen TVs use three times more power

Flat-screen TVs and digital radios use up a lot of energy. The trend towards larger screens means we're using three times as much electricity to power them than older cathode-ray tube models.

Texting while driving slows reaction times

Texting while driving may be more dangerous than being under the influence of drink or drugs, an RAC research study has found.

Identity theft on increase

People using social networking sites risk having their identities stolen, a consumer group reports.

Children exposed to offensive images

Three out of four children have seen images on the Internet that disturbed them, according to an NSPCC poll.

Techno addiction on the rise

Evidence is emerging that an increasing number of people are addicted to their mobile phones, BlackBerries and PDAs. Techno addicts regularly check for messages in the middle of the night, say researchers.

Online networking may be bad for you

While social networking sites aim to improve our social lives, the lack of face-to-face contact may be bad for our health.

Airbrushing ads should be banned

e-component

Airbrushing should be banned in advertisements aimed at children to help protect them from trying to achieve a perfect look that is really impossible. Look at **Website 6.14** to get a better idea of what airbrushing is and the results it achieves.

In this chapter you are going to have a look at how technology can have an effect on our health and well-being. You will be considering both the positive and negative impacts of technology and how it affects our heath, self-esteem, confidence and outlook on life.

You will not be meeting any new topics in this chapter – the tasks are designed to help you revise what you have learned in the previous five chapters.

You will be looking at news articles based on the topic of health and well-being. You will be able to use your knowledge to answer the questions after each article and to do the practical tasks.

e-component

Is technology having a positive or a negative effect on our health and well-being? What do you think? Have a look at some of the headlines on this page to help you decide.

BBC News has published articles on all these topics – you can read them in Websites 6.1–6.13.

6 Let's revise! Health and well-being

In this chapter you will consider...

- Health and safety.
- Online safety.
- Password protection and security measures.
- Reliability of websites.
- Games safety.
- Data protection.

By completing this chapter you should be able to achieve the following learning outcomes...

- Understand that technology has both positive and negative impacts on health and well-being.
- Have a better understanding of the different topics covered in the book so far, as you revisit them.

Functional Skills...

In this chapter there is information and activities that will help you to practise the following Functional ICT Skills:

Level 1

Using ICT

- Select and use software applications to meet needs and solve straightforward problems.

Finding and selecting information

- Use search techniques (search engines, queries) to locate and select relevant information.

Developing, presenting and communicating information

- Apply editing, formatting and layout techniques to meet needs, including text, tables, graphics, records, numbers, charts, graphs or other digital content.
- Process numerical data in a graphical format.
- Display numerical data in a graphical format.
- Enter, search, sort and edit records.
- Combine information within a publication for print and viewing on-screen.

Level 2

Using ICT

- Select and use software applications to meet needs and solve complex problems.

Finding and selecting information

- Use appropriate search techniques (search engines, queries and AND/NOT/OR, >,<,>=,><=, contains, begins with, use of wild cards) to locate and select relevant information.

Developing, presenting and communicating information

- Apply a range of editing, formatting and layout techniques to meet needs, including text, tables, graphics, records, numerical data, charts, graphs or other digital content.
- Process and analyse numerical data.
- Display numerical data in appropriate graphical format.
- Analyse and draw conclusions from a data set by searching, sorting and editing records.
- Organise and integrate information of different types to achieve a purpose, using accepted layouts and conventions as appropriate.

The files you will use in this section are listed here:

Interactive activities:

1. 6.1 Revision.swf
2. 6.2 Revision.swf
3. 6.3 Revision.swf
4. 6.4 Revision.swf
5. 6.5 Revision.swf
6. 6.6 Revision.swf
7. 6.7 Revision.swf

Files:

1. Meals 6.3.mdb

Websites:

1. Website 6.1 – BBC News
2. Website 6.2 – BBC News
3. Website 6.3 – BBC News
4. Website 6.4 – BBC News
5. Website 6.5 – BBC News
6. Website 6.6 – BBC News
7. Website 6.7 – BBC News
8. Website 6.8 – BBC News
9. Website 6.9 – BBC News
10. Website 6.10 – BBC News
11. Website 6.11 – BBC News
12. Website 6.12 – BBC News
13. Website 6.13 – BBC News
14. Website 6.14 – YouTube
15. Website 6.15 – BBC News
16. Website 6.16 – Food Standards Agency Calorie Calculator
17. Website 6.17 – BBC News
18. Website 6.18 – Guardian
19. Website 6.19 – BBC News
20. Website 6.20 – BBC News
21. Website 6.21 – Mail Online
22. Website 6.22 – Times Online
23. Website 6.23 – BBC News
24. Website 6.24 – BBC News
25. Website 6.25 – BBC News
26. Website 6.26 – BBC News

Mobile phone with GPS to help blind people

Easy Walk is a new GPS service that has been developed to give blind people greater independence.

Blind users have a specially designed mobile phone with a Bluetooth GPS receiver and text-to-speech software called Talks. They can press one key to find out their exact location (spoken by Talks). They press another key to link to a call centre, where they will speak to a real person who can give them directions to where they want to go.

The system has been trialled in Italy, France and Switzerland, but it could be used anywhere in Europe. It gives blind people the confidence to get to where they need to go. It can also be used on trains, trams and other transport to help users know where to get off.

The service will cost approximately £300 per user per year, but the developers hope to offer the service free of charge to end users.

BBC News published an article, 'GPS navigation plan to help blind', on 20 March 2007. You can read the full article on **Website 6.15**.

e-component

Questions

Look back to chapters 1–5 of this book to find the information you need to answer these questions.

1. What is GPS technology? How does it work?
2. Describe ways in which GPS technology can be used as part of a fitness programme.
3. Explain the advantages for blind people of having a hands-free attachment to their phone.
4. Some people find mobile phone features difficult to use, such as those who are elderly or disabled. What can be done to make mobile phones more user friendly for these people?
5. Being blind or partially sighted could make you a target for mobile phone thieves. What steps should all mobile phone users take to prevent their mobile phone from getting stolen?
6. Prolonged use of mobile phones can have health implications. Give examples of these.
7. Bluetooth is used in the Easy Walk service. What are the limitations of Bluetooth?

What other wireless method could have been used to transfer data instead of Bluetooth?

 This service costs approximately £300 annually for each user. What are the social problems that could be associated with products and services that are expensive?

 A user wants to use the Easy Walk service while travelling through different countries. Explain why it might not work on their mobile phone.

Skills builder 6.1

e-component

Go to the Food Standards Agency Calorie Calculator on **Website 6.16**.

Enter the time it takes you to walk to school each day. As a class, you can record everyone's results. Then plot a graph to see who burns the most calories on their way to school and create a report.

Use Google Maps to look at your journey: enter your home postcode, click on the letter marking your street and choose 'Get directions'. Then enter the postcode of your school. This will give you directions and tell you the distance. Don't forget to change 'By car' to 'Walking'. See if you can find a different route that will take you longer. Add the new time to the Calorie Calculator and check how many more calories you would burn.

Be safe/be efficient

Only take safe routes that are well lit and regularly used by other people.

Health and safety for all

Home computer injuries on the rise

The number of computer-related injuries in the home has risen sharply, from 800 in 1995 to 2,100 in 2002.

According to the Royal Society for the Prevention of Accidents, a third of accidents in 2002 were to children under the age of 15. The under-fives were most likely to be injured, with the majority of accidents as a result of tripping over cables or being hit by falling monitors.

Most accidents are minor, but more serious injuries include a young boy burned by a fire which started when a drink spilt on to a computer.

BBC News published an article, 'Home computer injuries are rife', on 9 June 2009. You can read the full article on **Website 6.17**.

Increase in computer-related injuries

Between 1994 and 2006 in the USA, the number of computer-related injuries increased by 732% even though computer ownership only increased by 400%. The most common injuries were trips, falls, head injuries and strained muscles, and children were particularly at risk.

The *Guardian* published a similar article, 'Home computer-related injuries rise sharply', on 9 June 2009. You can read the full article on **Website 6.18**.

The articles above highlight that if computer equipment is not set up and used correctly, it can cause injuries. Injuries can occur not only at home but also in the workplace.

Questions

Look back to chapters 1–5 to find the information you need to answer these questions.

1. Write three pieces of advice on how to avoid accidents involving a computer.
2. What does 'ergonomic' mean?
3. Name three common health problems associated with computer use. How can these be prevented?
4. Discuss the possible causes for the increase in the number of accidents involving computers.
   a. Can the increase be explained by more computers in people's homes?
   b. Can the increase be explained by the fact that people are using computers differently?
   c. The use of wireless Internet and equipment is on the increase. Do you think this will have an effect on the number of accidents that occur?
   d. What sorts of injuries might be caused by new technologies such as the Nintendo Wii?
5. Can you think of examples of how digital technology improves people's health and well-being?

Skills builder 6.2

Produce a poster outlining five things people can do to avoid health problems caused by working at a computer.

Big brother is watching you!

Fingerprint technology part of healthy eating campaign

Fingerprint technology is in the forefront of a campaign to encourage school children to eat healthy foods.

One primary school in north-west England has introduced an electronic fingerprint scanner into the dining hall. By 'touching in', the scanner records what individual pupils have chosen to eat. Those selecting healthy options are awarded points, which are then converted into prizes at the end of the year.

At the same time, the scanner automatically deducts the cost of the meal from the pupil's lunch account.

The system has other advantages too. It can help identify food allergies, and parents can add money to their child's lunch account and see what their child eats.

BBC News published an article, 'School canteen takes fingerprints', on 9 January 2007. You can read the full article on **Website 6.19**.

Questions

Look back to chapters 1–5 to find the information you need to answer these questions.

1. In the primary school featured in the article, pupils are identified by their fingerprints. What is this type of identification called?
2. Apart from fingerprints, what other unique human features can be used for automated identification?
3. Why can't this kind of identification be used to make purchases online?
4. How else could fingerprint technology be used in school?
5. Parents in one school are kept informed of what their children are having for lunch via Twitter. Some people have dubbed this 'spy technology'. What do you think?
6. Describe one method that parents could use to top up the money in their child's lunch account.
7. Some secondary schools are introducing real-time web-based systems that will allow parents to check up on their children's attendance, grades and behaviour at the click of the button. Is this a good thing? Is it a breach of a child's civil liberty?
8. What security measures must schools put in place to prevent unauthorised access to students' records?

Skills builder 6.3

Using the database **Meals**, create a report that will give parents details of what their child ate for lunch at school. The database includes tables for: student details, main meal items, side dish items and pudding items.

1. Start by adding more details to the tables.
2. On the lunch table you can choose students and select which food items they chose.
3. Create a query that allows you to find out what individual students have eaten since the records began.
4. Create a professional-looking report that can be sent out to parents giving them details of what their child has been eating.
5. If you have time, try to create a parameter query that allows you to find all students who chose a certain food item.

Is the Wii more than just a game?

Whatever your age, using a Wii is proving to be more than just a game. Overweight children and the elderly are just two of the groups in society enjoying the health benefits of the console.

Many schools have bought a Wii to encourage children who regularly miss sports lessons to take part in a physical activity. A care home in Wales has also bought one to help residents stay physically and mentally agile.

In the USA, the Wii is being used to rehabilitate injured soldiers. Most find the Wii fun, and experts say it is just as beneficial as physiotherapy exercises.

But the health benefits of the Wii may have been exaggerated. According to research, people who played on the Wii burned only a few more calories than those who used other types of console games. People planning on doing a Wii workout have also been advised to do warm-up exercises.

BBC News published an article, 'Could the Wii be good for you?', **e-component** on 25 February 2008. You can read the full article on **Website 6.20**.

Questions

Look back to chapters 1–5 to find the information you need to answer these questions.

1. List three positive and three negative effects of playing computer games.

2. 'Nintendo thumb' is one form of repetitive strain injury (RSI) associated with playing computer games. What is repetitive strain injury? How can it be avoided? What other forms of RSI are associated with game playing?

3. When playing online, games often run more slowly. What factors can contribute to this?

4. Some games are moving away from being controlled by a hand-held games controller. Name other methods of controlling games.

5. Games are often sold illegally. What law are people breaking when they buy illegal copies?

6. What could happen to your computer as a result of installing illegal software?

7. What are the symptoms of someone who is addicted to computer games?

8. What is the benefit of using a network cable rather than a wireless connection for online gaming?

Do computer games affect the development of the brain?

New research carried out by Professor Ryuta Kawashima suggests that playing lots of computer games can result in parts of teenagers' brains being underdeveloped, which could in turn lead to violent behaviour.

The study suggests that playing computer games develops the vision and movement parts of the brain but not other important parts, such as the frontal lobe, which is associated with learning and self control.

By contrast, simple maths tasks stimulate the learning parts of the brain (including the frontal lobe) and could increase a teenager's ability to learn and control their behaviour according to the study.

Mail Online published an article, 'Are computer games damaging your child's health?'. You can read the full article on **Website 6.21**.

Are computer games responsible for rickets?

Twenty cases of rickets are diagnosed every year in Newcastle. Rickets prevents children growing properly and can result in bow legs, and is a disease normally associated with the developing world.

Rickets can be the result of a lack of vitamin D in the body, which can be caused by long periods without natural light and a poor diet. Some think that the rise in the number of rickets cases in Britain is due to the fact that children spend much of their spare time indoors watching TV and playing computer games. When our skin is exposed to sunlight it produces vitamin D but most children today spend little time outdoors.

Times Online published an article, 'TV and computer games blamed for return of rickets', on 22 January 2010. You can read the full article on **Website 6.22**.

Questions

Look back to chapters 1–5 to find the information you need to answer these questions.

1. Do you agree that playing computer games can make children more aggressive?
2. RSI and rickets are two of the possible health problems associated with playing computer games excessively. How many others can you identify?
3. What can people who play computer games do to avoid damaging their health?
4. Some teachers believe that computer games can help children to learn. Describe three examples of the use of computer games in education.

Safer Internet Day growing in popularity

More than 50 countries are expected to take part in the fifth Safer Internet Day, which aims to promote safe and responsible use of online technology.

Schools, youth groups and local authorities around Europe are running events to help educate parents and children about the risks of:

- sharing too much personal data
- virtual friends, who may not be who they say they are.

Organisers are keen to get the message across that people children talk to online might not always be other young people, and they should take care when planning to meet someone. Parents will be encouraged to oversee their children's online activity so they know who they are talking to.

According to a survey in the UK by Symantec, adults believed that 4% of children had been approached by a stranger – in fact, it was 20%.

According to Safer Internet Day organisers, being safe online involves more than installing anti-virus, firewalls and anti-spyware software. People also need to be aware of the way technology is used to carry out scams.

BBC News published an article, 'Internet Day highlights web risks', on 12 February 2008. You can read the full article on **Website 6.23**.

Pupils hack out of safe school networks

How secure are Internet filters on school computer networks? The filters are used to screen out risky websites, allowing pupils to surf the Internet safely.

But now, it seems, some filters do the job better than others, after pupils were found hacking out of their school network to access pornographic sites and violent computer games.

Research by the software company, Zentek, appears to confirm this concern. It monitored Internet usage at 70 schools and found that at some schools pupils accessed 4000 'unauthorised' pages every day.

In the majority of cases, pupils visit social networking sites, but there is still a long way to go to ensure online safety in school and at home.

BBC News published an article, 'Pupils can beat safe net filters', on 3 December 2008. You can read the full article on **Website 6.24**.

Questions

Look back to chapters 1–5 to find the information you need to answer these questions.

1. What are the different ways that you can communicate using the Internet?
2. Most email users receive spam mail. What is this and why is it a problem?
3. Using email could mean that you are targeted by phishing websites. What does 'phishing' mean?
4. How might you be able tell if a website is not legitimate or if an email is bogus (a phishing email)?
5. What advice would you give to someone who receives suspicious messages from a stranger while instant messaging? Give practical steps that should be followed.
6. What does a firewall do?
7. What does anti-virus software do?
8. Filters are used to protect young people from the dangers of the Internet. What dangers are associated with the Internet?
9. How can parents prevent their children being exposed to the dangers of the Internet?

Skills builder 6.4

Design and create an interactive presentation to inform children about Internet safety to be displayed on an information point.

It must give details of things to look out for when using the Internet and how to deal with problems that arise.

Keeping personal information safe

The social networking site Facebook has come under fire after it was alleged that users' personal details and those of their friends could be stolen.

The site has become very popular because of the wide range of applications users can add to their profile pages, including games, quizzes and IQ tests. But anyone who has a basic understanding of web programming could write a malicious program to collect data, and pretend it was a harmless application.

To maintain online security when using the site, experts advise users not to use applications and erase any that are on their profile.

BBC News published an article, 'Identity "at risk" on Facebook', on 1 May 2008. You can read the full article on **Website 6.25**. Facebook has now taken steps to prevent this problem but it just shows how careful you need to be.

Questions

Look back to chapters 1–5 to find the information you need to answer these questions.

1. What are the advantages of social networking?
2. What are the disadvantages of social networking?
3. State one way you can control who can view your photos on a social networking website.
4. People sometimes exchange personal information with people who they have only met online. Give two reasons why this is not a good thing to do.
5. Sometimes posting personal information on social networking sites can have unforeseen consequences. Can you think what these consequences might be?
6. When creating a password, how would you make it strong?
7. What is social bookmarking?
8. Data loss from computers is very common. What media can you use to save data to avoid this happening?
9. Explain primary and secondary storage.
10. Give three reasons why it is important to back up data regularly.

Watermarking your photos is a good way to stop people copying them

Cyberbullying comes under attack

Information and communications technology has brought great benefits, but it also has a dark side – cyberbullying.

The government now officially describes cyberbullying as the use of a mobile phone or the Internet to 'deliberately upset someone else'. Along with the definition, it's provided a set of guidelines for schools to tackle the problem.

First, pupils need to recognise how serious such bullying is and the pain it can cause the victim.

Schools are advised to:

- create policies on how school computers should be used
- record any incidents
- keep evidence, such as abusive texts, for investigations
- make efforts to track down the cyberbully
- have the same type of sanctions as for physical bullying
- confiscate mobile phones if they are being used to break behaviour rules.

Head teachers can also take action over abusive material posted on websites or sent from mobiles outside of school. Some forms of cyberbullying may be treated as a criminal offence.

Many schools already use software to monitor pupils' computer use. The software can provide screenshots as evidence.

BBC News published an article, 'What can stop cyberbullying?', **e-component** on 21 September 2007. You can read the full article on **Website 6.26**.

Questions

Look back to chapters 1–5 to find the information you need to answer these questions.

1 What is cyberbullying?

2 Mobile phones can be used to cyberbully victims. What other methods do culprits use to cyberbully?

3 Give examples of situations where use of a mobile phone is prohibited.

4 Modern mobile phones are multifunctional devices. What does this mean? Give some examples.

5 What is a responsible way of disposing of your old mobile phone?

6 What are the different methods of getting information from a mobile phone on to a website?

7 What does VoIP stand for and what is it used for? List the equipment that you need in order to use VoIP.

8 Companies like to communicate with their customers online. What are the different methods that they can use to do this?

9 Some software is known as open source. What does this mean?

10 Software does not always need to be purchased – it can be hosted. What are the advantages of hosted software?

11 Sometimes a company or organisation will store information online. What are the advantages and disadvantages of this method?

exam zone

Unit 1
Living in a Digital World

In Unit 1 you have explored the ways in which digital technology impacts on the lives of individuals, organisations and society. You have learned about current and emerging digital technologies and their use in a range of contexts. You have developed an understanding of the risks that are inherent in using ICT, as well as learning the features of safe, secure and responsible practice.

So how will I be tested?

The assessment for this unit is an exam paper lasting 1 hour and 30 minutes. The exam questions will test your knowledge and understanding of the content of Unit 1, as well as the skills that you have developed by completing the Tasks and Skills builders.

Unit 1 can be part of a single or a double GCSE qualification in ICT and the exam is worth 40% of the single award and 20% of the double award.

What will the exam paper look like?

The exam paper will be in a question-and-answer booklet like the one below. There will be five compulsory questions.

The exam will last 1 hour and 30 minutes

Write your name here
Surname
Other names

Centre Number
Candidate Number

Edexcel GCSE

Information and Communication Technology
Unit 1: Living in a Digital World

Sample Assessment Material
Time: 1 hour 30 minutes

Paper Reference
5IT01/01

You do not need any other materials.

Total Marks

Instructions

- Use **black** ink or ball-point pen.
- **Fill in the boxes** at the top of this page with your name, centre number and candidate number.
- Answer **all** questions.
- Answer the questions in the spaces provided
  – there may be more space than you need.

Information

- The total mark for this paper is 80.
- The marks for **each** question are shown in brackets
  – use this as a guide as to how much time to spend on each question.
- Questions labelled with an **asterisk** (*) are ones where the quality of your written communication will be assessed
  – you should take particular care on these questions with your spelling, punctuation and grammar, as well as the clarity of expression.

Advice

- Read each question carefully before you start to answer it.
- Keep an eye on the time.
- Try to answer every question.
- Check your answers if you have time at the end.

Turn over ▶

S37842A
©2009 Edexcel Limited.
2/

edexcel
advancing learning, changing lives

The quality of your written communication will be assessed in parts of some questions

The paper contains five questions, worth a total of 80 marks. The marks each question is worth is shown in brackets

Each paper starts by setting a scene that will be used throughout all of the questions. It will provide you with a context that will help you connect with the questions. Here is an example from the Sample Assessment Materials.

The Lee family

Jon and Manjit Lee have three children, Gia, Mark and Layla.

Digital devices play an important part in the daily lives of the Lee family. They keep in touch with friends and family using mobile phones and VoIP.

They use ICT in learning, leisure and socialising – sometimes connecting through the Internet to resources and sometimes using standalone devices.

The scene set provides a good starting point but you will not have to keep referring back to it during the exam. Each question will remind you of any relevant information you need in order to help you give good answers.

What will the questions look like?

There will be a range of different styles of questions on the paper, including multiple-choice, short answer, open response and extended writing questions.

MULTIPLE-CHOICE QUESTIONS

Multiple-choice questions require you to select one answer from a number of alternatives, usually four.

2 Manjit is opening a social networking account. She wants it to be secure.

   (a) The account requires a password.

      (i) **Figure 2** shows that the password she has chosen is not very secure.

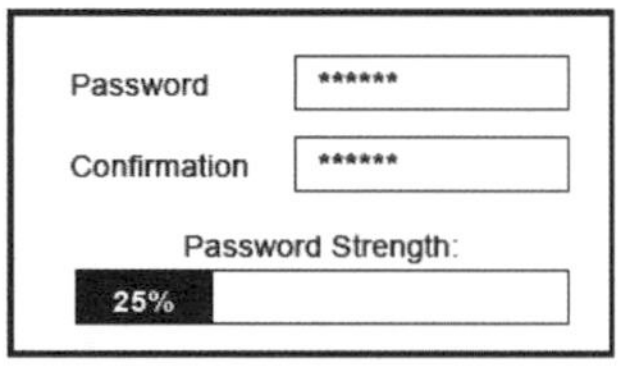

Password	******
Confirmation	******

Password Strength:

`25%`

Figure 2

Which one of these passwords is the most secure? (1)

    A seahorse ☐

    B C-hor4se ☐

    C Chor4se ☐

    D C-horse ☐

In the example multiple-choice question shown here, a screen shot has been used to help you understand what is required. The question is testing whether you know, and can use, the ways of making passwords secure.

SHORT ANSWER QUESTIONS

Short answer questions will ask you to *name*, *give*, *state*, *identify* or *select* a number of *reasons*, *disadvantages*, *benefits* or other responses. Sometimes the answers will be words, sometimes phrases and sometimes sentences. Normally, each response will be worth one mark.

This is an example of a short answer question.

(ii) Some of Manjit's friends exchange personal details with people they meet online. Give two reasons why this might not be a good thing to do. (2)

1 ....

....

2 ....

....

Note that the question asks you to give two reasons. The space provided for the answer makes this clear. So, to get two marks, you must give two reasons. Don't worry if you don't use all of the space provided.

OPEN RESPONSE QUESTIONS

Open response questions range from more open-ended short answer questions that will ask you to describe or explain something, to those asking for a justification, a more detailed explanation, a discussion or an extended response.

Open-ended short answer questions

Here is an example of an open-ended short answer question.

(ii) The online shop must keep the customer database secure. Explain two ways of preventing unauthorised access to the database. (4)

1 ....

....

....

2 ....

....

....

In this case, the two marks are given for showing links between the security measure you are describing and how it prevents unauthorised access to the database, e.g. Encrypt the data (1 mark) so that it cannot be read (1 mark).

EXTENDED WRITING QUESTIONS

Here is an example of an extended writing question.

*(e) Some people claim that playing video games is beneficial. Make a reasoned argument to support this point of view. (6)

....

....

....

....

In an extended writing question like this one you need to organise your thoughts carefully. You need to use your knowledge to support the claim about video games. The asterisk (*) also indicates that the quality of your written communication will be assessed in your response.

So you should:

● Ensure that your writing is legible and that your spelling, punctuation and grammar are accurate so that meaning is clear.

● Select and use an appropriate form and style of writing.

● Organise information clearly and coherently, using specialist vocabulary when appropriate.

How to do well in the examination

The five questions in each exam paper will be structured so that the parts of each question generally become harder towards the end of the question, and the questions become more difficult as the paper progresses.

So how should I approach the questions?

Firstly, keep calm. The examiners are not trying to catch you out. The questions have been written to ensure that they allow you to demonstrate your knowledge and understanding. You must read the questions carefully though to ensure that you answer the question that has been asked.

You have 90 minutes to answer the five questions, so that is about 18 minutes for each question. Keep your eye on the time but don't panic about the time and try to answer questions so quickly that you do not get full marks for work that you know well. These marks are just as valuable as the marks that you may get for the harder questions at the end of the paper. A good strategy is to try to pick up all of the easier marks and leave enough time to tackle the open response questions towards the end of the paper. You should also leave some time to read through your answers before the end of the exam.

Read the scenario carefully – it should help you get into the right frame of mind to tackle the questions. Then start question 1.

The different styles of questions will need slightly different approaches.

Multiple-choice questions can be tricky. In the Unit 1 exam paper they are not all in one section, but are spread throughout the paper and used when this style of question is most appropriate. Do not guess the answer at this stage, but if you think that you know the answer mark the correct box. Leave enough time to go back and try any multiple-choice questions that you left unanswered when you first looked at them.

For short answer questions underline the command word, such as *state* or *identify* to remind yourself of how you are expected to answer. Then give the number of responses that the question asks for. If the question asks for two reasons for doing something you lose half of the marks if you only give one reason. Make sure that the two answers are different and that you have not used an answer that was given in the question. Don't worry if you don't use up all of the space provided for the answer in the question-and-answer booklet.

More extended answers require careful planning. In questions marked with an asterisk (*) the quality of your written communication will impact on the mark that you receive.

The mark scheme for the 6-mark question on page 155 is shown below. In this type of question the content of your answer is allocated a mark in a band and then this is adjusted, **within the band**, on the basis of the quality of your written communication.

Mark scheme for the question 'Some people claim that playing video games is beneficial. Make a reasoned argument to support this point of view. (6)'

Criteria for level 1 answer, worth 1 or 2 marks

Criteria for level 3 answer, worth 5 or 6 marks

Possible points that could be made as part of the answer

Criteria for level 2 answer, worth 3 or 4 marks. If a mark of 4 is awarded in terms of the points given in the answer but the quality of the written communication (QWC) is weak, then the mark will be reduced to 3. If the QWC is good, then the original mark of 4 remains unchanged

Question Number	Answer
4 (e) QWC (1-11)	Indicative content to support the benefits of playing video games • Improves hand-eye coordination • Can be an effective tool for learning / cognitive development / thinking / problem solving skills / reasoning / memory • Stops young people getting into trouble on the streets • Multiplayer games encourage social interaction • Some games provide fitness/exercise programmes • Encourage interest in particular subject / research / develop interest • Developing language skills • Games can mirror real life and allow players to make mistakes without harming themselves • Whole brain activity occurs when playing games

Level	Mark	Descriptor
	0	No rewardable content
Level 1	1-2	The student will produce brief responses, making a limited number of simple statements, probably with limited reference to the benefits of video games. Responses produced by the student will be generalised and will cover a limited range of benefits. They have used everyday language but their response lacks clarity and organisation. Spelling, punctuation and the rules of grammar are used with limited accuracy.
Level 2	3-4	Student's responses will be mostly accurate and will include a number of relevant benefits. Candidates will have discussed the benefits that they identify. Limited attempt to argue the case. They have used some specialist terms and their response shows some focus and organisation. Spelling, punctuation and the rules of grammar are used with some accuracy.
Level 3	5-6	The student will produce a factually accurate response that includes the discussion of a range of appropriate benefits. The benefits identified are appropriate and the case is well argued. They have used appropriate specialist terms consistently and the response shows good focus and organisation. Spelling, punctuation and the rules of grammar are used with considerable accuracy.

Don't worry about this too much though. When you tackle these questions make sure that you:

● Focus on the question that has been asked and not on the similar one that you have prepared.

● Don't extend the question. Giving drawbacks as well as benefits in your answer to the question at the top of this page will not gain more marks and will waste valuable time.

● Organise your thoughts. A reasoned argument needs to be more than a list of ideas to get to level 3.

How should I prepare for the exam?

This Student Book provides many activities and ideas for investigations as you develop your understanding. The more experience that you have with the content of this unit, the easier you will find it to answer the questions, whatever context is used in the exam paper. The ability to transfer knowledge between contexts is an important higher order skill.

The questions will be set in an everyday context such as learning and earning, leisure, shopping and money management, health and well-being, and on the move. In the exam you will need to use your knowledge of digital technologies to determine appropriate ICT solutions for specific users and situations. You will also need to consider the benefits and drawbacks of alternative options and be able to identify potential threats and dangers associated with using ICT and how these can be overcome.

So what about other forms of revision?

If you have access to the checklists provided which identify the content for you, you can assess how well you know each part and tick it off when you understand it so that you always spend your time on your weakest areas.

You could also use the questions in chapter 6 of this unit, which will help you to check your understanding.

Your teacher may also guide you towards sample assessments and papers from completed exam series.

Another way would be to take each of the chapters that are written around the contexts of learning and earning, leisure, shopping and money management, health and well-being, and on the move, and to use spider diagrams to identify the content that may be associated with each context and how it is linked. Or try other techniques like note-taking, flashcards, pictures and colour-coding to provide variety and keep you focused!

Create a revision plan – you'll have many subjects to revise so make sure you timetable enough time in for each of them. Aim to study in 30-minute slots so that you don't lose concentration, and build up your revision over a number of weeks. Try not to cram a few nights before, which can cause you to panic.

Take time to relax in between revision sessions to avoid becoming too stressed!

What happens next?

After the exam all completed papers are sent to the Edexcel Processing Centre for scanning. Your work will then be marked online by a team of examiners. They are trained to mark accurately using an agreed mark scheme in a process known as standardisation. Their work is overseen by senior examiners and checked at regular intervals. You can help the process by writing your answers in the identified areas of the question-and-answer booklet and making sure that your work is easy to read. When all of the exam papers have been marked the marks required for each grade are agreed.

What about re-sits?

You should try to get the best mark that you can the first time that you sit the Unit 1 exam but, if you think that you could do better, you can re-sit the unit once and the higher mark will count. There are some new rules that mean that if Unit 1 is part of the 40% terminal requirement then the mark achieved then will count.

Unit 2
Using Digital Tools

Overview

Unit 2 is a practical unit. In this unit you will broaden and enhance your ICT skills. You will work with a range of digital tools and techniques to produce effective ICT solutions in a range of contexts.

The assessment for Unit 2 is a Controlled Assessment task. The task is specified in a Controlled Assessment Brief (CAB). The Controlled Assessment task has replaced what was traditionally referred to as coursework. Sixty per cent (60%) of your overall marks for your GCSE are for work on the CAB.

So how is the assessment 'controlled'?

The assessment is controlled in a number of ways.

THE TASK IS CONTROLLED

The task is set by Edexcel in a Controlled Assessment Brief (CAB). A new CAB will be published on the Edexcel website each year. This brief can then be used in the four examination windows starting in June of the next school year. The CAB is an interactive digital publication, designed to be viewed onscreen. You will submit digital evidence of your work for assessment and moderation. The CAB will be made available to you by your teacher.

THE TIME ALLOWED IS CONTROLLED

The maximum time allowed for completing the supervised part of the CAB is 40 hours.

THE WAY THE TASK IS 'TAKEN' IS CONTROLLED

Your work on the Controlled Assessment task, except for some of the research and information gathering activities, must be done in a supervised environment. This is not an exam: you will not have to work in silence but you will be formally supervised at all times. You will be working on the CAB over many weeks. At the end of each supervised session, the materials that you are working on, paper based and electronic, will be collected and stored securely. You will not be able to access them until the start of the next supervised session. The materials that you can take into a session will also be controlled.

You will complete the Controlled Assessment task in controlled conditions

The CAB

The CAB provides a context or scenario within which you will work. It identifies a number of activities that require you to use a range of digital tools and techniques to produce effective ICT solutions. The brief concludes with an evaluation of the outcomes and of your own performance.

The Unit 2 CAB is broken down into four activities. Each activity has a different focus, although in every activity you will be expected to produce at least one **digital product** and carry out a review of your work. Each CAB will include these activities, although the context and the nature of the digital products will vary.

Activity 1 involves gathering information, using a database, and creating one or more digital products.

Activity 2 consists of a modelling activity using a spreadsheet, and creating digital products, which will include information generated from the model.

Activity 3 requires you to produce a design for an interactive digital product, to create it and to test it to demonstrate its effectiveness.

Activity 4 involves evaluating the products you have produced and reflecting on your own performance.

All digital products have some degree of interactivity. A product like an **e-card** has only limited interactivity – 'Click here to open this card'. A fully interactive

> ***Digital product*** – a product produced using ICT tools and viewed onscreen. It does not need to be printed out.
>
> ***e-card (electronic card)*** – a digital greetings card or postcard created and sent to someone via the Web.

digital product, such as a computer game or a virtual tour, is one in which the user is in control.

This is a practical unit, so you'll be spending a lot of time putting your ICT skills into practice. You will need to know how to use software to create digital products such as spreadsheet models, information points, presentations, e-posters and virtual tours.

But that is only part of it. A key part of the CAB is showing that you can think *creatively*, *logically* and *critically*.

Skills builder 1.1

Look out for digital products online that you come across. To help you become digitally aware you should think about:

- the purpose of the product
- design features that have been used
- the effectiveness of the product.

What will the CAB look like?

There is a contents list on the left-hand side of each CAB.

Click here to print the page.

The Overview provides the scenario for the CAB and a summary of the activities in it.

Figure 1.1 The Overview screen of a sample CAB

Figure 1.1 shows the Overview screen of a sample CAB. The CAB is a digital publication designed to be viewed onscreen. It provides the instructions you need to complete the task. You should read through the whole CAB before you start work on Activity 1, so that you have an overview of the work involved. Then you should work through the activities in order.

Starting work on the CAB

This page of the CAB helps you to organise your work. Remember that an examiner will be assessing your work. He or she needs to find the required evidence to be able to award marks.

Test buddy – you need one and you will be one for someone else.

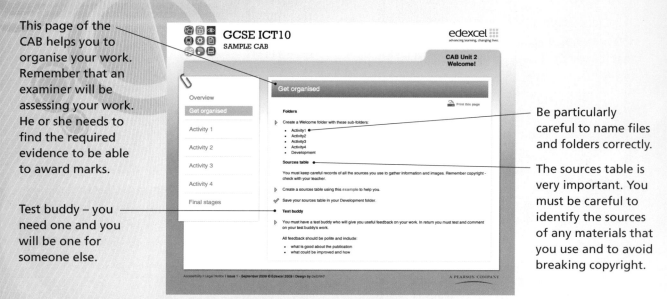

Be particularly careful to name files and folders correctly.

The sources table is very important. You must be careful to identify the sources of any materials that you use and to avoid breaking copyright.

Figure 1.2 The Get organised screen of a sample CAB

The screen after the Overview screen will always help you to organise yourself. An example of the Get organised screen is shown in Figure 1.2. You will set up the folders you need, start thinking about sources and find a test buddy.

Managing your files

One of your first tasks in the CAB will be to create folders to organise the files you are going to create – one folder for each activity, a Development folder for development work such as research and surveys and an Ideas folder.

TIPS FOR MANAGING YOUR FILES

- Make sure you use sensible names for all your files. There is nothing worse than having to open dozens of files called Pete1, Pete2, Pete3... until you find the one you want.
- Use names that give you a good idea of what is in the file: for example, PlayPoster would be a good file name for a poster you are creating to advertise a school play.
- Use version numbers if you decide you do not want to overwrite an earlier version of a document: for example, PlayPoster1 and PlayPoster2 might be two versions of the poster.
- Save your work regularly.
- Keep a backup copy of your files in a separate folder, in case you accidentally corrupt or delete a file.

Skills check... make sure you know how to:

- create folders and subfolders
- move around a folder structure
- find a file by searching
- save a file in a folder or subfolder
- copy, move and delete a file or folder
- change a file or folder name.

Skills builder 1.2

Create a folder in your school user area for the work you will do in the Skills builders in these chapters and name it GCSE ICT Task.

Inside this folder create five more folders called Activity1, Activity2, Activity3, Activity4 and Development. Add another folder called Ideas.

Planning your work carefully

Where do you start? Tasks are more likely to be successful if they are properly planned. First of all, read through all of the activities in the CAB carefully, to make sure you understand exactly what is required. There are a number of key questions you need to ask yourself, including:

- What do I have to produce?
- Who is the intended audience?
- What is the product for?
- How will I judge the success of what I produce?
- Who will review my work and when?

Make a list of every task that the CAB mentions in Activity 1, and then break down each task into smaller tasks. The smaller the task, the easier it will be to plan how long it will take. Remember, you only have about 10–12 hours to complete Activity 1. Look at a calendar and make a note of when it has to be finished. You do not have to hand in your time plan but it will help you to get everything done in time.

CREATING A TIME PLAN

Although you do not have to submit your time plan for assessment, that does not mean you should not make one. Having a thorough time plan will help you get everything done in time. If you produce a plan for your practice tasks, you will have a better idea of how long each task is likely to take when it comes to the real thing. Creating a time plan involves taking the following steps:

- Decide on a suitable method of creating a time plan, and then create a blank time plan with headings.
- Add the tasks and subtasks to the plan.
- Find out all holiday and term dates.
- Insert dates, allowing enough time for each part.

For your time plan, you could create a table in a word-processing or spreadsheet program. Alternatively, you could use a calendar, such as the one shown in Figure 1.3, and use the spaces in the calendar to write comments explaining your progress.

Figure 1.3 An example calendar downloaded from Microsoft's online Excel spreadsheet templates

Reviewing your work

As you develop a digital product you need to review its design, the way that it is developing and the quality and effectiveness of the final version. You should do this yourself but it is helpful to have someone else to give feedback to you as well. In Unit 2 you will use a **test buddy**.

> *Test buddy* – someone who provides feedback on the digital products that are being developed. They tell the developer what is good about the product and what should be improved.

WHAT IS A TEST BUDDY AND WHAT WILL THEY DO?

While you are completing the Controlled Assessment task, someone will act as a test buddy for you and you will act as test buddy for someone else.

Any feedback that you give should be polite but, in order to be helpful, it must identify areas for improvement as well as commenting on things that are good. The comments of a test buddy should help improve the digital product. It is important that a test buddy tells the truth. There is no point them saying a product is brilliant when, in fact, there are lots of things that can be done to improve it. When you are a test buddy you should think about the target audience and how the product will be used. A teacher may also comment on your work.

1 Gathering and presenting information

In this chapter you will be practising the skills that you will need in order to complete Activity 1 of the Controlled Assessment Brief (CAB).

Activity 1 consists of a number of tasks based on the scenario given in the CAB. Here are some examples of the types of tasks you might be asked to do in Activity 1.

BUILD UP A PROFILE THAT GIVES YOUR OWN INTERPRETATION OF THE SCENARIO

In the sample CAB you are told that there are 80 visiting students and that they have a basic knowledge of English. You now need to identify your own target audience.

In order to do this, the sample CAB asks you to identify:

- their age range
- the number of girls
- the number of boys
- the place they come from
- the place they are visiting
- their interests.

You will then base your research around your target audience.

Other CABs will use different scenarios and the profile that you need to produce will be different.

GATHER INFORMATION FROM SOURCES

Once you have built up a profile based on your interpretation of the scenario given in the CAB, you will have to gather the information you require from a range of sources. These will include all or some of:

- the database that is provided in the CAB
- the Internet
- other primary or secondary sources from your own research.

USE THE DATABASE PROVIDED

You will need to be able to:

- search the database for information that matches specific criteria
- produce reports detailing the results of your searches
- add records to the database.

CREATE DIGITAL PRODUCTS WITH LIMITED INTERACTIVITY

The CAB may ask you to create digital products with limited interactivity, such as a digital poster to display in a suitable location. It is extremely important to consider where your product will be used or displayed. A digital poster for each of the following locations would have different requirements:

- reception area of your school
- wall next to an escalator on the London Underground
- a computer screen at parents' evening.

Think about what the requirements might be for each location.

REVIEW YOUR WORK

You will need to review your work and answer questions about this activity. You will need to show that you have:

- gathered useful information
- checked that your digital product is fit for purpose
- asked for and received feedback
- responded to feedback.

Here are two sample tasks to get you started.

Skills builder 1.3

You want to find out the nutritional content of a meal that you like to eat. Where could you look for this information? If you are using the Internet as one of your sources, list the website addresses of two specific sites that you find.

Skills builder 1.4

Your school wants to let parents know about an upcoming school play. What methods of providing information can you think of? What are the advantages and disadvantages of each?

Presenting your information

In Activity 1 of the CAB, you will be given a database to work with. You will search the database to find information. You will then use this information in digital products, in this or later activities. This section will help provide some ideas for the sort of tasks you will be asked to do and how they relate to each other.

In order to practise the skills required for Activity 1 of the CAB, you will look at a number of different scenarios and attempt various different Skills builders throughout this chapter. These will be similar to the scenarios and activities in the CAB.

Query an existing set of data to find specific information

Field:	Name	Category	Type	Location	Postcode	Region	Phone	Web address	Entry cost	Opening time
Table:	Destinations	Destinations	Destinations	Destinations	Destinations	Destinations	Destinations	Destinations	Destinations	Destinations
Sort:	Ascending									
Show:	☑	☐	☐	☑	☑		☐	☐	☑	☑
Criteria:						"London"			<20	
or:										

View the results of your query

Name	Location	Postcode	Entry cost	Opening time
BFI London IMAX Cinema	Waterloo	SE1 8XR	£12.50	10:00
Britain at War Experience	London Bridge	SE1 2TF	£10.45	10:00
British Airways London Eye	Westminster	SE1 7PB	£15.50	10:00
Buckingham Palace and Houses of Parliament Tour	St.James Park	SW1A 1AA	£8.75	09:45
CBBC Tour	Wood Lane	W12 7RJ	£7.00	10:00

Create a report based on your results

London Activities under £20

Name	Location	Postcode	Entry cost	Opening time
BFI London IMAX Cinema	Waterloo	SE1 8XR	£12.50	10:00
Britain at War Experience	London Bridge	SE1 2TF	£10.45	10:00
British Airways London Eye	Westminster	SE1 7PB	£15.50	10:00
Buckingham Palace and Houses of Parliament Tour	St.James Park	SW1A 1AA	£8.75	09:45

Create a symbol, emblem or similar graphic

LONDON TOURS

Select relevant information from your reports and create a digital poster or advertisement using your symbol

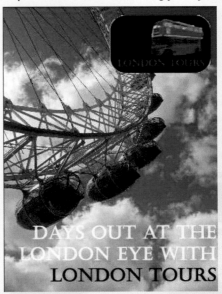

DAYS OUT AT THE LONDON EYE WITH LONDON TOURS

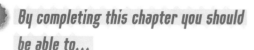

1 Gathering and presenting information

By completing this chapter you should be able to...

- Plan and organise your work.
- Gather useful, accurate and unbiased information from primary and secondary sources.
- Record and acknowledge sources of information.
- Sort and search a database for useful information.
- Create suitable lists or reports from a database.
- Add records to an existing database, using a data entry form where necessary.
- Create simple digital products that are fit for purpose and audience.

Functional Skills...

In this chapter there is information and activities that will help you to practise the following Functional ICT Skills:

Level 1

Using ICT

- Select and use software applications to meet needs and solve straightforward problems.
- Select and use interface features effectively to meet needs.
- Adjust system settings as appropriate to individual needs.
- Work with files, folders and other media to access, organise, store, label and retrieve information.

Finding and selecting information

- Use search techniques (search engines, queries) to locate and select relevant information.

- Recognise and take account of currency, relevance, bias and copyright when selecting and using information.

Developing, presenting and communicating information

- Use field names and data types to organise information.
- Check for accuracy and meaning.
- Evaluate own use of ICT tools at each stage of a task and at the task's completion.

Level 2

Using ICT

- Select and use software applications to meet needs and solve complex problems.
- Select and use a range of interface features and system facilities effectively to meet needs.
- Select and adjust system settings as appropriate to individual needs.
- Manage files, folders and other media storage to enable efficient information retrieval.

Finding and selecting information

- Recognise and take account of copyright and other constraints on the use of information.
- Evaluate fitness for purpose of information.

Developing, presenting and communicating information

- Use appropriate field names and data types to organise information.
- Analyse and draw conclusions from a data set by searching, sorting and editing records.
- Work accurately and check accuracy, using software facilities where appropriate.
- Evaluate the selection, use and effectiveness of ICT tools and facilities used to present information at each stage of a task and at the task's completion.

In Activity 1, you will be assessed on how well you have:

- Used a range of appropriate sources, including the database provided in the CAB, to select relevant information for use in your products.
- Used effective techniques to refine your searches.
- Developed the specified products, using appropriate content and features.
- Tested your work and made appropriate modifications.
- Responded to feedback received from your test buddy.
- Reviewed the outcomes of Activity 1 and explained how you acted on feedback received.

The files you will use in this section are listed here:

Files:

1. Profile.rtf
2. Sources_table.rtf
3. Food.mdb **or** Food.accdb

Websites:

1. Website 1.1 – Edexcel

Skillsbank

Use a database:

- search and sort to retrieve information
- sort records on single or multiple fields in ascending or descending order
- add and amend records in a flatfile database
- use a given data entry form to add and amend records in a relational database.

Generate a database report:

- customise report headings
- add headers and footers
- choose appropriate titles
- select which fields are to be displayed in your report, avoiding redundant data
- adjust field widths
- add subtotals and totals where required.

Researching and customising the brief

In the CAB, you will be given a brief scenario and told what tasks you have to do for each of the four activities. However, detail will be left out of the scenario, so it will be up to you to decide how to customise the brief. In the sample CAB, you had to customise the brief by building up a profile of the visiting students, deciding on factors such as how old the students were and where they were from.

Customisation can involve building a profile of the target group as it does in the sample CAB, but it may involve other things. Here's an example scenario.

Scenario 1: Producing promotional materials

You have been asked to produce promotional materials for a play.

The play will run for three nights at a local venue.

You will create some digital products for the organisers, including a digital poster.

Customising the requirements

One of the first things you need to do is to flesh out this scenario. This is something you can do away from class – do not waste precious time starting off on the wrong track before you have thought it through properly. You need to ask yourself:

- Who is putting on the play? Is it an amateur or a professional production?
- What sort of play is it? Is it a pantomime suitable for small children, a comedy, a Shakespearean tragedy that is one of the set books for an English exam?
- Who will the audience be?
- Where is it taking place – in a school, at a local theatre, out of doors?

Skills builder 1.5

With a partner, come up with a list of other questions that you need to answer in order to:

- build a clear **audience profile** for your products:
  > age group > gender > reading ability > degree of interest
- decide what information your product needs to contain
- clarify the purpose of the product
- decide where the product will be displayed or seen.

Audience profile – a description of the people your products are aimed at. It could include their age, the language they speak, their special needs, or any other characteristics relevant to the scenario you are given.

You will need to do some research to help you set the task firmly in a realistic context.

Look at the document called **Profile**. This document is supplied to you as part of the CAB and is designed to help you build up a profile of the visiting students. How could you adapt it for the 'Producing promotional materials' scenario above?

Gathering information

Research involves gathering data or information for particular purposes such as:

- increasing knowledge
- getting ideas
- supporting decision making
- helping to make recommendations.

The information that you collect may be used in items that you produce or to give you a steer about what to work on. For example, if someone is anaemic, you can find out what products contain iron and design digital recipe cards to help them make meals.

To create your promotional products, you will need to:

- collect background information
- look at other people's posters for ideas
- collect material to use in your own products.

This poster was designed to advertise a production of the Shakespeare play
A Midsummer Night's Dream

IMAGES

When designing a poster to advertise the play, as you're asked to do in Scenario 1, you need to consider what images you will use on your poster. You need to consider whether you can:

- use existing photos
- find suitable images on the Internet
- take some photos yourself.

You need to choose images that give a feel for the play.

Primary and secondary sources

When gathering information, you can use a wide range of sources. These might include both **primary sources** and **secondary sources**.

Primary sources include:

- interviews
- photos you have taken yourself
- audio recordings you have made
- surveys that you have conducted.

Secondary sources include:

- paper-based sources, e.g. newspapers, directories, books and maps
- digital sources, e.g. the Internet, web pages, blogs, social networking sites, databases, TV and radio.

You will have to select the most appropriate sources, by asking yourself questions such as:

- Does the source have a particular **bias**?
- Is the information accurate? Information sources such as wikis are not always checked for accuracy.
- Is the source current (up to date)?
- Is the source reliable? Can you confidently make decisions based on it?

BIAS

Information is said to be biased if it is one-sided or does not reflect the entire situation or event that took place, or does not contain all of the relevant information. The person giving the information might omit information that conflicts with what they want you to believe, or that does not support the message they want to get across.

For example, a company selling double-glazing may come up with figures showing that you will save thousands of pounds in heating costs, but can their figures really be trusted? Do they take everything into account?

Primary source – information or data that you have collected yourself.

Secondary source – information or data that has been produced by someone else.

Bias – prejudice towards one viewpoint or against another.

> According to my calculations, you'll make average savings of £375 a year.

Figures put together by a company that wants to sell you something may well be biased

It is a good idea to do your own research and to find out what other people think of the company. It would be sensible to ask people who'd already bought double-glazing from the company questions such as:

- what are your average savings since the double-glazing was installed?
- have you experienced any problems with the double-glazing?

Skills builder 1.7

Search the Internet for websites or news articles that have an obvious bias. Why has the information been presented in this way? How could the information be amended to present a more balanced and unbiased view?

ACCURACY, CURRENCY AND RELIABILITY

Is the information source accurate? Some information dates very quickly, while other information may never date. For example, if you are researching a company and find information saying that its share prices rocketed six months ago, that is not a reliable indicator of how the company is doing today. An historical document, however, will never date – even if it was written 100 or more years ago – because it provides a permanent record of life at that time. Always check when the information you have found was written. Is it up to date, or in other words, current? You should also check whether the information is likely to be reliable. Official documents should be more reliable sources than a wiki, for example.

Using and recording information sources

Let's look at another scenario and how you might find information to use in Activity 1.

Researching information

First, you will need to customise the scenario for yourself. You should decide on answers to questions such as:

- Which countries does the airline fly to?
- Is the airline a no-frills operator, or an upmarket company with many first-class passengers?

Once you have done this, you will be ready to start your research.

Skills builder 1.8

Start by finding out about different special dietary requirements. You could use the Internet, as shown in Figure 1.4, you could read newspapers and magazines, or you could try asking people you know.

Collect your information carefully, especially when using Internet searches. It is easy to collect so much information that it becomes very difficult to identify what to use and what to ignore. Use the information you find to identify three special diets that your airline catering company is going to provide for.

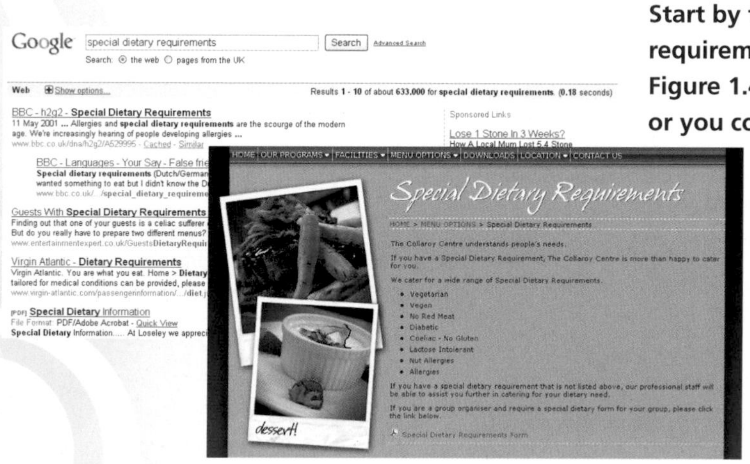

Figure 1.4 Using Google to research special dietary requirements and then selecting a relevant website

Skills check... make sure you know how to:

- use an Internet browser and a search engine
- bookmark a page
- copy and paste a link
- copy and paste information.

Copyright

Normally, it is all right to use text and images that you have copied from a book, CD or the Internet in your own work, so long as you are using them for educational purposes, and you do not intend to publish your work or to make a profit out of it. You must always respect the author's copyright and include the source of any material you use. You should never claim that something is your own work if it is not.

If you intend to publish or publically display work containing text or images produced by someone else, you must get their permission. You may have to pay a fee in order for them to agree to allow you to use their text or images.

In the CAB you need to consider copyright issues carefully and show that you understand any legal constraints. If you are designing products that are, in theory, intended for display in a public place and/or commercial use, you should flag up the fact that some or all components would need to be replaced or that permission would have to be obtained from the copyright holders prior to use.

Recording your sources

Details of any information you find and use must be recorded in a separate file of your sources.

For each image or piece of information you find on the Internet, you should typically record the following source information:

- document title or description
- author, if known
- date of publication
- URL – the full web address, copied from your browser window, to ensure there are no errors
- permission details and copyright holder, where necessary
- date accessed.

You need to follow these guidelines for all paper-based sources too, and add details of the publisher. It is important to record your sources for your own use as well as for an official record. Imagine you needed to go back to one of the really useful web pages you previously visited but have forgotten which site it came from. A list of sources will act as a permanent reminder and is likely to save you time and frustration.

HOW TO RECORD SOURCES

e-component

Edexcel provides a template as part of the sample CAB in which you can record your sources – see Figure 1.5. Open **Sources_table** to familiarise yourself with the document or go to **Website 1.1**.

I found a fantastic picture of airline food last week, but I can't find it now...

Keeping a record of sources is good practice for more than one reason

Information/Image	Where found/source	Where used	Details of permission if required

Figure 1.5 Edexcel sources table

Using the Internet safely

The internet is a fantastic source of information, but as a savvy user you must be aware of its dangers.

- Never give out personal information such as your phone number.
- Even innocent keywords can sometimes bring up inappropriate information – if this happens let someone know.
- Make sure you know how to report anything suspicious or offensive.
- If in doubt, log off.

Working with databases – searching and adding new records

> **Flatfile database** – a database held as a single table. It is structured with a row for every record.
>
> **Relational database** – a database that uses more than one table. Tables are linked together by common data items, such as ID number, known as keys.

A database is a collection of information stored in an organised way, so that, whether you have five records, or five million, you can find what you are looking for immediately. The database provided in the CAB could be a **flatfile database** or a simple **relational database**.

Searching a database

Databases are a useful way of recording information because, no matter how many records you have, you can quickly search for all the records that satisfy any criteria. Consider the database shown in Figure 1.6.

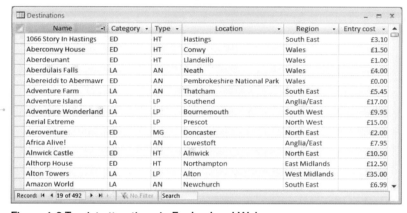

Name	Category	Type	Location	Region	Entry cost
1066 Story In Hastings	ED	HT	Hastings	South East	£3.10
Aberconwy House	ED	HT	Conwy	Wales	£1.50
Aberdeunant	ED	HT	Llandeilo	Wales	£1.00
Aberdulais Falls	LA	AN	Neath	Wales	£4.00
Abereiddi to Abermawr	ED	AN	Pembrokeshire National Park	Wales	£0.00
Adventure Farm	LA	AN	Thatcham	South East	£5.45
Adventure Island	LA	LP	Southend	Anglia/East	£17.00
Adventure Wonderland	LA	LP	Bournemouth	South West	£9.95
Aerial Extreme	LA	LP	Prescot	North West	£15.00
Aeroventure	ED	MG	Doncaster	North East	£2.00
Africa Alive!	LA	AN	Lowestoft	Anglia/East	£7.95
Alnwick Castle	ED	HT	Alnwick	North East	£10.50
Althorp House	ED	HT	Northampton	East Midlands	£12.50
Alton Towers	LA	LP	Alton	West Midlands	£35.00
Amazon World	LA	AN	Newchurch	South East	£6.99

Record: 19 of 492 — No Filter — Search

Figure 1.6 Tourist attractions in England and Wales

The table below shows the criteria you might use to find specific data stored in the database in Figure 1.6.

What you want to find	Criteria
Finding a specific region	**Region="South East"** finds all records with South East in the Region field
Finding a number greater than a given value	**Entry cost>10** finds all records with an Entry cost greater than £10
Finding a number less than a given value	**Entry cost<10** finds all records with an Entry cost less than £10
Finding a value in a particular range, e.g. finding all the activities with entry costs of between £5 and £10	**Entry cost>=5 AND<=10** finds all records within this range
Finding all values except a particular value, e.g. all activities outside Wales	**Region=NOT Wales** finds everything except Wales

> ## Skills builder 1.9
>
> Look at examples of databases on the Internet. You could choose an online site such as Amazon, Ocado or the itunes store. Try searching them to identify the information stored about particular items.

Skills builder 1.10

Use the database shown in Figure 1.6 to answer these questions.

a) How many records satisfy the criteria Entry Cost<£8.50?

b) List the names of all attractions in East Anglia.

c) Which attractions satisfy the criteria Entry Cost>£5 and Region="South East"?

In the CAB, you may be asked to add information to the database that is personal to you. When adding records to an existing database, you must make sure that you have all the information needed and that it is accurate. To do this you need to know the record structure being used.

Skills builder

Following on from your work for Scenario 2 on page 171, think of three special dietary requirements (vegetarian, nut-free, etc.) and gather details of two meals that would be suitable for people with these dietary requirements. You can use the Internet, magazines or look on the packets of existing specialist meals in supermarkets as part of your information gathering.

Open the database file called Food to see what data you need to find.

Look at the fields in the database and think about where you could look for this sort of information and how you can make sure that the information you find is accurate. Remember to record the sources of your information in **Sources_table**. Figure 1.7 shows how you might source a web page.

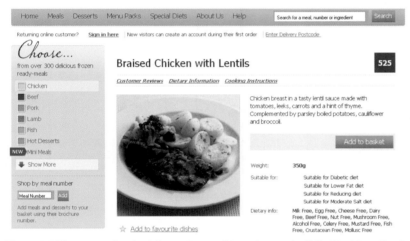

Figure 1.7 The source for the information on this web page is: Wiltshire Farm Foods, http://www.wiltshirefarmfoods.com/frozen-ready-meals/chicken-ready-meals/ braised_chicken_with_lentils_525.asp, accessed on 29 June 2009.

Adding data to the database

To add new data to a flatfile database, simply open the database table, scroll to the end of it and type in the new records. To add new data to a relational database, you will need to use the data entry form provided. Enter the values required in the **Food** database. Test out the validation to see if it prevents you from entering invalid data.

Skills builder

Open the database file called Food and find the Meal table. Insert three new records at the bottom. These could be three records from the six you have researched in Skills builder 1.11. Make sure the information is accurate and not made up. Then save the amended database in your Activity1 folder.

Record the sources of your information in Sources_table and save it.

If you are using database software, you need to design a query to extract information from the database.

Make sure that you have the database file called **Food** open and ready to work on.

e-component

You can search the data in the database to find a list of the meals that match your requirements. You can add criteria to any of the fields in order to find all the records that you are interested in.

Field:	Description	Hot or Cold	Meat Type	Contains Nuts
Table:	Meal	Meal	Meal	Meal
Sort:			Ascending	
Show:	☑	☑	☑	☑
Criteria:				"No"
or:				

Figure 1.8 Query to find all the meals in the database that do not contain nuts

The query shown in Figure 1.8 shows the criteria that will find all the meals in the database that do not contain nuts. It will also sort the results in ascending order of Meat Type.

When you run the query, you should see the results shown in Figure 1.9.

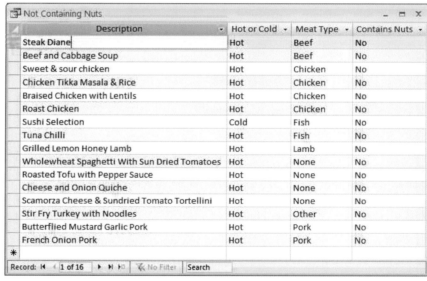

Description	Hot or Cold	Meat Type	Contains Nuts
Steak Diane	Hot	Beef	No
Beef and Cabbage Soup	Hot	Beef	No
Sweet & sour chicken	Hot	Chicken	No
Chicken Tikka Masala & Rice	Hot	Chicken	No
Braised Chicken with Lentils	Hot	Chicken	No
Roast Chicken	Hot	Chicken	No
Sushi Selection	Cold	Fish	No
Tuna Chilli	Hot	Fish	No
Grilled Lemon Honey Lamb	Hot	Lamb	No
Wholewheat Spaghetti With Sun Dried Tomatoes	Hot	None	No
Roasted Tofu with Pepper Sauce	Hot	None	No
Cheese and Onion Quiche	Hot	None	No
Scamorza Cheese & Sundried Tomato Tortellini	Hot	None	No
Stir Fry Turkey with Noodles	Hot	Other	No
Butterflied Mustard Garlic Pork	Hot	Pork	No
French Onion Pork	Hot	Pork	No

Record: 1 of 16   No Filter   Search

Figure 1.9 Results of the query for meals that do not contain nuts

Choosing the fields you need to display

You can specify which fields are to be included in your query results: for example, if you are not interested in whether the meal is hot or cold, you can deselect the 'Show' box in the 'Hot or Cold' column, and this field will not appear when you run the query.

It is good practice to choose meaningful names for all your queries and reports so that you can easily identify them later.

Sorting a database table

Often, you will want to display records in a database in a particular order, to make it easy to find particular information: for example, you might want to sort the meals according to the number of calories or the type of meat they contain. Figure 1.10 shows the records ordered by the type of meat they contain.

Meal ID ▾	Description ▾	Calories ▾	Fat ▾	Carbohydrates ▾	Protein ▾	Hot or Cold ▾	Meat Type ▾	Contains Da ▾	Contains Nu ▾	Contains Whe ▴
16	Beef and Cabbage Soup	204	8	18	14	Hot	Beef	No	No	No
25	Meatballs in Onion Gravy	345	5	23	16	Hot	Beef	No	Yes	No
22	Steak Diane	330	19	7	33	Hot	Beef	Yes	No	No
23	Chicken Tikka Masala & Rice	499	9	75	29	Hot	Chicken	Yes	No	Yes
21	Coq au Vin	505	27	16	49	Hot	Chicken	No	Yes	No
5	Roast Chicken	272	12	1	39	Hot	Chicken	Yes	No	No

Figure 1.10 Meal table sorted in ascending order of meat type

If presented with a database containing information about people, you might want to sort the records alphabetically by surname or first name, by year group, by age or by some other category.

SECONDARY SORTS

It is possible to sort on two fields at the same time using a query.

The fields in the table need to be in a particular order for sorting on multiple fields – the main sort field has to be to the left of the secondary sort field. If they are not in the right order, you need to move the secondary sort field before doing the sort.

How to...

... move a field.

Click in the column header (e.g. just above Meat Type in the query shown below) and then drag the selected field to where you want it. Remember that this will vary depending on the software you are using.

Imagine you want to specify a main sort field of Meat Type (ascending), and a secondary sort field of Calories (descending). Your sort query will look like the one in Figure 1.11.

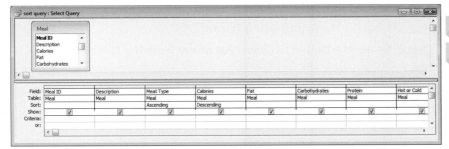

Figure 1.11 Sort query

To make full use of your searches and sorts, you now need to put all the results into a neat and tidy report.

When you start to prepare a report for the CAB, you will need to refer back to Activity 1 to remind yourself of the brief and to make sure you know the answers to the following questions:

● Who is the report for?
● What data needs to be included?
● Are any subtotals or averages required at the end of the report?
● Does the report need to include a date?
● What is the most appropriate heading for the report?
● In what order should the fields appear?

Database software has the facility to generate reports automatically using a **wizard**, which allows you to customise the look of the report. This can be a good place to start when creating your report.

Here are some tips for making sure that you produce a high quality report:

● Make sure that your report has an informative title.
● Do not include unnecessary fields.
● Make sure that all the information is clear and easy to read.

Wizard – part of a program that helps the user to create a new document, chart, etc. A sequence of dialogue boxes guides the user through the steps needed to create the item required.

Skills builder 1.15

 e-component

Open the database called **Food** and follow steps 1–11 below to create a report from your query 'Under 10 Grams Fat' that you made in Skills builder 1.13 (see Searching a database, page 176). The instructions below assume you are using Microsoft Access.

Step 1: In Microsoft Access, make sure that the Database window is visible, and select Reports.

Step 2: Click Create Report using Wizard.

Step 3: Select the Under 10 Grams Fat query from the Queries option box.

Step 4: Click the double right-facing arrow to put each of the fields from the query into the report (see Figure 1.12).

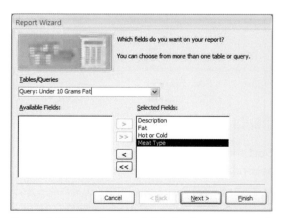

Figure 1.12 Selecting the fields for the report

Step 5: Click Next. Adding a grouping level divides the results up from the query by subcategory.

Step 6: Select Meat Type and click the right-facing arrow (see Figure 1.13).

Step 7: Click Next again. You can specify up to four sort fields for the report here.

Step 8: Sort by Fat grams. Click Next again and select a style.

Step 9: Click Finish to view your report (see Figure 1.14).

Step 10: Edit your report if necessary – you can change the title, change the style or make room for some of the longer data in your fields. In the report in Figure 1.16, the Description field needs to be made wider.

Step 11: Click Save to save the report. Save the report in your Activity1 folder.

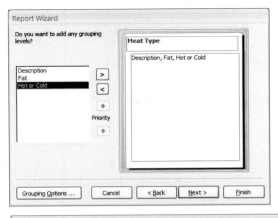

Figure 1.13 Adding Meat Type as the grouping level

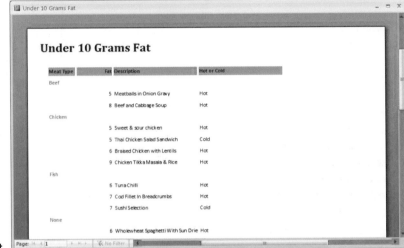

Figure 1.14 The finished report

Skills builder 1.16

 e-component

Using the database called **Food**, create reports for the other two queries that you made in Skills builder 1.13 (see Searching a database, page 176). Make sure you format these reports to match the first one you did.

Does my report have a sensible title and sensible column headings?

Is the information clear and easy to read?

Have I left out unnecessary fields?

It is important that you think carefully about what information to include in your report

Skills check... make sure you know how to:

- customise report headings
  > include the correct date for rapidly changing information
  > use sensible titles
- select which fields are to be displayed in your report
- adjust field widths
- remove repeated data
- add subtotals and totals where required
- add page numbering on multipage reports.

Creating digital products

Activity 1 will involve the use of a database and research using the Internet and other sources. You will also have to create digital products such as posters, presentations, e-cards and advertisements.

You need to plan the layout and **functionality** of your digital products carefully before you start to create the products themselves. It is very unlikely that your finalised product will be exactly the same as your initial designs, but getting your ideas down in the first place will give you vision and save you time. Test your products as you work on them and use feedback from your test buddy during development as well as getting their feedback on the completed product. Review your completed products carefully.

You will need to create or gather components that you can use in your digital products. You may want to consider using:

- logos and other symbols
- digital photos
- video files
- sound files
- animations.

Logos and symbols can be very powerful and are often used to represent companies, groups of people or countries.

Here are some of the main points to consider when creating a digital product:

- What is it for?
- Who is it for?
- How is it going to be used?

Designing digital products

In Activity 1 the digital products that you will be asked to create will be fairly straightforward, with limited interactivity. However, it is still best to plan their design carefully. A well designed product will meet all the requirements and will be fit for audience and purpose. This means that it will gain more marks.

Even a single screen requires choices to be made:

- What content will be included?
  - › images
  - › sound
  - › text
  - › animation
- How will the content be arranged?
- What colour scheme will be used?
- What fonts, styles and formatting will you use?
- Will there be any automated features?

Functionality – the different things that you can do with a website or other product, e.g. click on link to go to another page, select check boxes, submit an online form.

Use a simple **storyboard** to plan your design, such as the one in Figure 1.15, which is the design for a poster advertising a school production of *Jack and the Beanstalk*. The storyboard needs to show details of every screen in the product and explain the design decisions that you have made. You may wish to include this information on a separate sheet accompanying your designs. There is a more detailed discussion of storyboards in Chapter 3.

> *Storyboard* – a series of illustrations or images shown in sequence for the purpose of planning a movie, animation or website interactivity.

School logo

Beanstalk border graphic

Lewis School is proud to present...

Jack and the Beanstalk

Location: Lewis School Hall
Dates: 8–10 March 2010
Tickets: Adult £6
Children £3

Tickets available from reception

Pale background so text is legible

One font for all text apart from title of the pantomime, which is dark green to match the beanstalk border, and is the largest text on poster

Figure 1.15 Storyboards are a useful way of planning products and should capture all details and design decisions

Skills builder

Look at several websites on the Internet that are aimed at the audience you identified in your audience profile in Skills builder 1.6. Find examples of the use of different images, colours and fonts. Copy and paste the ones you like into an 'ideas' document for easy reference later. Save this in your Ideas folder. Similarly, look out for good and bad examples of the use of sound, animation and video.

Using test buddy feedback

Good use of feedback from your test buddy will ensure that your product evolves from initial design to finished product successfully. You should ask your test buddy to comment on your initial designs and modify them as appropriate. This should help you to produce a better product and save time in the long run.

Designing a web page, digital poster, banner, e-card or any other digital product involves making decisions about several basic elements including background, fonts, colours and images.

Background style

Whichever type of product you have to produce, you will need to give consideration to the background. Ask yourself these questions:

- Will the background be a solid colour?
- If so, what colour will it be?
- Will the background be an image?

A white background such as the one in Figure 1.16 gives a clean-looking screen and plenty of flexibility regarding the layout of objects on top of the background. A solid colour background gives some additional life to the screen if you feel you need an extra splash of colour.

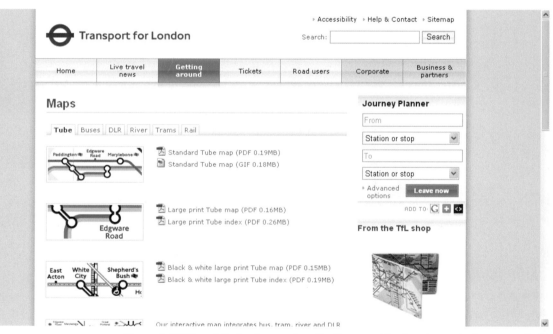

Figure 1.16 The white background on the Transport for London website means that the text and images are clearly visible, and that the page does not look cluttered

An image set as the background can add to a screen but only if chosen very carefully. More often than not, an image as a background makes a screen look cluttered and difficult to read, and sometimes the most important parts of the photo get covered by other objects such as text or other images.

FADING THE BACKGROUND IMAGE

Most programs will allow you to select an image and then fade it. For example, in Microsoft PowerPoint, you select the image, then select Washout from the Picture menu – see Figure 1.17.

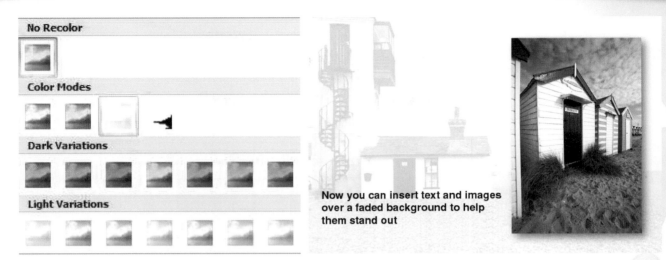

Figure 1.17 Fading out a background image in Microsoft PowerPoint

WHITE SPACE

If you are using an image for the background, you need to be aware of **white space**. White space is a blank or plain area on a screen. In the example in Figure 1.18, there is a lot of empty space in the image to the right of the car. This draws your attention towards the car while also leaving an area over which you could add text, without it covering the main object of the picture.

> *White space* – the blank (not necessarily white) area between screen components such as text and images. White space is an important design element.

Figure 1.18 Blank space in a background image is a good place to position your text

Fonts, colours and sizes

Remember to:

- limit yourself to just a few colours
- use one or two main fonts
- keep the font sizes consistent.

Font colours must also stand out against the background. You should choose dark-coloured text on a light background, or vice versa. If you are putting text over an image, you might find that no colour is really suitable because the background image has areas of different colours. In this case, you could insert the text in a tinted box, as in the picture of the car in Figure 1.18. You could make the box semi-transparent to allow some of the detail of the image to come through.

Titles and subtitles should be bigger than the rest of the text but should always be the same size on each screen. For example, you might decide to use 16 pt for all headings and 12 pt for all main text.

Skills builder `1.18`

Have a look at the colour schemes shown below. Discuss with a partner which of these colour schemes work and why.

| **Sample Text** | **Sample Text** | **Sample Text** |

Skills check... make sure you know how to:

- format and align text
- use text boxes
- use images as backgrounds.

Making sensible decisions

You should always be able to explain and justify the rationale behind your design decisions. For example, if you are creating a school website and the school colours are blue and yellow, it makes sense to choose these colours for particular areas of the site, headings, links, etc. If you are designing a website for a musician, you might choose to include clips of music they have recorded and maybe an animation with musical notes dancing across the page, and so on.

Using images

You will need to choose your images with care. They must be relevant to the information on the screen and enhance the design, rather than cluttering it or distracting the reader's attention away from the text.

RESIZING

Never resize an image without constraining its proportions. Always use the corner handles and keep the Shift key pressed to avoid the image getting distorted, which is what has happened in Figure 1.19.

Skills builder `1.19`

Choose colours, fonts and at least one image to be used in a web page providing information about a forthcoming event taking place at your school. Create all the text that is to go on the page. Write an explanation of your design decisions.

Figure 1.19 This photo has been resized incorrectly, producing a distorted image. Make sure you always use the corner handles to resize images

CROPPING

Rather than resizing an image awkwardly to fit an area by distorting its original proportions, you can use the Crop tool on the Picture toolbar of software applications and crop the image, as shown in Figure 1.20.

Figure 1.20 Crop a picture to select the part of the picture that you want or to make it fit the space available

IMAGE RESOLUTION

Images downloaded from the Internet are already at their optimum resolution of 72 dpi (dots per inch). You cannot make them much bigger (or smaller) without degrading their appearance. This degradation is called **pixelation** and should be avoided. An example of a pixelated image is shown in Figure 1.21. If resizing an image has this effect and you cannot use the image at its original size, then you should avoid using it at all.

> *Pixelation* – an effect caused by displaying a bitmap or a section of a bitmap at such a large size that individual pixels (small single-coloured squares that the image is made of) are visible to the eye.

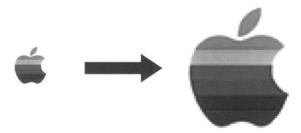

Figure 1.21 Resizing a downloaded image will reduce the quality of the image

How to...

... resize an image.

You do not need to use high resolution images if they are only to be viewed onscreen. If you have a photo that you want to use in your work, use a graphics package or utility program to optimise the image size.

Skills check... make sure you know how to:

● import and position images
● crop and resize images
● optimise images for onscreen viewing.

Sound, video and animation

You may want to use multimedia in your products, and it is important to know in what format to store your media in order for it to work.

Sound

There are several sound file formats available. Each of them has particular advantages and disadvantages in any given application. Here are three sound file formats that you may be familiar with, but there are others too:

- CD Audio
- WAV
- MP3.

CD AUDIO

As the name suggests, this format is music or sounds recorded on CDs. To use this in a **multimedia** presentation, you will need to convert the CD Audio track to WAV or MP3. You can do this by using one of thousands of freely available **ripping** programs available on the Internet.

WAV

WAV files are commonly used for smaller sound samples such as the noises that Microsoft Windows makes when you do something wrong or shut down your computer. There are thousands of samples available on the Internet for almost anything you could imagine. Many of these are free to use, but check for any issues before downloading any sound or music clips.

MP3

MP3 files work well in presentation software and Web-based publications and, as they are compressed, are best for longer music clips. You can find programs available to convert any of these sound formats into almost any other format you need.

You could choose to use a sound effect in a Flash animation, a music track playing in the background of a presentation or a short sample of a tune playing when viewing a page on a website.

> *Multimedia* – a combination of different content types such as text, audio, still images, animation and video.
>
> *Ripping* – the process of copying audio or video content to a hard disk, typically from removable media such as a CD.

Skills builder

Think about how many of the websites you have visited use sound or music. Revisit three of them or find three new ones. Which uses of sound or music work and which are annoying? Try to explain why. In your opinion, should the user be able to turn off the sounds if they want to?

Write a list of key points on how sound is best used in a website or multimedia presentation.

Video

Like sound samples, video clips come in a variety of formats. The most commonly supported formats are MPG, WMV (Microsoft Windows only), AVI or 3GP (mobile phone video format). With the exception of 3GP, all of these formats are supported by Microsoft products, but if in doubt, use the MPG format as this is the most universal.

USING YOUR MOBILE PHONE VIDEO CAMERA

If you wish to capture a video on your mobile phone, it will be saved on your phone's memory as a 3GP file. You can find software to convert 3GP to MPG on the Internet.

USING A DIGITAL CAMERA

Most digital cameras capture videos and automatically store these as MPG files. You can use these directly without any conversion and, if you want to edit them, you could import them into a video editing program.

EDITING A VIDEO

A video consists of a combination of text, audio and images. It runs for a fixed amount of time during which the content is constantly changing. There are usually several things happening at once in a video – a soundtrack can be playing while a series of pictures is displayed, along with a text narrative. A **timeline storyboard** is used to plan what happens when.

Windows Movie Maker is an example of an easy-to-use program with enough features to produce a short, edited video, with titles. Once you have imported your video files into Windows Movie Maker, you can rearrange the clips, trim unwanted footage and add effects and titles.

Timeline storyboard – a series of screens shown in sequence used for planning a movie or an animated sequence.

Animation

Animation can be included in your products, either as an animated GIF image or as a Flash movie. You may need to create an e-card, digital advertisement or website banner and you might want to include some animation to help attract people's attention.

 Remember

Clever use of technology does not always result in effective digital products. In addition to having the technical skills to develop digital products, you also need to develop your design skills and to have an understanding of what works and what does not.

Here are a few tips for designing effective digital products:

- Keep it simple.
- Do your research – look at other digital products like the one that you are planning to design and decide what you like and don't like about them.
- Pause to reflect on your design and come back to it later to see if you still like it.
- Use your test buddy to test your ideas.

Creating a symbol

Symbols are important components of digital products. They convey an easily recognisable, unambiguous message, often without any words. A good symbol is simple with a clear outline.

Skills builder

Search for examples of effective symbols on the Internet. Try doing a search for vegetarian symbols using Google Images.

An emblem or logo is a special sort of symbol that represents a group of people, an organisation or a country. Find some examples of emblems and save these in your Ideas folder.

When designing a symbol, follow this advice:

- Rough out several design ideas to organise your thoughts before getting started.
- Write down all of the concepts that you want to portray, e.g. modern, rustic, eco-friendly, healthy or helpful.
- Choose styles and colours that help to reflect these concepts.

Remember, the simplest ideas are often the most effective.

Choosing a colour scheme

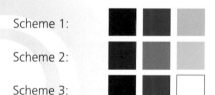

Figure 1.22 Possible colour schemes

You can try putting blocks of colour next to each other to test out how they look together, as in the examples in Figure 1.22. You might find it easier to keep each of your colour schemes separate. This makes it easier to judge which one you like the best.

Selecting a font

Many symbols convey their meaning without using any text at all. If you do decide to use text as part of your symbol, select your font with care. Are you looking for something that is solid and reliable, or frivolous and fun? Do you want it to be traditional or modern? Take a look at the example fonts in Figure 1.23.

Font 1   Font 2   *Font 3*   Font 4

Figure 1.23 What mood or image does each of these fonts convey?

Choosing your software

You should use a graphics package to create symbol and logos. This is so that it becomes an image file that you can import into any document at a later date.

Making your designs fit for purpose

Think about the requirements for each symbol:

- Does it need to be instantly recognisable?
- Does the information need to be easily read, in a large or small font?

- Would colour aid recognition and add to the suitability of the designs, given that they are part of a series?
- How big do the symbols need to be?
- Do the symbols need to look similar so that they are recognisable as part of a series or set?
- Who is your audience? For example, think about age, nationality, good/impaired vision, reading ability.

Getting feedback

You will find it helpful to show your colour schemes and ideas to your test buddy and ask them for their opinion. They may have some useful feedback.

It is important to continue getting feedback as your symbols develop to make sure they do their job as effectively as possible. This is important as they may be used on a number of products in Activity 2 and Activity 3 as well as in Activity 1.

Planning your symbols using a few clear objectives

You will need to plan your designs carefully before you begin to create them. Use the answers to the questions above to make a short list of the requirements of your symbols. You can use these points later to assess whether you achieved your objectives.

Once you have some ideas, try sketching out your designs. For this type of exercise, you will need to keep them very simple.

Figure 1.24 Examples of stickers for special airline meals

Once you have created one symbol, the fastest way to create another similar symbol is to save the first symbol again under a new filename. You can then edit this to become your new symbol instead of starting from scratch. This also helps to ensure the symbols look like they belong together as part of a set.

Symbols might be used instead of words to get the point across. Is this a good symbol?

> *Consistency* – in design terms, this means that all elements of the design (e.g. fonts, colour schemes, positioning of objects and buttons, animation styles) remain the same throughout the product.

Skills builder

Continuing with your work on Scenario 2, create a set of symbols for three special dietary requirement meals. For this task, imagine that you have chosen vegetarian, low-fat and nut-free as your three special meals to promote.

You need to create a small symbol to go on each of the meal cartons to identify them as they are served.

The symbols will be printed on a sticker and attached by the cabin crew to the foil lid of each meal before it is served on the aircraft. You need to remember that the people who will see this symbol are flight attendants and, more importantly, the passengers (customers). The symbols should be designed to give the customer confidence that the meal they have in front of them fits their special dietary requirements. You will need to make sure the symbols are fit for this purpose.

Given that the designs will all be part of a 'set', you should also give careful consideration to **consistency** of design. You could try making all the symbols similar, using colour to help differentiate the different meal types.

Shops, estate agents and the London Underground are among the many businesses and organisations that make use of digital posters. Digital posters are timed presentations involving more than one screen that are used to give information. Digital posters may be used to advertise products or services as well as providing information. The screens are displayed continuously using timings that have been pre-set.

Skills builder

Look for examples of digital posters. What design features have been used to make the screens work together? Is there a common colour scheme? Are the same fonts and styles used throughout? Is there any use of common components?

Digital posters are often used in London Underground stations, positioned on the walls next to the escalators

You could use a graphics program to create the screens for a digital poster. It is important to bear in mind that the screens need to form part of a set, using a common design and having some shared elements, such as a border, logo or emblem. Once you have created the images, you will need to use presentation software to set up a timed presentation to display them on the screen.

Remember what and who your poster is for. Posters aim to do two things:

- attract the attention of people passing by
- get a message across with very few words.

Figure 1.28 shows one idea for a digital poster advertising the airline's meals that cater for those with special dietary needs.

Using a storyboard to design the poster

Before you start designing your digital poster, use a storyboard to plan each screen of the poster.

Choosing the correct resolution

Resolution is measured in pixels per inch (ppi). For posters designed to be viewed on screen, you do not need high-resolution images. The highest resolution your screen can display is 72 ppi, so if your product will only ever be viewed on a screen, use 72 ppi. This will make the file size much smaller.

Skills builder 27

Remind yourself of Scenario 2 on page 171. Produce a design for a digital poster consisting of three screens to advertise the airline's new meals for people with special dietary requirements, like the ones shown in Figure 1.28.

- Decide on the look and feel of the digital poster. What content and elements of the layout will be common to all three screens?
- Use the design to work out what content you need to gather. Will you use images, sounds, animations?
- Gather the content you have decided to use.
- Prepare the content and write any text that you need to include.

Creating a timed slideshow

Once you have collected all the content you need for your digital poster, you need to set up a timed slideshow. There are many different types of software that you could use to create a slideshow. Using presentation software, follow these steps:

1 Open a blank presentation and add three new slides.

2 Insert one of the images into each slide.

3 Set the timings to a few seconds for each slide.

4 Get some feedback on whether others think your timings are about right.

Reviewing digital posters

There are a number of things you should consider when reviewing your own, or someone else's, digital poster. Ask yourself these questions:

- Are the screens consistent? Do all the screens have similar feels and communicate a consistent message?
- How much time do you think people will need to look at each screen? It should be long enough for them to take in the message, but not so long that they lose interest before the next screen appears.
- Where will the digital poster appear? The digital poster shown in Figure 1.31 is intended to be displayed in the airline check-in area or on the screens on board the aircraft itself.

It is extremely important to consider where your digital poster will be displayed as this will influence how much information you include. For example, displaying your digital poster in London bus shelters would be a complete waste of time as they do not include enough information for people to know what they are advertising. However, if displayed in an airline's check-in area or on board a flight, airline passengers will know what the digital poster is promoting.

Figure 1.28 A digital poster advertising the airline's new low-fat, nut-free and vegetarian meals

These people wouldn't be able to understand the digital poster produced for use in an airport or on board an aeroplane

As you design and develop a digital product such as a poster, a presentation or a website, you need to test it yourself, and you also need to get some feedback from your test buddy and maybe your teacher too. Once your product is complete, you need to review it. How well does it meet the requirements? What further improvements could you make?

Testing

Everything that you create for the CAB activities must be thoroughly tested. Remember that you are testing not only to find any mistakes but also to improve fitness for purpose. You should constantly be asking yourself whether your products suit the audience they are aimed at. The effectiveness of your testing will affect the quality of your products.

You should provide evidence that your work has been tested by someone else and that you have acted on any comments or suggestions for improvement that they have made. This evidence does not have to be separately recorded and reported. It should be included in your review where you should discuss any feedback you were given and the actions you took. The outcomes of these actions will be seen in your products.

What do you need to test?

You should:

- make sure that your digital product works as you intended
- check that your digital product meets all the requirements specified in the CAB
- check that the content is correct
- identify and correct typing and spelling errors
- make sure that any animations, sounds and videos work smoothly.

You should also test for impact and effectiveness. Ask yourself:

- Does my digital product get the message across?
- Is the audience convinced by my digital product?
- Does my product achieve what I intended it to?

REVIEW AND FEEDBACK

Here are some important questions to ask:

- Does the digital product work as intended?
- Does it meet all the stated requirements?
- Is it suitable for the intended audience?
- How can it be improved?

Sometimes you may not see the mistakes or shortcomings on something you have been working on for a long time, but instantly find mistakes or shortcomings in someone else's work. Remember this when you act as a test buddy for someone else.

EFFECTIVE TEST BUDDIES

When the time comes to give feedback to someone else on their efforts, you need to work to some kind of structure. It's fairly pointless if your friend just asks you, 'Hey, what do you think of this?' and you reply, 'Yeah, it's OK' or 'Well, I think the colours are awful.'

One method of getting useful feedback on what you have produced is to ask your test buddy to tell you:

- specific things they like about the product
- specific things that they think could be improved.

Feedback from a test buddy can be very useful in helping you to improve your product. Ask them to tell you what they like about you product and what they think could be done better

Using the Activity Review in the CAB

There will be a checklist in the CAB for you to complete. Here is part of one from the Sample Assessment Material.

ACTIVITY 1 REVIEW

Digital poster

Why did you choose the images you have used?

What useful feedback did you get from your teacher and your test buddy?

How did you make use of the feedback?

What could you do to make the digital poster more exciting?

Test buddy feedback

What feedback did you give your test buddy during Activity 1?

How did your test buddy make use of your feedback?

Remember to save the Activity Review checklist in your Activity1 folder.

Activity 2 Overview

In Activity 2 you will be working with a **spreadsheet model**. These are often used to help with planning and forecasting and to explore 'What if… ?' scenarios.

Spreadsheet model – a simulation of a real-life situation. For example, a spreadsheet model might be used to help plan an event like a school trip or concert. The organisers could use a model to help them decide how much they need to charge to cover their costs.

Models are used in all sorts of ways. Consider the uses of modelling described below.

Architects build 3D models of proposed new developments so that prospective investors can visualise what they will look like.

Engineers build models of aeroplanes, cars, submarines and spacecraft and test them out in wind tunnels, pools and other environments under different extreme conditions.

Have you ever been in a simulator such as a motor-racing or flight simulator? It gives you a feel for the real thing without putting your life in danger.

Spreadsheet models help business people to look into the future and see what might happen in different situations, for example if costs rise or fall, if income goes up or down, if demand for a product changes or if a disaster strikes. Health experts use spreadsheet models to predict the spread of epidemics (within single countries) and pandemics (around the world). Environmentalists use spreadsheet models to predict the likely fate of an endangered species, the need for new housing or the availability of fresh water in a few years' time if a current trend continues.

In Activity 2, you do not have to develop a spreadsheet model from scratch. Rather, you will be given two basic models: one of them is very basic and the other one is more complex, allowing you to take several factors into account and more accurately model reality. You can choose which model to develop, depending on how confident you are at using spreadsheet software. Once you have developed the model, you need to:

- explore options, using 'What if… ?' scenarios, and make recommendations
- include charts, relevant images and explanatory text in a presentation of your results, to back up your recommendations.

Flight simulators allow pilots to practise flying planes without even being in the sky

Using a spreadsheet model to support decision making

In Activity 2 of the CAB you will be given a choice of spreadsheet models to work with. The information provided by the model you develop needs to be reliable because you will have to make decisions based on it. You will be asked to present your findings in various ways to your audience. In the sample CAB you are asked to produce a presentation, but other types of digital products may be required in other CABs. This chapter should provide you with some ideas about the sort of tasks you will be asked to do and how they relate to each other.

Start by using a spreadsheet model that is provided in the CAB

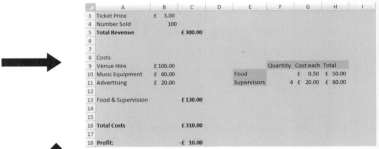

Develop the model so that it is more detailed and provides more accurate information than the one you were given to start with

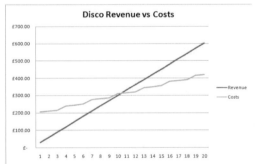

Create meaningful graphs and charts from your model

Present your recommendations to your audience. You can include important figures and graphs in your presentation

Create simple digital products such as invitations or adverts. They will be designed to be read on-screen so you may want to include animations or sound. (Refer back to Design workshop 1, pages 181–4, for more information on including animations and sounds in digital products.)

In order to practise the skills required for Activity 2 of the CAB, you will look at a number of different scenarios and attempt various different Skills builders throughout this chapter. These will be similar to the scenarios and activities in the CAB.

2 Modelling

By completing this chapter you should be able to...

- Adapt and enhance spreadsheet models:
  - › Gather and validate data.
  - › Enter and organise numerical data.
  - › Format numerical data and other information.
  - › Use formulae, functions and variables.
  - › Use validation techniques.
  - › Enhance clarity and presentation.
- Use spreadsheet models to explore ideas:
  - › Ask 'What if... ?' questions.
  - › Try out alternatives.
  - › Create and develop charts and graphs.
  - › Verify that results are accurate and reasonable.
  - › Interpret results and base recommendations on them.
- Design and develop digital products that are fit for purpose and audience:
  - › Combine different types of digital content, e.g. charts and images, into a presentation or other type of digital product.
  - › Test for functionality and usability.
  - › Make use of test buddy feedback.
  - › Discuss any improvements made as a result of feedback.

Functional Skills...

In this chapter there is information and activities that will help you to practise the following Functional ICT Skills:

Level 1

Using ICT

- Use ICT to plan and organise work.
- Select and use software applications to meet needs and solve straightforward problems.
- Work with files, folders and other media to access, organise, store, label and retrieve information.

Developing, presenting and communicating information

- Apply editing, formatting and layout techniques to meet needs, including text, tables, graphics, records, numbers, charts, graphs or other digital content.
- Process numerical data.
- Display numerical data in a graphical format.
- Use field names and data types to organise information.
- Evaluate own use of ICT tools at each stage of a task and at the task's completion.

Level 2

Using ICT

- Use ICT to plan and analyse complex or multi-step tasks and activities and to make decisions about suitable approaches.
- Select and use software applications to meet needs and solve complex problems.
- Manage files, folders and other media storage to enable efficient information retrieval.

Developing, presenting and communicating information

- Apply a range of editing, formatting and layout techniques to meet needs, including text, tables, graphics, records, numerical data, charts, graphs or other digital content.
- Use appropriate software to process and analyse numerical data.
- Display numerical data in appropriate graphical format.
- Use appropriate field names and data types to organise information.
- Analyse and draw conclusions from a data set by searching, sorting and editing records.
- Work accurately and check accuracy, using software facilities where appropriate to ensure fitness for purpose.
- Evaluate the selection, use and effectiveness of ICT tools and facilities used to present information at each stage of a task and at the task's completion.

How you will be assessed...

In Activity 2, you will be assessed on how well you have:

- Selected appropriate data to use in your model.
- Developed a spreadsheet model that generates reliable and meaningful information and enables you to make informed decisions.
- Tested your model.

- Used your model to explore alternatives and make recommendations.
- Used effective content and features to show your findings and recommendations in digital products.
- Used your test buddy to give feedback on your work and identify things that need to be improved.
- Made suggestions for improvement.
- Reviewed your own work.

The files you will use in this section are listed here:

Files:

1. Sources_table.rtf
2. Solar panel1.xls
3. Hoodies model.xls
4. Solar panel2.xls
5. Solar panel3.xls

Websites:

1. Website 2.1 – Heat my Home

Skillsbank

Using a spreadsheet model:

- enter and format labels and numbers
- create formulae using relative and absolute addresses
- put a validation check on input data
- use a table lookup function
- use an IF function
- lay out a model so that it is easy to find answers to 'What if... ?' questions.

Creating a graph or chart:

- select the figures and labels that you want in a chart
- use a wizard to chart or graph a series of numbers
- select the appropriate type of graph or chart
- add a suitable title, axis labels and legend, and data values if required
- select non-adjacent columns (columns that are not next to each other) from which to create your graph or chart
- customise chart titles, labels and legends
- change fonts and font sizes after your graph has been created.

A simple spreadsheet model

Imagine you decide to set up a stall selling ice creams at the school fête. There are some important decisions to make before the day arrives. You want to make sure your stall does not make a loss.

You will need to research information on costs and plan for different conditions on the day of the fête.

Skills builder 2.1

Use the spreadsheet in Figure 2.1 to answer these questions.

a) Which cells in the spreadsheet might contain **formulae**? Can you say what these formulae might be?

b) Which cell contains your best guess about what will happen on the afternoon of the fête?

c) What are the possible consequences if your guess is wrong?

d) Why might it be important for the school to keep records of how many people attended the school fête, what the weather was like and how much each stall made?

e) What information might you keep about what happens on your stall to help you make accurate estimates for the ice cream stand at next year's fête?

Spreadsheets are often used for financial calculations, such as estimating whether a new business will be profitable and how much profit it is likely to make. It is not worth starting a business if it is always going to make a loss.

Here's an example scenario to get you started. What do you think the characters below are thinking?

'Making predictions is difficult – particularly about the future' (Sam Goldwyn, US film producer)

	A	B	C	D	E
1		Ice Cream Sales			
2					
3	Cones	£0.17		Selling Price per Ice Cream	£1.50
4	Ice Cream per Cone	£0.10			
5	Flake	£0.70		Expected Sales	100
6					
7	Total Cost per Ice Cream	£0.97		Total Revenue	£150.00
8					
9	Total Cost of all Ice Creams	£97.00		Profit	£53.00
10					

Figure 2.1 The ice cream sales spreadsheet model that you are given with the scenario

Enter the data shown in Figure 2.1 into a spreadsheet program. Don't forget to use formulae where appropriate. Use the spreadsheet to answer these questions:

f) How much profit will you make if you sell 150 ice creams?

g) What are the weaknesses of this model? Suggest ways of improving it.

This example gives you some idea of the skills you will need for this part of the project.

Gathering and validating data

You may be asked to research some new data to put into an existing model, or to check that data already in the model is reasonable. So, within the context of the Ice cream sales scenario, you may need to do your own research to check if the costs of cones, flakes and ice cream are accurate.

SOURCES OF INFORMATION

There are various sources of information you could use to find new data or to check the data already in the spreadsheet model. You could:

- use the Internet – but make sure you check the accuracy of your data by looking at several different websites and making sure that they are up to date
- use printed paper sources, including books, advertisements, newspapers, magazines and flyers that come through the letterbox – but make sure you check your facts using more than one information source
- use primary sources such as observations you have made yourself.

To make sure that the data you collect from the Internet is current, look carefully at when the data was produced. Websites often include the date that they were last updated. Companies usually provide up-to-date information, but their prices may change frequently, so you need to be sure.

Imagine you search the Internet and find a site like the one shown in Figure 2.2. This company is selling packs of 24 ice cream cones for £3.95, which works out at nearly £0.17 per cone, the figure used in the model. It looks as though the model is spot on.

Figure 2.2 Researching the cost of ice cream cones

You shouldn't give up there though. It would be advisable to find at least two more sites selling the products you are interested in to make sure you have got the best price.

Remember to record all your sources in **Sources_table** in your Development folder. *e-component*

The Internet does not have all the answers. In this situation you would need to look somewhere else for information to help you estimate how many ice creams you are likely to sell. For example, the school Bursar or Treasurer may have records of how much money the ice cream stand made at last year's fête or how many people usually attend the fête each year.

> *Formula* (plural *formulae*) – a statement or equation that automatically calculates a result based on values entered in the formula or in other cells.

Skills builder 2.2

Use the ice cream model spreadsheet in Figure 2.1 to research and answer the following questions.

a) **Cell B3 contains the cost to you of buying a single cone. Where do you think this data came from? How can you check that it is accurate and up to date?**

b) **Which other cells contain data that you should check before using the model?**

c) **How would you find out what is a reasonable price to charge for an ice cream?**

d) **What will happen to your profit if you are left with too much stock?**

e) **What recommendations could you make for dealing with leftover stock?**

f) **How can you build these possibilities into your model?**

Using different data sources

A spreadsheet model needs to contain accurate data in order to be useful. You will need to look at a range of sources to find all of the data that you need and to ensure that the data supplied is correct. Always check data to ensure that it is reasonable.

Solar panels in the roof of a house

Skills builder 2.3

Look at Figure 2.3. What information does the solar panels spreadsheet give?

Discuss with a partner what recommendations you would make about using solar power to heat your home.

How could you make this model more useful?

How can you ensure that the information generated by a model is reliable and meaningful?

Scenario 2: Solar panels

Imagine that your neighbour, Sandra, a keen environmentalist, has asked you to look into the financial advantages of installing a solar panel for providing hot water in her four-bedroom house. She is worried about climate change and wants to do something to reduce her carbon footprint. She has already put some figures into a basic spreadsheet model, and is dismayed to find that it will apparently take up to 41 years to recover the cost of installing a solar panel.

Figure 2.3 shows the spreadsheet Sandra gives you.

	A	B	C	D	E	F	G
1	How long will it take to recoup the cost of a solar panel?						
2							
3							
4	Current rate for gas	3.3	pence per kilowatt hour				
5	Average annual consumption for hot water	3000	kWh				
6	Annual cost of hot water	£99.00					
7	VAT	£4.95		VAT rate	5%		
8	Total cost	£103.95					
9							
10	Cost of solar panel	£2,150					
11							
12	Percentage of hot water supplied by solar panel	50%	55%	60%	65%	70%	
13	Total annual saving	£51.98	£57.17	£62.37	£67.57	£72.77	
14							
15	Payback period in years	41.4	37.6	34.5	31.8	29.5	
16							

Figure 2.3 Sandra's spreadsheet model on recovering the cost of a solar panel for hot water

Before doing anything else, you need to check the figures in rows 4, 5, 7 and 10.

Sandra gives you her gas bill to look at – see Figure 2.4. You can see that she used 1538 kWh (kilowatt hours) in 24 days at a cost of 6.862p per kWh for the first 176 kWh and 3.43p per kWh for anything over that. Gas is used for central heating, hot water and cooking.

Gas you've used this period

30 Sep 2008 – estimated	37850	
23 Oct 2008 – actual	37988	We read your meter
	- 138 metric units over 24 days (actual)	
Gas units converted	- 1538.45 kWh used over 24 days	
	First 176.00 kWh x 6.862p -	£12.08
	Next 1362.45 kWh x 3.434p -	£46.79

Figure 2.4 Sandra's gas bill

She also tells you that she looked at various websites to check the other figures.

Skills builder 2.4

Use the spreadsheet **Solar panel1** for this activity.

a) Look at the pie chart in Figure 2.5. Make an estimate of what proportion of gas is used to heat the hot water. Write this as a percentage of total gas consumption.

Breakdown of Energy Costs

Figure 2.5 Energy costs

b) Sandra uses about 2000 kWh per month for all of her gas consumption. Based on this, does the figure of 3000 kWh seem reasonable for Sandra's annual gas consumption for heating the water? If not, what would be a more reasonable figure?

c) Replace the figure in cell B5 with your own estimate.

Go to **Website 2.1** to read some useful information about solar panels.

Skills builder 2.5

Research the current costs for gas (per kilowatt hour) and for installing solar panels and replace the figures in blue in the spreadsheet with ones that you find.

You may find the report of estimated running costs shown in Figure 2.5 useful, but remember that this is not Sandra's house, so you need to treat the figures with caution.

Update **Sources_table** to show where you obtained your costs.

Save your amended spreadsheet in your Activity2 folder.

Did you know?

Many power companies, including British Gas, encourage you to fill in a simple online form and they will then display an Energy Report for you, showing what proportion of your energy bill is spent on heating, cooking, etc.

Figure 2.6 shows a sample Energy Report for a large, poorly insulated house. A similar report could be a useful source of information for Sandra in working out how much of her annual gas consumption is used on heating water.

Figure 2.6 An example of a breakdown of gas running costs

Finding good sources of information for your project is one of the points you'll be assessed on – and it's something you can work on at home. You need to be sure to save the links you find so you can look up an information source again any time you want to go back to it.

Here's another scenario. Think about how you would find out the information you need to put into the model, and how you would use the model to help find the answer to a question.

Scenario 3: Hoodies for school leavers

You will be part of a Year 11 team that wants to do something special to celebrate the end of the year. You have decided to offer hooded sweatshirts for sale to everyone who would like one. The tops will have the school logo and the sentence 'Class of 2XXX' (insert your own year) printed on the front.

You have been asked to find out:

- how much the sweatshirts will cost to buy from a manufacturer
- how many people are likely to buy one
- how much they should be sold for.

To complete this task, you will need to:

- research different companies selling hooded sweatshirts to find information about prices and bulk discounts
- estimate the number of people likely to buy one
- put the information into a basic spreadsheet model and use it to calculate a reasonable selling price.

The quality of the information that goes into a model has a direct impact on the quality of the information you get out of it: remember GIGO – Garbage In, Garbage Out. For example, if you are trying to model your income and expenditure in order to save for something, it would be foolish to exaggerate your income as this would give unreliable results. Your information must be as accurate as you can make it, so use several sources to ensure that it is reliable.

Figure 2.7 shows one of the many websites that sells the type of product you are looking for in wholesale quantities. It contains details of prices per hooded top, the discount information for ordering in bulk, information on the cost of adding your own lettering, such as a school logo and custom slogan, and **VAT** rates.

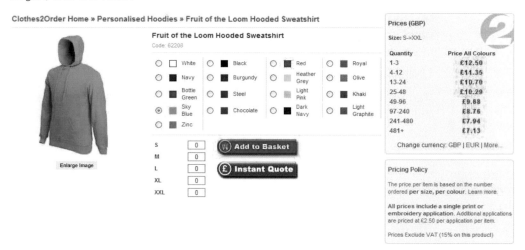

Figure 2.7 Website selling hoodies

Skills builder 2.6

Using the Internet, find at least one site selling personalised hooded tops and compare the prices to those shown in Figure 2.7.

a) **How many sites do you think you should look at to compare different prices?**

b) **Is it good enough to use the first site you come across?**

c) **Is the cheapest always best?**

> **VAT (Value Added Tax)** – a charge added to most goods and services in the UK. The standard rate of VAT charged is currently 17.5%. However, the rate of VAT does sometimes change so it is important that it is easy to change this in your spreadsheet.

Skills builder 2.7

Use the data in Figure 2.8 to answer the questions below.

	A	B	C	D	E	F	G
1	Hooded Tops						
2							
3		Prices	VAT rate 15%			Discounts	
4	Hooded Top with School Logo	£ 10.29	£ 11.83			Quantity	Discount price per top
5	Addition Printed Lettering "Class of 2XXX"	£ 2.50	£ 2.88			1	£12.50
6	**Total Cost**		£ 14.71			4	£11.35
7						13	£10.70
8	Expected Sales	27				25	£10.29
9	Total Cost of Hoodies		£ 397.13			49	£9.68
10						97	£8.76
11						241	£7.94
12						481	£7.13
13	Total Delivery	6.95	£ 7.99				
14	Total Cost including Delivery		£ 405.12				
15							
16	Cost per Hooded Top		£ 15.00				
17							

Figure 2.8 Spreadsheet for Scenario 3

a) **Which cells contain data that needs to be researched?**

b) **Which cells contain formulae?**

c) **Does the spreadsheet show how much you will sell each hooded top for?**

d) **Which cell contains a figure that is an estimate? How would you arrive at such an estimate?**

e) **It won't be easy to change the VAT rate in this spreadsheet. Have you got any ideas for improvement?**

Developing a simple model

Before you start developing your chosen model for Scenario 3 on page 203, you will need to be sure you understand how it works.

Using a lookup table in a spreadsheet

The price table from the website in Figure 2.7 on page 204 has been copied and pasted into cells G5 to G12 of the spreadsheet. A minor change has been made to the quantity column to enable you to use a table lookup **function**. You will notice that the more tops you order, the cheaper the unit price becomes. To calculate the price of a single top, you need to refer to the price table in Figure 2.9.

> *Function* – a formula used in a calculation, such as IF or SUM.

Quantity	Price per top
1	£12.50
4	£11.35
13	£10.70
25	£10.29
49	£9.68
97	£8.76
241	£7.94
481	£7.13

Figure 2.9 Price of hoodies according to quantity ordered

Skills builder 2.8

Use the price table in Figure 2.9 to find out the price of each top if you order:

a) 50 tops; b) 100 tops; c) 241 tops.

Spreadsheets have a useful function which enables you to look up data in a table. In Microsoft Excel this function is called VLOOKUP. To use this function, you need a lookup table in the format shown in Figure 2.9 – it shows the minimum number of tops you have to buy to get a particular price.

Skills builder 2.9

Open the Hoodies model spreadsheet. Look at the formula in cell B4 of the spreadsheet. It is:

$$=VLOOKUP(B8,F5:G12,2)$$

Work out what this formula calculates.

Which cell contains the figure you are looking up in the table?

> *Tip:* the last parameter, 2, signifies that the price is found in the second column of the lookup table.

Using data validation

Figure 2.10 Using the Data Validation dialogue box to specify that the number entered must be between 1 and 200

Validation is the process of checking data when it is input into the spreadsheet to make sure that it is sensible or reasonable. For example, it is possible that you could accidentally type 270 instead of 27 into the Expected Sales cell. This would give you a wrong overall price. Using validation techniques you could specify that the cell can only contain a value between 1 and say 200 – the total number of students in your year – and therefore the maximum number who could order a hoodie (see Figure 2.10). If you accidentally enter a number outside the range 1 to 200, the spreadsheet will produce an error message for you.

Making your model useful

Developing a model means trying to make it as useful and realistic as you can. For the **Hoodies model** spreadsheet, developing the model in some or all of the following ways would make it more useful.

- There may be other factors, such as a delivery charge, which you need to take into consideration in your model.
- You can alter the model so that it is easy to adjust for changing circumstances such as a change in the rate of VAT.
- You can add data validation to the cells holding data that users will change when they use the model, to help prevent mistakes.
- You can format individual cells, so that they are easier to read, by using different currency or date formats, colour, text sizes and orientation, etc.
- You can include **conditional formatting** to identify when an action produces a particular outcome.
- You can add headings or move things around so that the model is clear and easy for someone else to use.
- You may be able to expand the model so that it works for more than one product, venue or other circumstance, or compares more than one possibility.

Skills builder 2.10

Develop the **Hoodies model** spreadsheet in the following ways.

a) Make no charge for delivery for orders over £300.

b) Change the model so that it can easily reflect a change in the VAT rate.

c) Add validation to the cells containing Expected Sales, Total Delivery and VAT rate.

d) Make the text in cell C9, the Total Cost of Hoodies cell, turn red if it is above £1000.

The more detailed and complex your model, the more realistic it will be.

Asking 'What if… ?' questions

A 'What if… ?' question involves changing variables in your model. For example, asking 'What if we only sell 20 hoodies?' would mean changing Expected Sales to 20 to see what effect this has on the price.

You may find it a good idea to create a larger table under your existing model which shows the price for a wide range of different sales quantities. For example, you might set out some of the data as shown in Figure 2.11.

19	Quantity Bought	Price excluding VAT	Price including VAT	Lettering	Total Cost	Cost per Top
20	10	£ 11.35	£ 11.35	£ 2.88	£ 150.24	£ 15.02
21	20	£ 10.70	£ 10.70	£ 2.88	£ 279.49	£ 13.97
22	30	£ 10.29	£ 10.29	£ 2.88	£ 402.94	£ 13.43
23	40	£ 10.29	£ 10.29	£ 2.88	£ 534.59	£ 13.36
24	50	£ 9.68	£ 9.68	£ 2.88	£ 635.74	£ 12.71
25	60	£ 9.68	£ 9.68	£ 2.88	£ 761.29	£ 12.69
26	70	£ 9.68	£ 9.68	£ 2.88	£ 886.84	£ 12.67
27	80	£ 9.68	£ 9.68	£ 2.88	£ 1,012.39	£ 12.65
28	90	£ 9.68	£ 9.68	£ 2.88	£ 1,137.94	£ 12.64
29	100	£ 8.76	£ 8.76	£ 2.88	£ 1,171.49	£ 11.71
30	110	£ 8.76	£ 8.76	£ 2.88	£ 1,287.84	£ 11.71
31	120	£ 8.76	£ 8.76	£ 2.88	£ 1,404.19	£ 11.70
32	130	£ 8.76	£ 8.76	£ 2.88	£ 1,520.54	£ 11.70
33	140	£ 8.76	£ 8.76	£ 2.88	£ 1,636.89	£ 11.69
34	150	£ 8.76	£ 8.76	£ 2.88	£ 1,753.24	£ 11.69
35	160	£ 8.76	£ 8.76	£ 2.88	£ 1,869.59	£ 11.68
36	170	£ 8.76	£ 8.76	£ 2.88	£ 1,985.94	£ 11.68
37	180	£ 8.76	£ 8.76	£ 2.88	£ 2,102.29	£ 11.68
38	190	£ 8.76	£ 8.76	£ 2.88	£ 2,218.64	£ 11.68
39	200	£ 8.76	£ 8.76	£ 2.88	£ 2,334.99	£ 11.67

Figure 2.11 Prices for a wide range of sales quantities

Skills builder 2.11

Using the **Hoodies model** spreadsheet, answer the following questions.

a) What would be the price per top if all 200 students in the year bought one?

b) How many tops would you have to order in order to keep the price below £15 each?

c) What if the VAT rate increased to 18.5%?

d) How much would one top cost if a quarter of the year (50 students) bought one?

Let's return to Scenario 2: Solar panels (see page 201) to examine a more complex model and find out how it could be developed further.

In the Edexcel CAB, you will typically be given two spreadsheet models for the same scenario, one more complex than the other. Here are the criteria for getting top marks for developing a model:

The student has **selected** relevant data, developed a **complex** spreadsheet model that generates **sufficient** reliable and meaningful information to **fully** inform the decision-making process. **Effective** testing has been carried out.

Skills builder 2.12

Open the **Solar panel2** spreadsheet and save it in your Activity2 folder. Part of the spreadsheet is shown in Figure 2.12.

	A	B	C	D	E	F	G	H
8	Total cost	£103.95						
9								
10	Cost of solar panel	£2,150	(Source: xxx)					
11								
12	Percentage of hot water supplied by solar panel	50%	55%	60%	65%	70%		
13	Total annual saving	£51.98	£57.17	£62.37	£67.57	£72.77		
14								
15	**Payback period in years**	**41.4**	**37.6**	**34.5**	**31.8**	**29.5**		
16								
17								
18	Now assume that the price of gas rises by 10% per annum							
19						Potential saving with solar panel		
20		Cost of hot water	Cumulative cost	50%	55%	60%	65%	70%
21	Year 1	£103.95	£103.95	£51.98	£57.17	£62.37	£67.57	£72.77
22	Year 2	£114.35	£218.30	£109.15	£120.06	£130.98	£141.89	£152.81
23	Year 3	£125.78	£344.07	£172.04	£189.24	£206.44	£223.65	£240.85
24	Year 4	£138.36	£482.43	£241.22	£265.34	£289.46	£313.58	£337.70
25	Year 5	£152.19	£634.63	£317.31	£349.04	£380.78	£412.51	£444.24

Figure 2.12 Part of the spreadsheet

The spreadsheet has been developed a little further than the one you used to complete Skills builder 2.3 on page 201 (**Solar panel1**). The original spreadsheet calculated that it would take at least 29.5 years to recoup the £2,150 cost of installing a solar panel, even if it provided 70% of all Sandra's hot water. But is that really fair? Gas prices go up almost every year and, as they rise, Sandra will save more because her use of solar energy will mean she uses less gas.

Skills builder 2.13

a) **Do some research to find out how much gas prices have risen over the past three years, and estimate how much they are likely to increase in the future or look at what other people are predicting.**

b) **Put your own figures into the spreadsheet Solar panel2. You can include figures from your amended Solar panel1 spreadsheet if you saved them.**

c) **How many years might it take for Sandra to recover the cost of installing the solar panel?**

Remember to save the sources of all your figures in **Sources_table** in your Development folder.

Absolute cell referencing

The **Solar panel2** spreadsheet makes extensive use of absolute cell referencing, so make sure you know how to enter a formula with an absolute reference. For example, look in cells B13 and C13.

- The formula in cell B13 is =B12*B8
- The formula in cell C13 is =C12*B8

Inserting the dollar sign ($) before both the column and row reference ensures that when you copy this formula to another cell, the reference to cell B8, which contains the total cost of the hot water, remains unchanged.

Skills builder 2.14

Answer the following questions to show your understanding of absolute cell references.

a) **What will the formula =D$20*$C21 be if you copy it to E21?**

b) **What will the formula =D$20*$C21 be if you copy it to D22?**

Use the spreadsheet to check if you were right.

Extending the model

The new model in **Solar panel2** is a bit more realistic, but does it 'fully inform the decision-making process?' In other words, have you taken all the relevant facts into consideration?

Here is where you really have to use your imagination. Can you think of any other relevant factors? For example:

- Will Sandra's gas boiler last longer with less use?
- Do solar panels require expensive maintenance?
- Could she get a government grant for installing a solar panel?

Another thing you could consider is what might Sandra do with the £2,150 if she does not spend it on a solar panel? If she puts it into a bank account, she could be getting interest on it every year. That would make a big difference to the calculations, and would be well worth including in the model.

Should I spend the £2,000 I've saved on a solar panel or on a more economical car? Or perhaps I should put it in a savings account?

Might Sandra be able to reduce her carbon footprint and save money by investing in something different?

Skills builder 2.15

In a small group, discuss each of the factors described in the section 'Extending the model'.

a) **How would you expect each of the factors to influence the payback time on Sandra's investment?**

b) **Would they increase or decrease the payback time? Why?**

c) **Would you be able to show this in the spreadsheet if you had time?**

Charts and graphs can make information and data easier to understand, so it is important to know when to use each type of chart and how to make the chart as easy to interpret as possible. The wrong type of chart used in the wrong situation can make information misleading or impossible to understand.

Skills check... make sure you know how to:

- select the figures and labels that you want in a chart
- use a wizard to chart or graph a series of numbers
- select the appropriate type of graph or chart
- add a suitable title, axis labels, **legend** and data values, if required.

Legend – a key that explains the patterns or colours that represent the different data series or categories in a chart.

Choosing the right type of chart

Charts can make figures much easier to understand and interpret. A suitable chart can help to show at a glance which products or holiday months are most popular, or whether sales figures or exam results are better or worse than previous years. A chart can be used to show a trend or to forecast figures in future months or years.

There are several types of chart that you can choose from including line graph, bar chart and pie chart. Different types of chart are appropriate in different circumstances. The question you need to ask is: 'Does the chart make the data clearer than a table of figures?' Choosing the right chart for the job is crucial. A pie chart is useful for showing percentages or proportions of a total, whereas a bar chart would be less clear for this purpose.

Data table

Average temperatures in Barcelona	
January	10°C
February	13°C
March	13°C
April	14°C
May	18°C
June	21°C
July	25°C
August	25°C
September	22°C
October	18°C
November	16°C
December	12°C

Chart

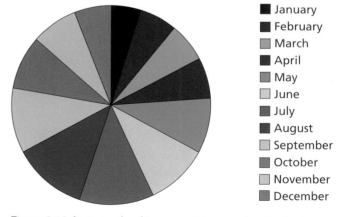

Figure 2.13 An example of inappropriate use of a pie chart

What information does the pie chart in Figure 2.13 convey? This pie chart does not tell you anything at all. It is totally inappropriate to use a pie chart to represent this information because the temperatures are not part of a total figure.

Remember

- ONLY use a pie chart to show parts of a whole
- NEVER use a line graph to show parts of a whole
- ALWAYS think about the purpose of the chart.

Skills builder 2.16

Look at the table of data in Figure 2.13 and decide what type of chart would be more appropriate and why.

Enter the data into a spreadsheet and create the chart you have recommended.

A company has five different products, and it has calculated the profit on each product, as shown in Figure 2.14.

Skills builder 2.17

You have been asked to show the figures in Figure 2.14 in a suitable graph or chart.

a) Which of the charts shown in Figure 2.15 are the most suitable? Why?

b) Which of the charts in Figure 2.15 are totally unsuitable? Why?

c) How could the suitable charts be improved?

d) What is a legend used for?

Product	Profit in £000s
Model A	12.57
Model B	4.60
Model C	6.50
Model D	1.34
Model E	10.24

Figure 2.14 Data table showing the company's profits on its range of products

Chart A

Chart B

Chart C

Chart D

Figure 2.15 Four different charts showing the same data

You must make sure your chart is fit for purpose – you will get no credit for an inappropriate chart.

Using a chart to present information

Skills builder 2.18

Let's look again at Scenario 2 on page 201. Sandra has received her Energy Report from the power company, and it shows a breakdown of her combined gas and electricity costs. The results are as follows.

Lights and appliances	£278
Cooking	£62
Heating	£1,526
Water heating	£137

Put these figures into a spreadsheet and create a chart that will give an instant picture of the figures. Try several types of chart and decide which one would be most effective in a digital presentation.

Remember to add a heading, labels if applicable and a legend. Try different font sizes and chart colours.

Showing exact values in a chart

You need to give some thought to how you are going to show the exact figures in a bar or pie chart.

Skills builder 2.19

What is missing from the chart in Figure 2.16? Think of at least three ways in which you could improve it. It is not worth a lot of marks as it stands now.

Breakdown of Energy Costs

- Lights and appliances
- Cooking
- Heating
- Water heating

Figure 2.16 Pie chart showing Sandra's breakdown of energy costs

Using a line chart to present information

Look again at the **Hoodies model** spreadsheet. Rows 19–39 (shown in Figure 2.11 on page 206) show how much an individual hooded top costs, depending on how many are ordered. Is this the best way of presenting the data?

It would probably be a lot easier to understand the information if it was shown in graphical form. A line graph would be best, with Quantity Bought set against Cost per Top Ordered – see Figure 2.17.

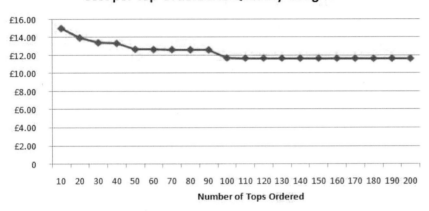

Figure 2.17 Line graph showing cost per hooded top for the different quantities ordered

Adding suitable headings is as important as the graph itself. You must always include a main heading and axis titles. If you have more then one series of data, you will also need a legend or key to show what each of them are.

Interpreting the results of a model

Looking at the chart in Figure 2.17, you can see at a glance that in order to get the best price for the tops and to be able to offer hooded tops to students most cheaply, you should aim to order at least 100 hoodies. It does not matter if you only get 100 because above this figure the price is not affected by the number of tops ordered.

Skills check... make sure you know how to:

- select non-adjacent columns from which to create your graph or chart
- customise chart titles, labels and a legend
- change fonts and font sizes after your graph has been created.

Presenting the information clearly

As your spreadsheet gets more and more complex, it may become harder for a user to understand. This section looks at ways of presenting your results clearly.

A complex spreadsheet is no use if no one can understand it

Here are some suggestions:

- List clearly the assumptions you have made somewhere on the spreadsheet.
- Make it clear, for example through the use of colour, exactly where the user has to enter data.
- Move all the detailed calculations to a different part of the spreadsheet.
- Summarise the results for the user.
- Use an appropriate cell format, e.g. there is no need to show the number of tops ordered to two decimal places – it would be better to have no decimal places.

Look at the spreadsheet in **Solar panel3**. The model has been developed a little further to show how the figures are affected by the loss of interest (if Sandra used the money to install a solar panel instead of investing it). But what does it all mean? Unless you are very familiar with the spreadsheet, it is almost impossible to interpret. The chances are that, unless you use the spreadsheet regularly, you will forget the assumptions you have made. It is a good idea to make the spreadsheet as self-explanatory as you can, so that you or anyone else can understand how it works and what assumptions you have based the spreadsheet on. Use comment boxes to note any assumptions or decisions you have made.

e-component

Communicating results

A graph or chart is often a better way of communicating important information from a model. Use titles, data labels, colours and legends to make a graph easy to understand.

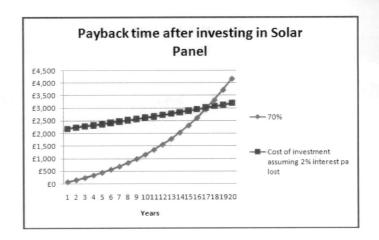

Figure 2.18 A graph of the relevant data from **Solar panel3**. How could it be improved?

Skills builder 2.20

Answer these questions using **Solar panel3** and 2.18.

a) How long is the payback time under the conditions specified in the graph in Figure 2.18?

b) Could you gather this information just by looking at the figures shown in the spreadsheet **Solar panel3**?

c) What other improvements could you make to the spreadsheet so that the results are easier to interpret?

Making changes to a chart

Sometimes you may want to make a minor change to a chart. You can do this by either right-clicking on the part of the chart you want to change or by using the Chart menu. For example, you might want to change the size or font of the chart title. Just right-click on it and select Format Chart Title. You can edit the text simply by clicking it and typing the new text.

If you want to change the text in the legend, instead of recreating the chart from scratch, you can do it like this:

1 Click the chart to select it.

2 From the Chart menu, select Source Data.

3 On the Series tab, click the data series name you want to change.

4 In the Name box, type the new legend – with an equals sign and between inverted commas, e.g. ="Savings assuming 70% of hot water supplied by solar panel".

You can also change the range of values to be charted in this window – see Figure 2.19.

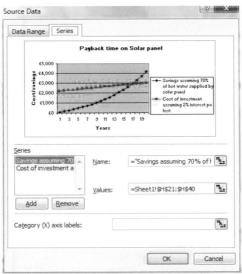

Figure 2.19 Use the Source Data window if you want to change the text in the legend

Just because a spreadsheet works does not mean that it is right. It is essential that your model gives you reliable information. You will make a lot of important decisions based on the information in your spreadsheet, so you must verify the spreadsheet for accuracy and plausibility.

Here are some things to consider when testing a spreadsheet:

- Some errors are easy to spot because they generate an error message, whereas others are harder to see.
- It is sensible to calculate some key figures manually and then compare these answers with the results in the spreadsheet.
- You could use test data to check that the results are what you expect.
- If using test data does not give the results you expected:
  › check that the formulae are correct
  › check that the ranges you have used are correct
  › check that you have entered the correct values.
- Get your test buddy to test your model – ask them to check for usability as well as accuracy.

Creating a test plan

No matter what you are testing, you need to be organised about your methods. Use a test plan and include space to compare the expected results of each test with the actual outcomes. Then you can explain how you fixed any errors in your evaluation. An example of a test plan is shown in Figure 2.20.

Test	Description	Method or test data	Expected result	Actual result
1	Make sure that the VAT is correctly calculated for the delivery	Manually calculate 17.5% VAT on £6.95	VAT should be £1.04, giving a total delivery charge including VAT of £7.99	Total delivery was £7.99
2				
3				

Figure 2.20 An example of a test plan

Do be careful though. Concentrate on the testing rather than the formulation of complicated plans and then trying to evidence them. Your teacher and the moderator will be able to see and use the model so they will be able to see for themselves how well it has been tested. The moderator will assess your tested model, not your test plan.

Skills builder

Look again at Scenario 3 on page 203. Use your calculator to work out the total cost of 100 hoodies from the costs given in the spreadsheet. You should break down the cost into price excluding (without) VAT and price including (with) VAT. Remember to add on the extra £2.50 per top for the printed lettering and as well as the delivery charge.

Now repeat the calculation for 50 hoodies. Do the results agree with your spreadsheet?

Suggest three other tests that you could carry out on your model to be sure there are no errors.

It is important to test manually some of the key calculations your model performs to see if you agree with the results your spreadsheet is giving

Receiving and acting on feedback

A crucial part of testing is end-user testing – getting someone else to try out your spreadsheet. You should ask your test buddy to use your model. By doing this, you will be able to see how well it fulfils its objectives. Your test buddy won't be able to give you useful feedback unless he or she has a good understanding of what you are trying to achieve. It should be possible for your test buddy or your teacher to use your model without you having to sit beside them explaining what they have to do and what the results mean, so keep quiet while they test it. Listen to their feedback carefully.

Think about questions such as:

- Did my test buddy find my model easy to use?
- Did my test buddy understand how to use my model without me having to tell them?
- Did my test buddy know where they were supposed to enter data, and in what format?
- What happened when my test buddy did something wrong?
- Did my test buddy find the results that my model gave useful and relevant?
- Has my test buddy got any suggestions as to how I could improve my model?

Having received feedback, you must decide what action to take. It would be foolish to ignore constructive criticism. You may decide to make the quick and easy improvements first. These could be as simple as correcting spelling mistakes, changing colours or font sizes to make figures more legible, or putting a box around important results to draw attention to them. Once you have made the easy improvements, you should then consider how to implement suggestions that may take longer but could result in a much more meaningful model and a better grade.

Reviewing your spreadsheet model

Once you are satisfied with your model, you will need to answer some questions about it. Here are some questions from Edexcel's sample CAB:

- Which given model did you base yours on?
- What did you do to improve the given model?
- Give some examples of 'What if... ?' questions that can be answered using your model.
- What useful feedback did you get from your teacher and your test buddy?
- How did you make use of the feedback?
- What could you do to make the spreadsheet even more useful?

Skills builder 2.2

Find someone else to test a spreadsheet that you have developed. Ask them to tell you:

- some things they like about your spreadsheet (identify its strengths)
- some things they think you could improve or add to (identify its weaknesses).

Write down their suggestions for a class discussion.

Having developed and tested your spreadsheet model, you are ready to move on to the next part of Activity 2, which is to design and develop digital products. It is likely that you will need to create a presentation for the audience you profiled in Activity 1, showing that you have considered alternatives to your final choices or results and that you have solid reasons to support your findings. As always, an important aspect of this is making sure that your digital products are fit for purpose and audience.

You should refer back to Design workshop 1 (see pages 181–4) for basic design ideas such as the use of images and text.

Planning a presentation

To deliver an effective presentation you must consider who your audience is and prepare your slides to suit them. Depending on the audience, you might use formal or informal language. You might use very simple language for an audience of young children or more complex language for a group of managers or teachers.

Whoever your presentation is for, here are a few basic guidelines:

- Start with a title screen showing what the presentation is about.
- Avoid including more than four or five points on a slide. People cannot concentrate on too much information at once.
- Keep each point short and simple. You can add more detail when talking about the points on the slide.
- Do not use too many words – use images and charts to get your message across.
- Do not use too many animations or transitions as these can be distracting.

As an example, we'll use Scenario 3 (see page 203) and look at how you could plan the content of four different slides to present to the Head and Deputy Head of Year. The purpose of the presentation is to explain:

- how the hooded tops will be advertised to students and parents
- how much students will have to pay for each top
- what each top costs the school to order
- how you arrived at that cost.

Figure 2.21 Example presentation to be presented to the Head and Deputy Head of Year

Skills builder

Look at the presentation shown in Figure 2.21. Think of at least three ways in which you would improve it. What effects or sound could you add to the presentation? Are there any mistakes in the figures used?

Using speaker notes

The best presentation in the world is of little use if the person delivering it is ill-prepared or a poor presenter. Remember that the presentation is not designed to run on its own – you will have to stand up and deliver it to an audience, talking about each slide as you show it. You will need to rehearse this. Make sure that:

- the transitions and special effects do not become boring
- any sounds added have a purpose and are not simply irritating
- the text is legible from the back of the room.

To help you remember what you need to say, you can produce speaker notes, which will be visible on your computer but which will not appear on the screen. An example is shown in Figure 2.22.

Figure 2.22 Speaker notes will help you remember what to say, but will not be visible to your audience

Fonts, colours and styles

The best advice is to keep it simple. Use only a very small selection of fonts – perhaps just two: one for the headings and another for the body text.

Choose only two or three colours plus black and white as your colour scheme and stick with them. Do not change your design from one slide to the next.

Figure 2.23 The number of fonts and colours used on websites is usually kept to a minimum to create a professional-looking style

Skills builder 2.24

Look at any three websites and count the number of fonts used on a page, and the number of colours used, excluding black and white. You will almost always find that the web designer has stuck to a surprisingly small selection of fonts and colours.

Did you find any WordArt, ClipArt or multi-coloured fill effects on these web pages? The answer is probably no. Why do you think this is?

You may have to create an email advertisement, invitation or another similar product as part of Activity 2.

You should refer to Design workshop 1 (see pages 181–4) for basic design ideas such as the use of images and sound.

A simple email advertisement

Email advertisements take many forms – most of them heading straight for the Junk Mail folder and then on to the Recycle Bin. How are you going to ensure that your advertisement reaches its intended audience, that the person who receives the advertisement reads it, and that the advertisement makes the right impact?

To: oliverchadwick@hotmail.com
Subject: Final Clearance Sale
From: jerry@BetterShoes.co.uk
Date: Fri, 17 Jul 2009 23:45:18 +0100

Hi Oliver,
We wanted you to be the first to know that BetterShoes is having a fantastic summer sale. **Don't miss savings of up to 70% in their final clearance sale.**
Order any shoes online for in-store collection and there will be no delivery charge!
Try BetterShoes Collect From Store Service:

1. Visit BetterShoes website and order some shoes to be sent to your nearest store
2. Receive an email or text when they arrive
3. Pop along to have them fitted correctly and pay in store

Figure 2.24 An example of a simple email advertisement

Skills builder

See if you can find any advertisements that you, your family or friends have recently received by email. Evaluate each email advertisement using the following questions.

- Who is the advertisement from?
- Did the person who received the advertisement respond to it?
- What format was the advertisement in? Did you have to open an attachment?
- Did the advertisement include graphics?
- What sort of language did the advertisement use?
- What was the subject line of the email?
- Was the advertisement fit for audience and purpose?

Organisations often use emails to send information out to their customers, as shown in Figure 2.25.

Your TV Licence is available

From: **TV Licensing** (donotreply@tvlicensing.co.uk)
Sent: 08 July 2009 10:43:13
To:

Dear

Thank you for renewing your TV Licence online.

Thanks also for choosing to receive your TV Licence by email.
To see your TV Licence, just click on the link below.

https://e.tvlicensing.co.uk/index.asp?id=4AAE96211DC7D06F2A537C8BA28147DA

Please save your TV Licence on your computer or print it off if you wish.

**Please don't delete this email. You will need the link above if you want to see
your TV Licence online again. You can do this as many times as you like.**

Figure 2.25 Example of an information email

Skills builder

Answer these questions about the email shown in Figure 2.25.

a) **What are the main features of this email?**

b) **Look at the subject line, the reply address and the instructions. Name
   another feature of this email.**

c) **Do you think it is an effective way of sending information to
   customers? What are its advantages?**

d) **Can you think of any disadvantages?**

e) **Is the email fit for audience and purpose?**

Getting the message across

If you want to boost the impact of your email, you may choose to:

- produce an advert as a JPEG in a graphics package and copy the
  image into the email
- produce a complete HTML email
- develop a short Flash animation.

Skills builder

**Create an email advertisement for Scenario 3 (see page 203) that can be
sent to all of the student email addresses in the year. The advertisement
will need to be bright, simple and informative.**

**Write a list of information that you will need to include in your email
advertisement. You can then begin sketching your ideas.**

To ensure that the digital products you make fulfil all of their objectives, you should test them to make sure that they are suitable for their intended audience.

Be aware of your audience

Demonstrating *a very good awareness* of your audience is essential in order to get top marks for your digital products. Look again at Scenario 2 on page 201. Remember what it said about Sandra: 'Your neighbour, Sandra, a keen environmentalist, has asked you to look into the financial advantages of installing a solar panel for providing hot water in her four-bedroom house. She is worried about climate change and wants to do something to reduce her carbon footprint.'

Sandra is keen to reduce her carbon footprint

You must take Sandra's characteristics into consideration when you plan the presentation of your results. Try to get inside Sandra's head. Is her primary motivation financial? Possibly not – but at the same time, she has asked you to look into costs, so she obviously wants to use her money wisely.

The best-case scenario, according to your model, might be that she will not recover the cost of the solar panel for around 20 years. Do not attempt to hide that result: instead, present the facts plainly, along with all the assumptions you have made. At the same time, try to present some positive news as well. Carry out some more research before you start creating the presentation. For example, you might want to look into the following and include some of your findings in the presentation you will give Sandra:

- When Sandra comes to sell her house, will it be worth more if she has installed solar panels?
- Are there any government grants or cash-back schemes for people who invest in clean energy?
- There are other cheaper ways of saving energy. Has Sandra considered loft or wall insulation, insulating her hot water tank more effectively, installing draught excluders on windows or using low-energy light bulbs?

If you make an effort to consider Sandra's specific needs and desires, you can present the *feasible alternatives* and *well-reasoned recommendations* needed for a mark in the top band.

Did you know?

A recent survey by MORI found that people are willing to pay up to £10,000 more for a home built to high environmental standards.

According to the Heat my Home website, estate agents devalue homes for sale with poor 'Energy Assessments' results.

Reviewing how well your products meet their objectives

Remember, you need to review the outcomes of each product in Activity 2, to:

- compare it with the requirements in the CAB
- identify strengths and weaknesses
- suggest possible improvements.

At the beginning of each activity you should have a clear idea of what you want to achieve. Having produced your model, presentation and any other products, you should review how well you achieved your original objectives and whether you could make any improvements, time permitting.

Obtaining feedback

You are also awarded marks for showing that you can collaborate with others, specifically to:

- choose suitable test users
- respond appropriately to feedback from others
- give constructive feedback to others.

You should try to obtain feedback from your test buddy. This could be in the form of a letter, a completed questionnaire, a brief chat or simply giving them a copy of the work for review so that they can make comments on it. You should be able to get plenty of ideas for improvement from their comments. It is quite likely that they will want you to do them the same for their work.

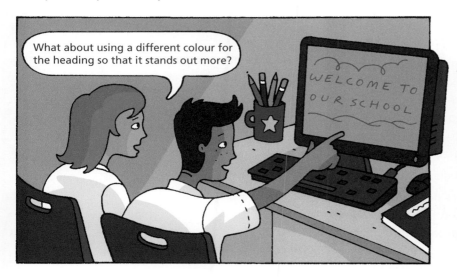

ACTIVITY 2 REVIEW

Model

Which given model did you base yours on?

What did you do to improve the given model?

Give some examples of 'What if… ?' questions that can be answered using your model.

What useful feedback did you get from your teacher and your test buddy?

How did you make use of the feedback?

What could you do to make the spreadsheet even more useful?

Test buddy feedback

What feedback did you give your test buddy during Activity 2?

How did your test buddy make use of your feedback?

Skills builder 2.28

Exchange work that you have completed in this chapter with a classmate or your test buddy to get some useful feedback. Use this feedback to improve your work.

Using the Activity Review in the CAB

There will be a checklist in the CAB for you to complete. Here is part of the Review for Activity 2 from the Sample Assessment Material.

Remember to save the Activity Review checklist in your Activity 2 folder.

Activity 3 Overview

The digital products that you have created so far have been relatively simple and have had limited interactivity. The emphasis in Activity 3 of the CAB is on designing a fully interactive product. This will extend the skills that you have developed in Activities 1 and 2. You will learn how to design an effective user interface and how to plan **navigation** carefully.

> *Navigation* – if a product is interactive, the user must be able to move around it easily. Navigational aids such as buttons and links are an important feature of interactive digital products.

In the sample CAB, the interactive digital product you are required to produce is a factfile, which must be viewable in a browser and allow the user to control how they move around the product. This is only one of many types of interactive digital products. You may be asked to design and build a website, a virtual tour, a digital story, an information point or even a simple game. This chapter will equip you with the knowledge and skills you need to produce any of these types of user-driven products.

When designing an interactive product, you will need to:

- decide how many screens are needed
- use storyboards to plan the content of each screen
- use a flow chart to show the paths through the product
- show that you have considered important aspects of the design
- explain important design decisions.

When developing an interactive product, you will need to:

- be clear about the requirements
- pay particular attention to your target audience and their needs
- decide on a suitable structure and user interface
- test your product thoroughly
- use feedback from others to test for interactivity and usability

Timing

There is a lot of work involved in producing a fully interactive digital product. Planning your work is key. Make sure you make the most of the time you have outside the classroom. For example, you could:

- think about your work at home and get your ideas sorted out before you enter the classroom
- practise some of the skills you will need to use at home, so that when you come into the classroom you are fully prepared.
- get ideas for your own product by looking at products designed by others.

All these steps will make working under supervised conditions much less stressful and will make you more efficient.

Developers always plan their products before they start creating them

Bringing it all together

In Activity 3 of the CAB, you will be using some of the work you have done in Activities 1 and 2 to help you produce an interactive digital product. This section should give you some idea of the sort of tasks you will be asked to do and how they relate to each other.

You will need to draw upon work you did in Activities 1 and 2 or reuse some of the products you developed

You might need to create an animation or a banner advert for your interactive product

You may be also be asked to create another type of digital product such as an online information page or an e-card

In order to practise the skills required for Activity 3 of the CAB, you will carry out Skills builder activities in this chapter all related to the production of an interactive factfile. But remember, the skills you are learning are transferable and can be applied to the production of any user-controlled digital product.

3 Digital publishing

In Activity 3, you will be assessed on how well you have:

- Designed your products.
- Commented on and justified important design decisions.
- Implemented your designs to produce the specified outcomes.
- Created effective content and features.
- Created an effective user interface, suitable for your target audience.
- Used testing and feedback from others to improve the outcomes.

Keep asking yourself 'what and who is this product for?' It does not matter how amazing your designs are or how much time and effort you put in to its development if the final outcome does not meet the specified outcome or is unsuitable for the audience.

The files you will use in this section are listed here:

Files:

1. Storyboard template1.pdf
2. Storyboard template2.ppt
3. Sources_table.rtf

Websites:

1. Website 3.1 – Ancient Nile
2. Website 3.2 – Edexcel

Skillsbank

Manipulating images to optimise them for the Web:
- cropping
- resizing
- changing the resolution.

Creating a website:
- use a web creation package such as Adobe Dreamweaver or Fireworks
- create a consistent interface
- make links that work
- include different types of digital content such as sound, video and animation.

Creating a user-controlled product

Scenario 1: Egypt trip factfile

You are going to design and create an interactive digital factfile for Year 12 and 13 students who are thinking about signing up for the school trip to Egypt. This is to be viewed in a browser.

The factfile will provide information about:

- preparing for the trip (what to take, medical information)
- three excursions
- overall anticipated cost of the trip, including extras.

The main task in Activity 3 is to create a user-controlled digital product viewable in a browser (a factfile). The product will draw on some of the work you did in Activities 1 and 2.

To create a digital product viewable in a browser, you will need to:

- analyse the user requirements
- identify the tasks that you will need to carry out in order to develop the product
- design the screens needed, identifying the content that you will use
- gather and prepare the content
- design the navigation and user interface.

As you can see from Figure 3.1, details of what should go in the factfile are given on a separate page of the CAB.

Gathering content

Whatever type of product you are asked to design, you can be sure that it will have a number of screens and that users can navigate easily from screen to screen in a non-predetermined fashion. Although you will be able to reuse some of the digital content you produced in Activities 1 and 2, you will almost certainly also have to create some additional material.

Make sure you understand exactly what is required before you start. This is a complex task. Break it down into a number of stages or sub-tasks and make sure you divide up your time appropriately between them. Don't make the mistake of thinking that up-front design is not essential. Plan your work carefully. How long will it take you to create your design? How much time do you need to allocate to collecting and preparing the content? How long will it take you to build the product? Don't forget to leave sufficient time for testing the product yourself and getting feedback from others and, of course, to action any changes that need to be made as a result of that feedback.

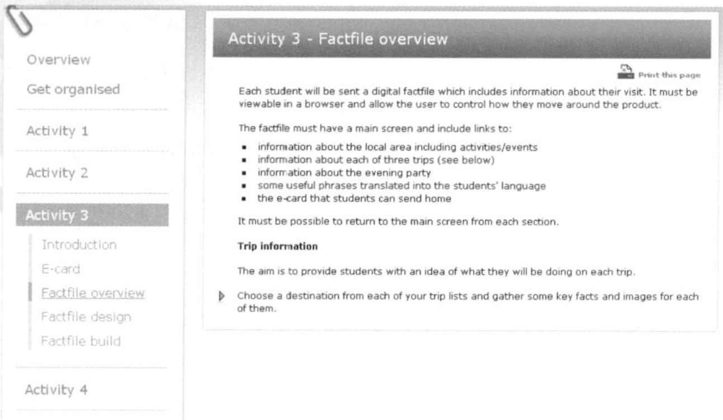

Overview
Get organised
Activity 1
Activity 2
Activity 3
Introduction
E-card
Factfile overview
Factfile design
Factfile build
Activity 4

Activity 3 - Factfile overview

Print this page

Each student will be sent a digital factfile which includes information about their visit. It must be viewable in a browser and allow the user to control how they move around the product.

The factfile must have a main screen and include links to:

- information about the local area including activities/events
- information about each of three trips (see below)
- information about the evening party
- some useful phrases translated into the students' language
- the e-card that students can send home

It must be possible to return to the main screen from each section.

Trip information

The aim is to provide students with an idea of what they will be doing on each trip.

Choose a destination from each of your trip lists and gather some key facts and images for each of them.

Figure 3.1 The page of the CAB that describes what should be included in the factfile

Up-front design

Almost half of the marks for this activity are allocated to your design work. This is because:

- interactive digital products are complicated and have lots of different types of content that have to work together
- there are many different ways of navigating around the product and links must go to the right place
- you won't know what you need to create or what content you need if you have not got detailed storyboards for each screen
- you need to gather all the content you need for a product before you can start to create it

Follow your designs carefully, but be prepared to make changes as your product develops.

The finished product is unlikely to turn out exactly as you planned it. Remember that there is not much point asking for feedback if you are not prepared to do anything about it. Your design work represents the first step on a journey that ends with a finished product which, hopefully, works properly, meets all the specified requirements and is tailor-made for the target audience.

Selecting effective content and features

Selecting effective content involves thinking carefully about the purpose of the product and the characteristics of your target audience. What does the audience need to know? Will an image or a diagram be more effective than text? Could a video clip get the message across? Will they be able to find what they are looking for quickly and easily? Your aim should be to make the user enjoy using the product and be eager to use it again and to recommend it to others.

What must go in it?

If you know who and what a product is for and where it is to be used, you can start to think about what must go in it. What information must you include? What other content will help to get the message across? You might decide to include a movie clip or a short piece of video footage.

Look back to Design workshops 1 (pages 181–4) and 2 (pages 217–8) to remind yourself how to prepare different types of digital content.

STILL IMAGES

If chosen with care, an image can convey a surprising amount of information. You can use:

- photos and drawings for illustrations
- symbols and buttons for navigation and user control
- logos and emblems to establish an identity or sense of belonging
- diagrams or charts to explain something.

VIDEO

Moving images can make the user feel part of the action. If you decide to include video in your product, keep it short. If you decide to use compression techniques, check that the quality is acceptable.

SOUND

You might consider using sound to add a commentary or voice-over, create a particular mood, add a welcome message or include appropriate sound effects.

ANIMATION

Animation is a great way of showing how something works, but it can also be really irritating. Only include animation if you can justify its use. Ask yourself 'What does this animation add?'

TEXT

It is not as easy to read text onscreen as it is on paper, so try to limit the number of words you use. Present it in short, easy-to-read chunks. Use crisp, clear words that suit the subject and will keep your audience interested.

Skills builder **3.1** **e-component**

Rewrite the information below to make it suitable for a single screen in the factfile for students who are planning to go on the school trip to Egypt.

Health and medical issues

There are potential health hazards when travelling in Egypt, however, it is fair to say that the vast majority of tourists suffer nothing worse than a bout of diarrhoea.

Although there are no requirements for travellers to have inoculations when visiting Egypt, we recommend that you discuss this and all your health requirements with your doctor.

Other potential hazards are heatstroke, exhaustion and dehydration. Drink plenty of bottled water and stay out of the sun during the hottest hours of the day.

Mosquitoes can be a problem. The worst time for getting bitten is after dusk.

Adapted from Ancient Nile's Travel Information – for the full text see Website 3.1

Think about the following questions:

- How much of this information is needed?
- What other content could you include on this screen?
- How will you arrange your content? Sketch out your ideas.

Creating a structure chart is a good starting point. It helps you to work out how many screens you need and how they will link together.

Creating a structure chart

Start by producing a list of all the items you need to include in your digital product. Does each item need a separate screen, or could some items share a screen? Which items relate to each other and which need to be separate? You need some sort of gateway into the product – a **home page** or welcome screen.

> *Home page* – this is the first screen of an interactive digital product. It usually has some sort of introduction to the product and a table of contents.

For the Egypt trip factfile (see page 227), you will need a home page plus a number of additional screens containing the following:

- planning information (what to take)
- medical information
- information about excursions 1, 2 and 3
- overall costs of the trip.

You can merge some of these into one screen. For example, you might decide to put the planning and medical information on the same screen. Some information might be best separated on different screens. For example, the information on excursions might need three screens, one for each trip.

To begin building the structure chart, start with the home page and consider what links you might have on it. In the example shown in Figure 3.2, the home page has links to three screens: Planning, Excursions and Costs.

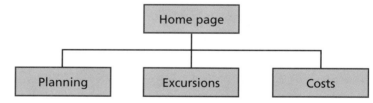

Figure 3.2 **Starting to map out the structure**

On the Excursions page, a further three links to each of the individual trips are needed – see Figure 3.3.

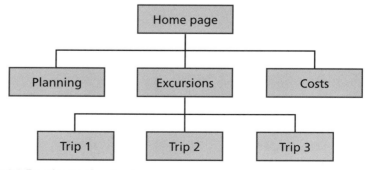

Figure 3.3 **Developing the structure**

Alternatively, you could have a different layout where you can navigate to each screen from every other screen, as shown in Figure 3.4.

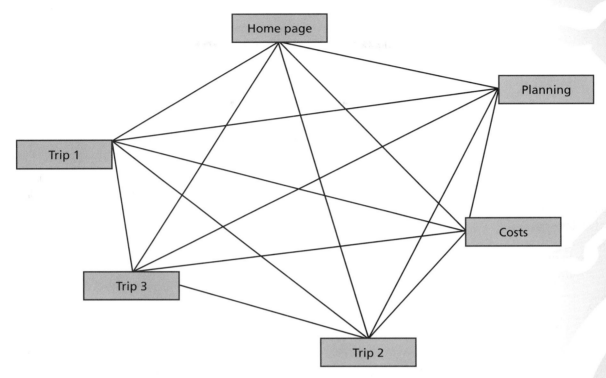

Figure 3.4 An alternative structure in which each screen links to all the others

Skills builder 3.2

 e-component

Look at the sample CAB on **Website 3.2**. Make a list of all the screens in it. Draw a structure chart showing all the screens and how each screen links to other screens.

If you were asked to evaluate this product, what would you pick out as being good design features? Is there anything you think could be improved?

Once you have established how many screens you will have, you should use a storyboard to plan the layout and content of each screen.

Producing a storyboard

A storyboard for a screen should include:

- notes about background and layout
- notes about font colours, styles and sizes
- notes about the content needed, e.g. text, images, sound effects, narration, video, animation, transitions
- navigation features and links.

The home page should set the look and feel of the whole product. The other screens should have a similar style, colour scheme and layout.

LAYOUT

Many sites adopt a typical layout for their screen design. This layout splits the screen into three sections. A typical layout is shown in Figure 3.5. There is:

- a bar across the top with the heading or company name, colour scheme and logo
- a **navigation bar** down the left-hand side with links to other screens within the product
- a main section where the content of the screen is displayed.

Navigation bar – usually placed along the top or side of the screen, this consists of a series of links to other screens. The navigation bar appears in the same position on every screen of the product, making it easy for users to find their way around.

Figure 3.5 The Bang & Olufsen website shows a typical screen structure

The first two areas usually do not change from one screen to the next, but the main section will display different content on each screen.

Producing a storyboard by hand

Some designers prefer to produce storyboards by hand. There are special templates available for this purpose.

Figure 3.6 shows an example of a hand-drawn storyboard sheet for the Egypt trip factfile (see page 227).

If you prefer to draw your storyboards by hand, you can use the file **Storyboard template1** provided. Remember, though, that if you use this method you will need to scan your hand-drawn storyboards so that they can be submitted in a digital format.

e-component

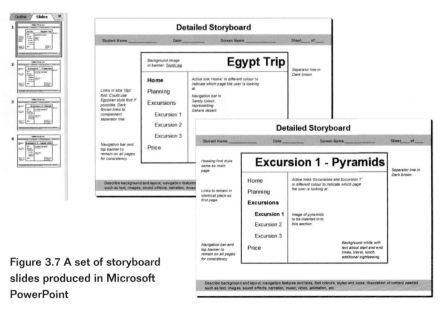

Figure 3.6 A hand-drawn story board describing the home page of the Egypt trip factfile

Using presentation software to create a digital storyboard

You could use presentation software to produce your storyboards, instead of creating them by hand. It is very easy to experiment with the positioning of content and, by default, the screens have the correct proportion and orientation. Figure 3.7 shows two digital storyboards for the Egpyt factfile.

Figure 3.7 A set of storyboard slides produced in Microsoft PowerPoint

Skills builder 3.3   e-component

You are going to use presentation software to create storyboards for the home page and one other screen in the factfile for the Egypt trip. Name the finished presentation Storyboards and save it in your Activity3 folder. A basic template has been provided for you to use called **Storyboard template2**.

Remember to include the names of the files that links lead to and the names of any content files needed.

Users need to be able to find their way around your product easily. The first rule is to keep the navigation simple and consistent. Some links will appear on every screen. Others will vary depending on what the screen is for.

Different types of links

Text is the simplest way to identify a link. Text links are usually blue and underlined. They perform an action when you click on them and can be made to change as you move over them.

Images and symbols are often used as links as they look more attractive than text.

Skills builder 3.4

Look for good and bad examples of navigation on the Internet. Ask yourself the following questions.

- Are some sites easier to navigate than others? If so, why?
- What features do you like?
- What features could you copy in your design?

Maintaining consistency

Most websites have a consistent design across all of their screens, which makes them look more professional. As a general rule, screens are consistent if all of the features in the list below remain the same on every screen:

- font styles and sizes
- the colour scheme
- the background style and/or colour
- the positioning of titles
- the layout
- the use of symbols
- the location and order of navigation links.

Although you need to achieve a consistent design for your product, the level of consistency that is appropriate will depend on the content of the individual screens. For example, one page may require more text than the others or a larger image. It is important to balance the need for consistency with the overall effectiveness of the product.

Skills builder 3.5

Look at the four pages of the website shown in Figure 3.8.

a) List the similarities between them all.

b) What are the differences?

c) How is colour used?

d) How do the images reflect the content of the page?

e) What might the *International* or *Trade* pages look like if you clicked on them on the first 'Home' page?

Write an explanation of the design decisions that the designer will have made when planning these pages.

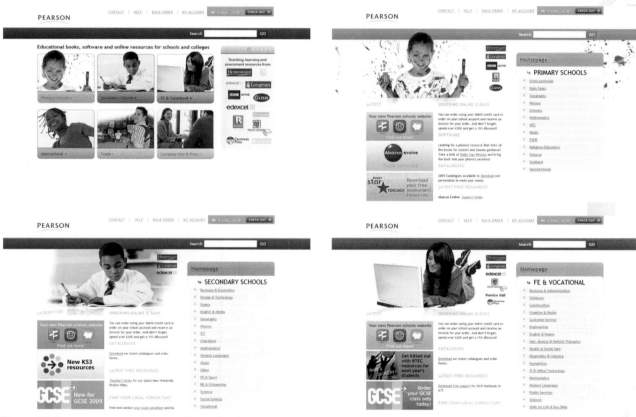

Figure 3.8 Four pages from Pearson Education's website

Justifying your design decisions

You will be expected to comment on and justify important design decisions. Make a note of:

- why you chose a particular colour scheme or font
- your reasons for choosing particular content items
- how your design is suitable for the target audience.

Using web authoring tools to build a user-controlled product

Web authoring tools are good for producing products that have a high degree of user control.

Setting up your folders

Before you begin to build your product, you need to get organised with your files and folders.

Everything you want to include in your product should be stored in a main folder. A lot of files are needed even for a simple interactive digital product, and you must keep track of all of them so that your links always work.

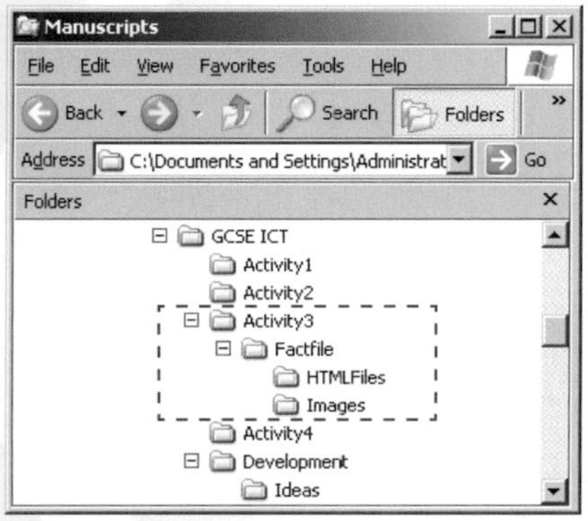

Figure 3.9 Your folder structure for the whole GCSE might now look like this – the red box shows the new folders for the website

Skills builder 3.6

a) Create a new folder called Factfile in your Activity3 folder.

b) Inside this create two more folders called HTMLFiles and Images.

e-component

As you collect the images you need for your factfile, put them into the Images folder. Some of them may need to be copied from Activities 1 and 2, and some may be new images that you need to collect or create for Activity 3. Remember to record all your sources in your document called **Sources_table** in the Development folder.

Using templates

By using a template you will make your products more consistent. A template should include all the content you want to appear on every screen.

ADVANTAGES OF USING A TEMPLATE

- Gives the product a consistent look and feel.
- Saves time as all objects that appear on every screen can go straight into the template.
- Makes the product more user-friendly.

Skills builder 3.7

Templates contain all of the elements common to every screen in a product. This means that they appear in the same place on every screen, in the same colour and style.

Look carefully at the web pages in Figure 3.10 and identify which objects may have been put on the web designer's template. Sketch out what you think the template might have looked like.

Skills check... make sure that you know how to:

- create web pages
- include different types of digital content such as sound, video and animation
- add lines and shapes
- use a table for page layout
- build a navigation bar
- create a template
- create text links, rollovers and hotspots.

Figure 3.10 Examples of pages from the Innocent Smoothies website

CREATING A TEMPLATE

To create a template in web design software, create a web page and then choose File, Save as Template.

All parts of the page are locked when you first create a template so, to make it useful, you have to make some regions editable.

Once you create a template, you can apply it to new screens. You can edit a template at any time, even if you have created screens based on it.

A template contains all the common elements that need to appear on every page of the website. Adding these objects to the template ensures that they are consistent in style, size, position and functionality.

Creating consistent screens without a template

You do not have to use a template. You could ensure consistency by following these steps:

1   Create the first screen, including all of the common elements and possibly some of the content unique to that screen.
2   Save the screen.
3   Click on Save As… to save the screen again but under a new filename, this time for the second screen.
4   Change any parts of the new screen that differ from the first screen by adding the relevant content.
5   Save the new screen to confirm the changes.
6   Repeat these steps to complete all of your screens.

As long as you are careful not to move any of the common objects, links, buttons or images on the first screen when you edit subsequent screens, this method is effective.

Skills builder **3.8**

Create the home page and one other screen in the factfile for the Egypt school trip, using the storyboard that you created in Skills builder 3.3 (page 232) as a starting point. You can create a template or use another method to ensure a consistent appearance. Insert some text and use at least one graphic. Would any other type of digital content be appropriate for this site?

Testing and review

A complex interactive digital product needs to be tested from a number of different viewpoints.

Functionality

You need to test the functionality of your interactive digital product.

In order to do this, you should ask the following questions:

- Is the content correct?
- Has everything been included?
- Has it been carefully proofread?
- Do all the links work?
- Do all the images load?
- Do videos play?
- Does the product work in different browsers?
- Is the navigation bar in the same place on every screen?
- Are the screens consistent?

Usability

You also need to test the usability of your interactive digital product. As well as checking the usability of the product yourself, you should complete a **usability test**.

In order to test the usability of your product, you should ask the following questions:

- Can other people use the product without help?
- Is it aesthetically pleasing? Does it have the 'wow' factor?

While you should plan to carry out functionality testing of your product yourself, you should arrange for your test buddy to carry out a usability test.

Watch how they get on when carrying out the usability test you have given them to do. Try not to prompt them or help them. If they cannot control the product and navigate through it by themselves, there is something seriously wrong with the design. Look for ways in which you can make the product easier to use to enhance the user experience.

Usability test – asks users to carry out a set of instructions using a given product.

Oh, I didn't expect the France link to take me to China!

You should always do a thorough check of your product's functionality before asking your test buddy to carry out a usability test

Review and self-evaluation

You need to review your work in Activity 3. As in Activities 1 and 2, a list of questions will be provided in the CAB to help you to do this. Save the Activity Review checklist in your Activity3 folder.

ACTIVITY 3 REVIEW

E-card

How did you decide what images to include?

What did you do to make it interesting to the visiting students' families?

What useful feedback did you get from your teacher and your test buddy?

How did you make use of the feedback?

Factfile

How did you decide what information to include?

What useful feedback did you get from your teacher and your test buddy?

How did you make use of the feedback?

What could you do to improve the leaflet?

Test buddy feedback

What feedback did you give your test buddy during Activity 3?

How did your test buddy make use of your feedback?

4 Evaluation

Activity 4 Overview

In Activity 4 you will evaluate the products you have produced for the CAB, reflect on your performance and suggest improvements you could have made. You should use the reviews you produced in Activities 1, 2 and 3 to help you.

A document is provided with the CAB to provide further guidance on key things you should consider. Try to include some worthwhile comments about what was good and what could have been improved.

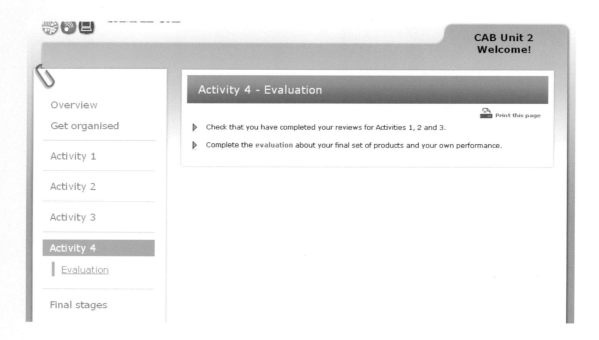

CAB Unit 2
Welcome!

Overview
Get organised

Activity 1

Activity 2

Activity 3

Activity 4

Evaluation

Final stages

Activity 4 - Evaluation

Print this page

▷ Check that you have completed your reviews for Activities 1, 2 and 3.

▷ Complete the evaluation about your final set of products and your own performance.

How you will be assessed...

In Activity 4, you will be assessed on how well you have evaluated:

● The products you have produced in Activities 1, 2 and 3 of the CAB.

● Your own performance, including your response to feedback.

The quality of your written communication will be assessed in the evaluation. You should be careful about your spelling, punctuation and grammar throughout the CAB, and especially in the evaluation.

As a savvy user you are expected to use specialist ICT terms where appropriate.

The products

For each product you produced, you should discuss:

- Its fitness for purpose – does it meet all the requirements specified in the CAB?
- Its suitability for the target audience you profiled.
- How feedback from others shaped the final outcome.
- Strengths and weaknesses – are there any ways in which it could be improved?

How did you perform?

Evaluating your own performance is probably the hardest thing to do. You need to be really honest with yourself. The idea is to learn from your experiences.

Ask yourself:

- How well did I manage my time?
- What skills were most useful to me in making my work successful?
- What difficulties did I encounter and how did I overcome them?
- What could I have done to make my work more successful?
- How good a test buddy was I? How could I have been more helpful?

Using collaborative tools to gather feedback

Your work on the CAB must be your own work but you need to work with your test buddy to get feedback. There are a whole host of tools available that will help you work collaboratively with your test buddy, and the student for whom you acted as test buddy.

Skills check... make sure that you know how to:

- share files
- mark up and comment on work
- arrange and hold meetings.

Functional Skills...

In this chapter there is information and activities that will help you to practise the following Functional ICT Skills:

Level 1

Using ICT

- Adjust system settings as appropriate to individual needs.

Developing, presenting and communicating information

- Check for accuracy and meaning.
- Evaluate own use of ICT tools at each stage of a task and at the task's completion.

Level 2

Using ICT

- Select and adjust system settings as appropriate to individual needs.

Developing, presenting and communicating information

- Work accurately and check accuracy, using software facilities where appropriate.
- Evaluate the selection, use and effectiveness of ICT tools and facilities used to present information at each stage of a task and at the task's completion.

You will need to save all of the work you have done for the CAB in one folder

Once you have finished everything, you need to put your work all together in one folder for assessment. This will include a central HTML document with links to all your files.

Putting your work together for submission

You will need to create one index page, viewable in a browser. In your index page you should create links to all of your work. The links will need to be organised and easy for your teacher and the moderator to find. You can choose any piece of software to create the index page, but it must be saved as an HTML page. You could use a word processing, desktop publishing or web authoring package for this.

Edexcel will give the exact details of what is required in the CAB.

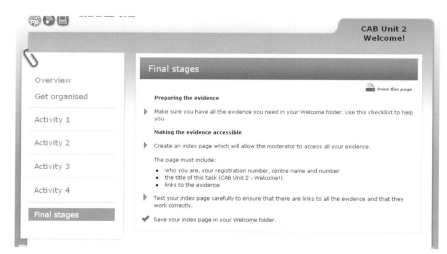

Skills builder 4.1

a) Organise your folders, making sure that they are named correctly and structured properly.

b) Save all of the files you have created in each of the sample activities and put them into the correct folders.

c) Show your file and folder structure to your teacher and ask them to check that your file management is suitable.

Organising your files and folders

Before your begin creating your index and adding links to your work, you must make sure that you have everything you want to be assessed and that it is all in the correct folders. If the work was for Activity 1, make sure that it goes in your Activity1 folder, and so on. If it is a more general file, such as a record of sources, make sure it goes in your Development folder.

What to include in your index page

You should ensure that at the top of the index page you include the following information:

- Your full name.
- Your registration or candidate number.
- The school or centre name and number.
- The title of the task in the CAB.

Below these details, you should create links to all of your work.

Planning the index page

The index page needs to include all the work that you wish your teacher and the moderator to see. You should organise it into Activities as set out in the CAB and keep things in the same order as you were asked to create them as part of the project. Your teacher may have some additional guidance on how to organise your files.

Create a rough plan on paper of all the files you will need to include in each of your folders and sketch out the overall plan of the index page on paper before you begin creating it.

CREATING AN INDEX PAGE IN A WORD PROCESSING PACKAGE

Whichever software package you use, you should make use of a table to structure the contents of the index page. You could create a table of 2 columns by 15 rows and use this as the basis of your index page. You can now complete the table by adding all the information and links to your work.

If you are using Microsoft Word, you can make the index look less like a table of contents and more like an index page by removing the border around your table cells (which is what has been done in Figure 4.1) by following these steps:

1 Highlight the entire table and right-click the selection. Select Table Properties…

2 Click on the Borders and Shading button.

3 Set the Border style to None.

4 Click OK.

Save the page as a web page by clicking Save As Web Page in the File menu. You should name your web page according to the following naming convention: your candidate number followed by your full name. So, the index shown in Figure 4.1 would be called 6027 Andrew Norris.html. Your teacher and the moderator will have many pieces of work to mark and this will make it much easier for them to find yours.

Before you can submit your work, you need to organise your files and folders and create an index page including links to all your work

---

GCSE ICT Coursework Submission Page – Unit 2

Name: Andrew Norris
Candidate Number: 6027
Centre Name: Highlands School
Centre Number: 11032

Task: Edexcel Unit 2 CAB Sample Task

Activity 1:   Profile Sheet
Digital Poster
Trip List reports created in a Database
Testing
Feedback
Review sheet

Figure 4.1 Part of a completed index page

Finally… test everything!

Before you submit your work for assessment, make sure that you test everything. Check that:

- it works on a machine that you are not logged in to
- you have included everything specified
- all the links work correctly.

Unit 2 is assessed using a Controlled Assessment Brief (CAB), which you will carry out in a supervised environment in a maximum of 40 hours. In the chapters in Unit 2 you will have developed the skills necessary to design and create effective digital products, and practised using these skills in the Skills builders provided. You should also have gained an understanding of how the CAB works, its structure and the likely content of the four activities.

Your success in the CAB will depend at least partly on how well you have prepared yourself for the Controlled Assessment. It is essential that you have acquired and practised all the skills that you will need before you start the assignment.

Remember that there is a lot of work you can do at home. Although you cannot create the files that will be assessed, you can do research, plan out your spreadsheet model and try out different designs for a digital product. You can also use your friends and family to get ideas. For example, if you need to create a product suitable for an eight year old, it would be helpful to ask someone you know who is around that age for background research and to obtain feedback on your ideas.

In summary, the Controlled Assessment Brief (CAB):

- Is an interactive digital product.
- Contains four activities.
  - Activity 1 involves the use of a database and the creation of one or more digital products or components of digital products.
  - Activity 2 involves the development of one of two spreadsheets provided in the CAB, and the design and creation of one or more digital products.
  - Activity 3 involves the design and development of digital products including a complex product that is fully interactive.
  - Activity 4 involves the evaluation of the products that you have created and of your own performance. To do this you will use the reviews that you carry out once you have completed each of the activities.

Monitoring progress

The importance of testing, feedback and review is stressed throughout the chapters in Unit 2. Testing your digital products as they are being developed, getting and using feedback, and reviewing the final product are all important processes in ensuring that you create effective digital products and that you develop your skills.

To help you to carry out a review of each activity, a series of prompt questions will be included in the CAB. These questions may vary slightly for different CABs and you can add to them if you wish.

Preparing the evidence

When your work on the CAB is finished you will need to prepare it so that it can be viewed and assessed on screen. This is an important part of the CAB and it involves creating an index page in which you can include links to evidence all your work. It is very important to check that all the links within your index work. You will be given instructions on preparing the evidence on the CAB screen called 'Final stages' as shown below. Make sure you follow the instructions on this screen very carefully.

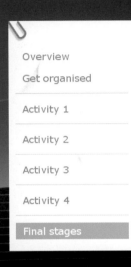

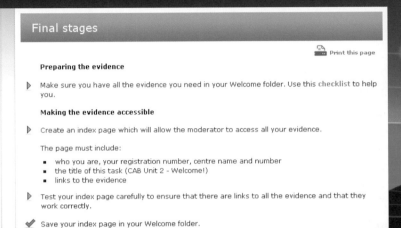

Final stages

Print this page

Preparing the evidence

▷ Make sure you have all the evidence you need in your Welcome folder. Use this checklist to help you.

Making the evidence accessible

▷ Create an index page which will allow the moderator to access all your evidence.

The page must include:

- who you are, your registration number, centre name and number
- the title of this task (CAB Unit 2 - Welcome!)
- links to the evidence

▷ Test your index page carefully to ensure that there are links to all the evidence and that they work correctly.

✔ Save your index page in your Welcome folder.

Overview
Get organised
Activity 1
Activity 2
Activity 3
Activity 4
Final stages

How much help can I have?

The work that you produce for the CAB must be your own work and you will be asked to confirm that this is the case when you submit your work.

Your teacher may give you feedback as you work on the CAB and you will also get feedback from your test buddy. You will see some of your test buddy's work but you must not copy their ideas. Remember that in Unit 2 of this book you will have tried similar tasks to those in the CAB and you may find it helpful to look back at work that you have already done between supervised sessions.

What can I do outside the supervised sessions?

To maximise the use of the time allowed in the supervised sessions you will need to do some work related to the CAB at home or between supervised sessions. Outside supervised sessions you will be able to carry out research and gather assets such as photographs, video footage and audio files. This 'raw material' must be brought into the classroom on a portable storage device and checked before you are allowed to use it. The files will then be deleted from the portable storage device.

You can also think about and plan the work you are going to do. You could devise strategies for searching a database, plan a product or sketch out some design ideas.

What will be assessed?

The products and other digital information such as your completed sources file (Sources_table.rtf), reviews and evaluation will be assessed. Do not include additional materials such as development versions of your products, time plans or test plans. They will not be looked at and may make it harder for your teacher and for the moderator to view your work.

How will be I assessed?

Your work will be assessed by your teacher using assessment criteria provided by Edexcel.

The general assessment criteria for Activity 1 of the CAB are shown below. These can be found in the specification and more detailed assessment information will be available for each CAB.

Activity 1

1a. Gathering information AO2 (10)

Gathering information involves the use of student identified sources and a given database. The information gathered must be relevant to the CAB and must include use of the Internet and email.

Better students will use efficient search techniques, using a range of self-identified sources, and will also make good use of the database. The information will be relevant to the publications they produce.

0	No rewardable content.
1-4 marks	The student has used some appropriate sources, including a given database, to gather information, some of which is relevant for use in their publications.
5-7 marks	The student has used a range of appropriate sources, including a given database, to select relevant information for use in their publications.
8-10 marks	The student has used a wide range of appropriate sources, including a given database, showing discrimination in their selection of information for use in their publications. They have used complex or efficient techniques to refine searches.

1b. Developing digital products AO1 (2), AO2 (8), AO3 (2)

The digital products are identified in the CAB. The effectiveness of testing is evidenced by the quality of the products that have been produced.

Better students will have produced products that are of high quality, with effective content and features.

0	No rewardable content.
1-4 marks	The student has developed the specified publications, with some use of appropriate content. They have carried out a limited review of their work but with few modifications.
5-8 marks	The student has developed the specified publications, using appropriate content and features. They have reviewed their work and made modifications some of which are effective.
9-12 marks	The student has developed the specified publications, using appropriate content and features effectively. They have reviewed and modified their work throughout its development, using feedback from others to improve the outcomes.

Using Activity 1 as an example, you can see that the general assessment grids do not refer to individual products within the activity.

Those assessing your work will be able to see the products you have produced and will therefore be able to tell if your testing of your products has been effective. There is no need to include separate evidence of your testing.

Note the importance of evidencing that you have used feedback effectively. You do not need to include the feedback from your test buddy or the updated version of your products in light of the feedback you received. Instead, you have to discuss what was said, how you changed your product and what difference you think these changes made. It would be useful to keep a log of this information to help you complete the review at the end of the activity. Remember that it should not be included in your final submission.

What if I want to improve my mark? Can I re-sit?

You should try to get the best mark that you can the first time you attempt the CAB but, if you think that you could do better, you can re-sit Unit 2 once and the higher mark will count. There are some new rules which mean that if Unit 2 is part of the 40% terminal requirement then the mark achieved then will count. In addition, a re-sit means that you must re-do the entire CAB. In some cases this will mean completing a different CAB to the one you used for your first attempt, which means a lot of extra work.

How many marks are there?

The CAB will be marked out of 80 marks. The different activities are worth different numbers of marks, as shown below:

- Activity 1: 22 marks
- Activity 2: 24 marks
- Activity 3: 22 marks
- Activity 4: 12 marks

How does moderation work?

Your CAB will be assessed in your own centre. Your centre will complete a form for each student, which gives the marks awarded and the reasons why marks have been awarded. This will happen for all students and these marks are submitted to Edexcel. Your centre will then be told which students' work must be submitted for moderation. Moderation is the process that Edexcel uses to identify whether adjustments need to be made to the marks that have been given to a student by their centre. This will ensure that all students taking the CAB are treated fairly and awarded the correct marks.

Edexcel uses trained moderators who review the marks given to a sample of student work in each centre. The moderators are 'standardised' by Edexcel so that they have a common view of the evidence needed for a particular mark to be awarded. This is not the overall mark awarded but the marks for each part of each activity. So in Activity 1 they would review the marks awarded for 1a Gathering information and 1b Developing digital products.

The moderator will check whether the marks given by the centre for the sample work can be agreed on the basis of the evidence in the CAB submission and any comments made by the centre. If they can, or if any changes would be very small, the centre marks are agreed. If this is not the case for all work in the sample, adjustments will be made to all marks from a centre.

What do I do if I'm short of time?

Firstly, try to manage your time carefully so that this does not happen. Make sure that you do some thinking outside the supervised sessions so that you can make full use of the time you have. You should know exactly what you plan to do as you go into each of the supervised sessions.

However, there is quite a lot to do in the time available. If you are short of time for an activity or for the CAB as a whole, despite managing your time carefully and planning outside of the supervised sessions, you will need to make some decisions about what to prioritise. You will need to be disciplined and use your time wisely. You need to get feedback on your work so plan the times when you will use your test buddy. Remember that they may be under pressure as well so you need to work together to ensure that you are asking for feedback at a time that is convenient for both of you. Do not forget your role as a test buddy to someone else either.

What if I leave out a product?

If you leave out a product you will lose the opportunity to gain some marks. How many marks you miss out on depends on how important the product is and how good your other products are. Remember that if you leave out a product that is then needed as part of another product in a later activity you risk losing more marks.

What if I don't do the last activity?

The last activity is the evaluation and this is important. If there is no evidence of evaluation you will lose the marks for this activity. As much of the basic work has already been done in the earlier reviews you would be foolish to leave this one out.

What happens if I don't add any extra records to the database in Activity 1?

It depends whether adding extra records is part of Activity 1 in the CAB. You will not always be required to add new records to the database. Most of work involved in this task is collecting the information that will make up the new records.

What happens if I don't complete a sources table?

The sources table is very important as it demonstrates the amount of research that you have carried out and that you have dealt with copyright issues properly. Your research marks will be very limited without a completed sources table.

What happens if I only use the simple spreadsheet model in Activity 2?

The spreadsheet that you choose to use does not impact on the mark that you might potentially achieve. It is what you do with the spreadsheet model that you use that is important. You might prefer to use the simple spreadsheet as a starting point and then make considerable additions to it to create a complex and effective model. It is the quality of your final model that is important rather than the one you start with.

What happens if I don't include any of my designs in Activity 3?

Design is an important part of all the activities as attention to design will help you produce better digital products. In Activity 3 there are marks available for the designs you produce. You cannot be awarded these marks without evidence.

What new things will I learn in the double award?

The double award focuses on using design tools and designing and developing products for other potential users. You can choose the products that you produce in Unit 4 and you can develop them using a range of different software tools.

Index